ISSUES IN CURRICULUM:
A SELECTION OF CHAPTERS FROM PAST
NSSE YEARBOOKS

Ninety-eighth Yearbook of the
National Society for the Study of Education

PART II

Edited by

MARGARET J. EARLY AND KENNETH J. REHAGE

19 NSSE 99

Distributed by THE UNIVERSITY OF CHICAGO PRESS • CHICAGO, ILLINOIS

The National Society for the Study of Education

The National Society for the Study of Education was founded in 1901 as successor to the National Herbart Society. It publishes a two-volume Yearbook, each volume dealing with a separate topic of concern to educators. The Society's series of Yearbooks, now in its ninety-eighth year, contains chapters written by scholars and practitioners noted for their significant work on the topics about which they write.

The Society welcomes as members all individuals who wish to receive its publications. Current membership includes educators in the United States, Canada, and elsewhere throughout the world—professors, researchers, administrators, and graduate students in colleges and universities and teachers, administrators, supervisors, and curriculum specialists in elementary and secondary schools.

Members of the Society elect a Board of Directors. Its responsibilities include reviewing proposals for Yearbooks, authorizing the preparation of Yearbooks based on accepted proposals, and appointing an editor or editors to oversee the preparation of manuscripts.

Current (1999) dues are a modest $30 ($25 for retired members and for students in their first year of membership). Members whose dues are paid for the current calendar year receive the Society's Yearbook, are eligible for election to the Board of Directors, and are entitled to a 33 percent discount when purchasing past Yearbooks from the Society's distributor, the University of Chicago Press.

Each year the Society arranges for meetings to be held in conjunction with the annual conferences of one or more of the national educational organizations. At these meetings, the current Yearbook is presented and critiqued. All members are urged to attend these meetings. Members are encouraged to submit proposals for future Yearbooks.

Issues in Curriculum is Part 2 of the 98th Yearbook. Part 1, published simultaneously, is entitled *The Education of Teachers*.

For further information, write to the Secretary, NSSE, 5835 Kimbark Ave., Chicago, Illinois 60637.

ISSN: 0077-5762

Published 1999 by
THE NATIONAL SOCIETY FOR THE STUDY OF EDUCATION

5835 Kimbark Avenue, Chicago, Illinois 60637
© 1999 by the National Society for the Study of Education

First Printing

Printed in the United States of America

Foreword

I was chair of the NSSE Board of Directors in 1997 when it requested the then Editor for the Society to make a selection of chapters from Yearbooks published during his tenure in that post for publication as Part 2 of the Society's 98th Yearbook. This volume was to be one of several publications planned by the Board in observance of NSSE's forthcoming Centennial.

Following consultation with Margaret Early, who was to become Editor for the Society and who was actively involved in editing several recent Yearbooks, an agreement was reached to select chapters that relate to the field of curriculum in order to give a particular focus to the book. The resulting collection fits neatly the goals I emphasize in curriculum workshops for teachers. I cue their memories with the acronym CIAO (curriculum, instruction, assessment, and organization). The integration of those four elements is essential for the evaluation and improvement of schooling.

Throughout its history, NSSE has focused on schooling. More than any other organization, the Society has managed a perspective that looks across a broad landscape. While individual volumes in the series of Yearbooks focus on particular issues, the genius of the present volume is that it brings together the various pieces so that the reader gains a sense of the whole.

I was especially interested in the last four chapters, each of which deals with the school as the organizational context for school improvement. Spanning more than a decade, these chapters convey a consistent message: efforts to "fix schools" are doomed to fail if critical organizational factors are ignored. This is important as society becomes increasingly "organizational." The assembly line is gone, and the factory model of school does not fit today's (and tomorrow's) style. It seems appropriate that the editors should have picked up that especially significant feature of contemporary schooling. By the juxtaposition of varied elements, they have produced a volume that merits careful study and review. It deserves a place on every educator's bookshelf.

ROBERT C. CALFEE

Preface

This part of the Society's 98th Yearbook is our response to a request from the Society's Board of Directors. The board asked us to bring together in one volume a selection of chapters from past Yearbooks. It was our choice, in which the Board concurred, to limit the selections to chapters relating to the field of curriculum.

The chapters we have selected deal with a variety of issues that have confronted the field of curriculum in recent years and continue to do so. Each chapter provides insights that help in understanding important aspects of the history of curriculum, a history that deserves to be taken into account in discussions of curriculum change. But the volume is not intended to be a history of curriculum development. Instead, we wanted it to be useful to teachers, curriculum specialists, and administrators as they confront and respond to proposals for change in the curriculum. Nevertheless, we could not escape history in this collection of essays.

The chapters in this book are themselves historical documents that reveal the nature of the discussion of curriculum issues when they were written. Some of the information provided is clearly dated and does not necessarily represent conditions today. We did not attempt to update such information, choosing instead to let each chapter stand as a valid description of situations existing when each was written.

The chapters chosen were selected not because the authors found some grand solution to the issues with which they were concerned. Rather, we chose chapters we thought could be helpful even today as guides to our thinking about curriculum problems.

We hope that others will benefit, as we have, from reading and rereading these selections.

THE EDITORS

Table of Contents

Introduction to Chapter I

We begin this collection of essays with an important piece of curriculum history—the efforts to redefine general education (i.e., education for all) in England and the United States in the light of profound social changes resulting from the Industrial Revolution. Herbert M. Kliebard recounts here the controversies in Victorian England when leading thinkers argued over the place of the humanities and the natural sciences in general education and also over how the curriculum should be determined. In the American context, a similar debate took place among leading educators. In the first quarter of the twentieth century, general education was being fundamentally redefined, while at the same time the increasing diversity among school populations forced attention to the need for differentiation in educational programs.

These two issues—the content of general education and the need for differentiation in school programs—have contemporary significance for American educators as dramatic social changes occur with ever increasing speed. Professor Kliebard's chapter will remind readers that today's curricular practices with respect to these issues have important roots in the not-too-distant past. As such, they are important aspects of the local school culture that must be taken into account as curricular changes are considered.

Herbert M. Kliebard is Professor of Education at the University of Wisconsin. His chapter is reprinted from the Society's 87th Yearbook, Part 2, Cultural Literacy and the Idea of General Education, *edited by Ian Westbury and Alan Purves.*

CHAPTER I

The Liberal Arts Curriculum and Its Enemies: The Effort to Redefine General Education

HERBERT M. KLIEBARD

Accounts of the rise of the liberal arts as an educational ideal usually begin, quite appropriately, either with the glories of ancient Greece or the revival of learning in Europe which we have come to call the Renaissance. While these time-honored beginnings of a kind of education that is supposed to exalt the human spirit and express many of the central values of western civilization have much to tell us about how that venerable ideal of education came to prominence, they are less illuminating on the question of how it fell into a kind of undeclared disfavor. (Hardly anyone is willing to admit being against a liberal education.) We know little about what the challenges to the liberal arts curriculum were or what accounts for its decline in twentieth-century American schooling. In the case of ancient Athens, the most potent challenger was reputed to be barbarism (which everybody is against) or perhaps Spartan education, and, in the Renaissance, it was probably scholasticism or even that great antagonist to sustained intellectual pursuit, Eros.[1]

The roots of the decline of the liberal arts curriculum are probably more proximate than either ancient Greece or the Renaissance. They are most likely to be found in the great controversies over educational policy that erupted in Victorian England. There is no question that education was then getting public attention. Controversy over educational policy tends to erupt as the perception of significant social change becomes acute, and it was apparent that the changes wrought by the Industrial Revolution in England were profound indeed. Not only were the lives of the working classes massively transformed, but the newly powerful middle class was beginning to flex its muscles.

By common agreement, education in England from at least the middle to late nineteenth century was a mess. The great figures of Victorian intellectual society—Thomas Carlyle, John Ruskin, John Henry Newman, John Stuart Mill, and Matthew Arnold—were aware of its shortcomings and frequently expressed their criticisms in their writings. One of the most potent of the critics of formal education in his time was Charles Dickens. Among other unflattering portraits of schooling in Victorian England, Mr. Gradgrind's address at the opening of his school in *Hard Times* conveyed Dickens's bitter impressions of the prevailing pedagogy of the day:

> Now, what I want is facts. Teach these boys and girls nothing but the facts. Facts alone are wanted in life. Plant nothing else, and root out everything else. You can only form the minds of reasoning animals upon facts; nothing else will ever be of any service to them. This is the principle on which I bring up my own children, and this is the principle on which I bring up these children. Stick to the facts, sir!

When "girl number twenty" (Sissy Jupe), a girl who has grown up with horses, is declared by Mr. Gradgrind to be unable to define a horse, he proceeds in his recitation until he finds one that satisfies him:

> Quadruped. Graminivorous. Forty teeth, namely, twenty-four grinders, four eyeteeth, and twelve incisors. Sheds coat in spring; in marshy countries sheds hoofs too. Hoofs hard, but requiring to be shod with iron. Age known by marks in mouth.

To that response, Mr. Gradgrind remarks triumphantly, "Now, girl number twenty . . . you know what a horse is." With accounts of education like this reaching hundreds of thousands of Dickens's readers, the controversy over the direction that education should follow was reaching beyond an inner circle of intellectuals. To be sure, what Dickens described in *Hard Times* and several other of his novels was anything but what a liberal education was supposed to be, but his criticisms, like those of his contemporaries, opened the way for a serious reexamination of the standard fare of the curriculum of his time.

What Knowledge Is of Most Worth?

Hovering over the brewing controversy as to the course that the curriculum of the Victorian school should take was the pervasive influence of Charles Darwin. While the theory of evolution was popularly conceived primarily as a challenge to the reigning theology of the day, its most lasting impact was in terms of what it said about science itself and what effect the new conceptions of science, as well as science's enormously increased status, would have on what knowledge people thought to be valuable. To a considerable extent, this reexamination had economic roots and is connected to the prominence of commerce and trade in industrial England. Increasingly, for example, critics of English society were observing that England no longer produced enough food for its citizens, and, to maintain its position of power and influence in the world, she needed to achieve preeminence in technology and manufacture. Classical studies, linguistic elegance, and masterpieces of literature as the centerpieces of the liberal arts curriculum were being challenged, and they were being challenged on a number of fronts. Illustrative of the kinds of challenges that were being directed at the traditional liberal arts were the positions of two of the most eminent Victorians who were also influential educational reformers: Herbert Spencer, whose "synthetic philosophy" was perceived to be at least consistent with Darwinism, and "Darwin's bulldog," Thomas Henry Huxley. The impact of their efforts to change the traditional curriculum of the time was ultimately to be felt in the schools of twentieth-century America.

Spencer, of course, is best known in the educational world for his essay, "What Knowledge Is of Most Worth?" (1859), that title having since been appropriated and paraphrased many times, practically taking on the status of being the most central of all the questions that can be raised about the curriculum. His answer to it, like that of many of his forebears as well as his contemporaries, was influenced by his interpretation of the theory of evolution. Spencer's speculative anticipation of Darwinian theory led him to carry forward the principle of natural selection into such areas as the development of knowledge and social relationships. Evolutionary theory, in other words, became not just a way of explaining the development of species in a biological world, but was actually the basis for a cosmic understanding of society, psychology, ethics, and education. Spencer's earlier essay, "On the Genesis of Science" (1854), for example, posited a kind of sympathy between the development of mental concepts within the individual and the evolution of knowledge. His main point was that everyday knowledge could not be distinguished in any significant way from scientific knowledge. The latter was merely the evolutionary extension of the former. Part of the appeal of that doctrine was that it made the lines between aristocratic and ordinary knowledge less distinct. As the study of the world around us, the natural sciences were not as arcane or as exclusionary as ancient languages and classical literature. Nor were they as specialized. "The sciences are as branches of one trunk," he said, "and . . . were at first cultivated simultaneously" with differentiation only occurring later. In fact, science may be said to have a "common root" with language and art as well. Spencer predicted that "whenever established, a correct theory of the historical development of the sciences must have an immense effect upon education."[2]

In that same year (1854), Spencer's "Intellectual Education" turned his theory of the evolution of knowledge into a principle of curriculum: "The genesis of knowledge in the individual must follow the same course as the genesis of knowledge in the race."[3] In general terms, that principle was a rough extrapolation of the commonly held scientific truth of the time that "ontogeny recapitulates phylogeny." The mental development of the individual, in other words, recapitulated the development of human knowledge over the course of history. This is one of the senses in which Spencer can be seen as an advocate of "natural education." According to this view, the course that the curriculum should take is one that follows scientific principles, which, when discovered and followed, lead inevitably to a desirable curriculum. This was an argument not simply in favor of a place for science in the curriculum but for a *scientific curriculum*. Education would proceed along evolutionary lines in the same way that the various plant and animal species, including the human species, proceeded.

Several versions of a scientifically determined curriculum rife in the latter part of the nineteenth century incorporated the idea of a recapitulation of human history within the child, thus setting out not only the sequence but actually the content of the course of study. Like Spencer's version, many of these were, potentially at least, antagonistic to the ideal of the liberal arts. Although the particular subjects that have been proposed as comprising the liberal arts have varied according to time and place, at a fundamental level the liberal arts ideal has always involved the conscious effort to select those elements of the culture that serve to make one fully human. Traditionally, the elements involved are presumed to make one sensitive to beauty, intellectually alive, and humane in outlook. For this liberal arts ideal, the idea of a natural education substituted the notion that education was deterministic in the sense that the search for the good curriculum did not involve casting about for the cultural elements of highest value. Rather, it consisted of *discovering* the laws that the human being followed over the course of development in the same way that Darwin discovered the laws that governed the descent of the human species. Once those natural laws of development were discovered, they could be used to determine the curriculum.

Spencer's "What Knowledge Is of Most Worth?," which first was published as a separate essay in 1859 and then appeared as the initial chapter of his *Education: Intellectual, Moral, and Physical*, offered an even more formidable challenge to the traditional conception of a liberal arts education. In his opening paragraph, Spencer noted with a suggestion of amusement if not condescension that "an Orinoco Indian, though quite regardless of bodily comfort, will yet labor for a fortnight to purchase pigment wherewith to make himself admired" and that an Indian woman would leave her hut unclothed but never unpainted. His point was to illustrate the curious phenomenon that "the idea of ornament predominates over that of use," and he then went on to argue that this principle seemed to hold true "among mental as among bodily acquisitions."[4] In English schools, for example, Latin and Greek, which had no functional value, were the equivalent of the Orinoco Indian's ornamental paint. And ornamental education predominated equally in the education of women: "Dancing, deportment, the piano, singing, drawing—what a large space do these occupy!"[5] "Before there can be a rational *curriculum*," he concluded, "we must settle which things it most concerns us to know," and, "to this end, a measure of the value is the first requisite."[6]

The requisite step in this process, according to Spencer, was to classify in their order of importance the activities that comprise human life. He listed them as follows:

1. Those activities which directly minister to self-preservation;
2. Those activities which, by securing the necessaries of life, indirectly minister to self-preservation;
3. Those activities which have for their end the rearing and discipline of offspring;
4. Those activities which are involved in the maintenance of proper social and political relations;
5. Those miscellaneous activities which make up the leisure part of life, devoted to the gratification of tastes and feelings.[7]

The substitution of these functional criteria for the development of curricula for those that emphasized criteria drawn from some conception of what comprised the great cultural resources of Western culture constituted nothing short of a major revolution in thinking as to how a curriculum should be determined. For one thing, Spencer set up an aim of education (self-preservation) to which education itself would be subordinate. Education, in other words, became an instrument to achieve something that lay beyond it. Specifically, there were categories of activities for which a good education prepared one to perform successfully. Music, poetry, and painting were no longer to be studied as the finest expressions of human aspirations and emotions but in order to "fill up the leisure left by graver occupations."[8] Leisure as an activity, ranking number five and last on Spencer's list of activities, was needed, and the study of certain subjects could help one perform that function successfully. But the task of developing a curriculum was seen in terms of "life as divided into several kinds of activity of successively decreasing importance; the worth of each order of facts as regulating these several kinds of activity, intrinsically, quasi-intrinsically, and conventionally; and their regulative influences estimated as knowledge and discipline."[9]

For Spencer, the subject most suited to the proper preparation for "complete living" was science. Although nature itself provided much of what is needed for self-preservation, deliberate education in the interest of self-preservation was also necessary. Nature could help us ward off such dangers as "want of food, great heat, [and] extreme cold" instinctively,[10] but the absence of "an acquaintance with the fundamental principles of physiology as a means to complete living"[11] led to all sorts of infirmities and chronic disabilities. "Hence, knowledge which subserves direct self-preservation by preventing this loss of health, is of primary importance."[12] Mathematics played a vital role in everything from ordinary carpentry to making a railway. Physics had given us the steam engine and has shown us how to make our smelting furnaces more efficient. Chemistry was vital to the work of the bleachers and dyers. Biology was intricately connected with the production of food. And the "Science of Society"[13] helped us to understand money-markets, to consider intelligently the chances of war, and improve mercantile operations. Science, in short, was the subject *par excellence* for maintaining the vital function of self-preservation in the modern world. According to Spencer, other subjects needed to be examined in similar fashion, in terms of their role in fulfilling the other vital purposes. Thus the absence of attention in the curriculum to the proper raising of children needed to be corrected. Spencer imagined, for example, that a future antiquary surveying the curriculum of the mid-nineteenth century would have concluded that "This must have been the *curriculum* for their celibates."[14] The functions of the citizen must be addressed not by

biographies of kings and queens but must be based on what is
necessary for the general welfare. As to poetry, that staple of the
liberal arts curriculum, Spencer would grant that taste could
conceivably be improved through its study, but "it is not to be
inferred that such improvement of taste is equivalent in value to an
acquaintance with the laws of health."[15] Those subjects that Spencer
called "the efflorescence of civilization" (the arts and *belles lettres*, for
example) should be subordinated to the knowledge really vital to our
civilization. Even the appreciation of the arts required such scientific
understanding as the theory of equilibrium and how the effects of
nature are produced. Referring to the fate of what we usually call the
humanities, he recommended, "*As they occupy the leisure part of life, so
should they occupy the leisure part of education.*"[16] Science, in its various
forms, was that subject that was associated with the real work of the
world, whereas the humanities were associated with mere leisure.

Spencer concluded his revolutionary essay in dramatic and
unequivocal terms:

What knowledge is of most worth?—the uniform reply is—Science. This is
the verdict on all the counts. For direct self-preservation, or the maintenance
of life and health, the all-important knowledge is—Science. For that indirect
self-preservation which we call gaining a livelihood, the knowledge of
greatest value is—Science. For the due discharge of parental functions, the
proper guidance is to be found only in—Science. For that interpretation of
national life, past and present, without which the citizen cannot rightly
regulate his conduct, the indispensable key is—Science. Alike for the most
perfect production and highest enjoyment of art in all its forms, the needful
preparation is still—Science. And for the purposes of discipline—intellectual,
moral, religious—the most efficient study is, once more—Science.[17]

Spencer's "What Knowledge Is of Most Worth?" turned the
traditional conception of the liberal arts curriculum on its head. In the
first place, the humanities, to which the liberal arts curriculum had
accorded the central place, were relegated in no uncertain terms to a
distinctly inferior position. Secondly, both the sequence and the
content of the curriculum could be determined scientifically rather
than merely representing a judgment as to the most valuable resources
of the culture. A "natural education" was one that followed the laws
that governed the process. And finally, the purposes of the curriculum
could no longer be described in such terms as "liberating the human
spirit" or "initiation into the life of the mind," but were to be seen in
terms of the curriculum's contribution to the performance of specific

and vital activities. In fact, the preservation of life itself became the supreme function of education. In Spencerian terms, education could no longer be seen as an adornment, like the pigment on the Orinoco Indian, but as an instrument necessary for the performance of life-preserving functions like the clothes that shield us from the vicissitudes of weather. The apparent good sense of such a position had an enormous appeal to the rising mercantile and manufacturing class.

The Prophet of Science

Spencer's contemporary, Thomas Henry Huxley, was a considerably more formidable public speaker and a more effective advocate of science than Spencer—and an even greater celebrity in the upper echelons of the Victorian scientific community—but, as an educational reformer, he was far less revolutionary. In a significant sense, however, his interest in educational reform was more abiding and more profound than Spencer's. He was, after all, a working educator for a good part of his life and took a particular interest in the education of the working classes. He had served as a professor of natural history at the Royal School of Mines, an examiner for the Government's Department of Science and Art, a member of the School Board for London and chairman of its influential Scheme of Education Committee, and was the author of several widely praised textbooks in science.

Huxley's best-known expression of his educational ideals is contained in the inaugural address he delivered when he became principal of the South London Workingman's College, an address he called, "A Liberal Education; and Where to Find It." As is implied in the title, Huxley took this occasion to redefine what was meant by a liberal education. Huxley reviewed briefly several of the extant justifications for providing a liberal education. For the politicians, educating the masses was essential because they would one day become masters; the clergy's hopes were built on the idea that education would halt the drift toward infidelity; the "manufacturers and the capitalists" claimed that "ignorance makes bad workmen" and that the market for English goods would suffer as a result. Huxley rejected these positions in favor of the view that "the masses should be educated because they are men and women with unlimited capacities of being, doing, and suffering, and that it is as true now, as ever it was, that the people perish for lack of knowledge."[18] Huxley's emphasis on the intrinsic need to know as the justification for education as opposed to purposes that lie beyond education made his position consistent with the *ideal* of a liberal arts education, although his notion of what the components of that education would be departed significantly from the traditional conceptions.

Huxley scorned the argument that education should be instrumental to some larger good. If the masses in power without an education would be so disastrous, why is it, he asked, that "such ignorance in the governing classes in the past has not been viewed with equal horror?"[19] As to the manufacturers' and the capitalists' position, he asked whether we really want the English educational system "diverted into a process of manufacturing human tools?"[20] Furthermore, Huxley went on, it was not simply the education of the masses that was a matter of concern. To him, it appeared that even the most exclusive of the English schools ought to be made to "supply knowledge" rather than simply performing their traditional function of inculcating "gentlemanly habits, a strong class feeling, and eminent proficiency in cricket."[21] The knowledge that Huxley sought to represent in a modern curriculum, included, to be sure, a strong dose of science, but one that was balanced by other factors:

Education is the instruction of the intellect in the laws of Nature, under which I include not merely things and their forces, but men and their ways; and the fashioning of affections and of the will into an earnest and loving desire to move in harmony with those laws. For me, education means neither more nor less than this.[22]

In Huxley's view, the main thrust of a liberal education could be found in the development of the intellect and not in something that lay beyond it, such as the production of high-quality workers, a course that the rising middle class of the time was advocating. The function of education was something much broader than "a process of manufacturing human tools, wonderfully adroit in the exercise of some technical industry, but good for nothing else."[23]

There is no question that Huxley was a passionate and, as it turned out, effective advocate for the introduction of a much stronger measure of science into the curriculum of his day. There were even times when his passion on the subject led to exaggerated claims for science and something close to a denigration of the traditional humanist curriculum. (Huxley's tendency toward hyperbole and embroidered rhetoric has even been the subject of some study.[24])

Unlike Spencer, however, he was not claiming that one study was actually more valuable than another. His position was that, given the prominence and significance of science in Western civilization, science was getting short shrift in the education of English youth. He was arguing for a redress of an imbalance found in the traditional liberal arts curriculum, not for a new set of criteria by which the worth of subjects would be determined. Opposition to the introduction of the sciences into the standard curriculum of Victorian England, in Huxley's view, came not only from business interests but also from the "Levites in charge of the ark of culture and monopolists of liberal education" who essentially ignored the significance of science in the modern world and its potential role in the liberal education of youth.[25] But despite his eagerness to give a major role to natural sciences in the curriculum, Huxley was not ready to assert unequivocally their superiority to the traditional humanities, or any of the other subjects.

Some indication of Huxley's basic moderation on the issue of redefining the general education of his time may be illustrated through his skirmish with his friend, Matthew Arnold, on educational policy. Arnold, of course, was one of the great defenders of high culture in Victorian society and, as one of Her Majesty's Inspectors of Schools, he was powerfully situated to influence the curriculum. His leadership in the defense of the traditional liberal arts against the onslaught of crass materialism in education was widely recognized. In his *Culture and Anarchy*, Arnold had sought to answer the question of what use is culture by arguing that real culture in its highest form not only "reminds us that the perfection of human nature is sweetness and light," but serves to infuse in us "the passion to make them prevail."[26] Rejecting the idea that culture must be adapted to the condition of the masses in order for them to appreciate it, Arnold argued passionately for what he called the "*social idea*" of culture. Culture, he said,

does not try to teach down to inferior classes; it does not try to win them for this or that sect of its own, with ready-made judgments and watchwords. It seeks to do away with classes; to make the best that has been thought and known in the world current everywhere; to make all men live in an atmosphere of sweetness and light, where they may use ideas, as it uses them itself, freely—nourished and not bound by them."[27]

It was in this sense that the upholders of true culture were "the true apostles of equality."[28]

In his response to Arnold, Huxley did not take issue with Arnold's well-known definition of culture as "the best that has been thought and known in the world." Culture, Huxley agreed, was something quite different from simply learning or a technical skill. But he took issue with the implication that culture was to be equated with the works of classical antiquity and a smattering of the modern classics. "The humanists," he argued, "take their stand upon classical education as the sole avenue of culture" despite the fact that, even in the Renaissance, that period commonly referred to as the "Revival of Letters," there was also a revival of science and learning generally.[29] Insofar as the ancients were concerned, Huxley went on,

we cannot know all the best thoughts and sayings of the Greeks unless we know what they thought about natural phenomena. We cannot fully apprehend their criticism of life unless we understand the extent to which that criticism was affected by scientific conceptions.[30]

Although he remained a passionate advocate of the sciences, and was even wont to exaggerate the merits of his case on occasion, Huxley's chief concern was that the monopoly on culture that had been traditionally exercised by the humanists had yielded a truncated version of "true culture" as the basis of a liberal education.

Arnold did find it ultimately necessary to reply to Huxley's attack on traditional humanism as the basis for the liberal arts curriculum, but his argument indicated a broader area of agreement with Huxley rather than disagreement on the nature of culture. He objected to the equation of humanism as a fundamental belief with superficial knowledge of *belles lettres*, but he went on to emphasize that "There is . . . really no question between Professor Huxley and me as to whether knowing the great results of modern scientific study of nature is not required as a part of our culture, as well as knowing the products of literature and art."[31] Rather, Arnold parted company with the reformers of the liberal arts when they proposed "to make the training in natural science the main part of education for the great majority of mankind . . . ."[32] The appeal to experience which the humane letters provided was for Arnold of a far more universal appeal than the desire to understand how the universe worked. Implicitly rejecting the approach that Spencer took in "What Knowledge Is of Most Worth?," he proposed instead: "Let us . . ., all of us, avoid indeed as much as possible any invidious comparison between the merits of humane letters, as a means of education, and the merits of the natural sciences."[33] Arnold's commitment to humanistic studies, however, eventually came through. He recalled from one of his own school reports that a young man in an English training college paraphrased the line in *Macbeth*, "Can'st thou not minister to a mind diseased?" as "Can you not wait upon the lunatic?" Arnold confessed in the end that he would rather have someone ignorant about the moon's diameter than someone who was unable to provide a better rendering of Shakespeare's line than that one.[34]

The Curriculum Debate in America

Both Spencer's radical challenge to the way the curriculum was traditionally structured and Huxley's advocacy of a balance in the liberal arts between science and humanities found their advocates in the American context. Both men, after all, had made triumphant tours of the United States. But the political and social climate of the times led Spencer's position to take root and flourish in late nineteenth-century America and to become a burgeoning movement in the twentieth century, strongly influencing the course that the American curriculum would take. Of special appeal to many Americans was Spencer's application of such biological principles as "survival of the fittest" to the conduct of social as well as economic affairs. With such ardent and influential disciples as John Fiske and Edward Livingston Youmans (the founder of *Popular Science Monthly*), Spencer soon became, in Richard Hofstadter's characterization, "the metaphysician of the homemade intellectual, and the prophet of the cracker-barrel agnostic."[35] The idea of a laissez-faire society that was somehow self-regulating made social legislation and economic regulation not only unnecessary but positively dangerous as an unwarranted intrusion on natural law and, therefore, an impediment to true progress. The law of the jungle became an accepted way of perceiving and justifying inequality in terms of wealth and differentiated social functions.

Through the work of such intellectual leaders as William Graham Sumner, one of the founders of American sociology and a professor of political and social science at Yale University, Spencer's social Darwinism achieved wide popularity. Like Spencer, Sumner saw not only the jungle but society generally as governed by the laws of survival. He argued, for example, that the struggle of various interest groups for their share of the fruits of industry should be left "to free contract under the play of natural laws" and that interference would result only in the diminution of the spoils that were left to be divided.[36] The choice, in Sumner's terms, was between "free social forces" on the one hand and "legislative and administrative

interference" on the other.[37] Such societal functions as the
concentration of wealth, should, according to Sumner, be seen as the
product of evolutionary forces. "The concentration of wealth," he
said, "is but one feature of a grand step in societal evolution."[38] In an
early version of "trickle down" economics, Sumner argued that "No
man can acquire a million without helping a million men to increase
the little fortunes all the way down through all the social grades."[39]
Millionaires were merely the "naturally selected agents of society for
certain work" and should be seen as much the product of natural
selection as Darwin's evolution of the species.[40]

 With Spencer's ideas enjoying such significant acceptance in social
and political worlds, it is not surprising that his conception of what
knowledge is of most worth should have gained popularity with
respect to the American curriculum. Basically, Spencer's conception of
a worthwhile curriculum is reflected in three directions that the
American curriculum began to take in the latter part of the nineteenth
century. First, there was the elevation of the natural sciences to a more
prominent role in programs of general education (although that
tendency in itself could easily have reflected Huxley's more moderate
as well as Spencer's more radical conception of how a curriculum
should be constructed). Second, there was the notion that the
curriculum was not merely to be a selection of the finest elements of
the culture, as Arnold or even Huxley would have seen it, but as a
reflection of natural laws governing both the course of human history
and the development of the individual. And finally, there was the
Spencerian conception of the curriculum as instrumental to some
purpose beyond itself. In Spencer's case, that purpose was self-
preservation first and foremost, and this made the development of
those functions that would achieve that purpose, rather than those
elements that would merely add to the stock of high culture, the most
desirable as elements in a program of general education.

 The new prominence that the natural sciences would enjoy was at
least symbolically represented by the elevation of Charles William
Eliot, a chemist and an admirer of Spencer's, to the presidency of
Harvard in 1869. Although some contemporary interpretations of
Eliot's work tend to depict him as a stodgy conservative who used the
Committee of Ten report[41] to impose college domination on the high
school curriculum, he was in his own time regarded as a radical
innovator and representative of the "new education." Eliot was not
simply interested in including a measure of science in the American
curriculum. He argued for the doctrine of the equivalence of school

subjects (a position that was incorporated into the Committee of Ten report). This meant that other subjects would have equal status with the time-honored triumvirate of the classical curriculum, Latin, Greek, and mathematics.

First of all, Eliot sought that status for English language and literature, which had had only a subordinate place in American schools and colleges in the late nineteenth century.[42] Second, he tried to achieve "academic equality" for French and German, arguing that there was no reason for modern languages to be slighted in favor of the classical ones.[43] Third, Eliot saw a larger place for the study of history and the social sciences in the form of political economy (or, as it was sometimes called, public economics).[44] And finally, Eliot sought the inclusion of the natural sciences in what he called "the magic circle of the liberal arts."[45] To some extent, as in the case of modern foreign languages, Eliot's arguments were somewhat utilitarian in character, but, for the most part, he framed his justification for the inclusion of new subjects into the liberal arts curriculum in terms of the doctrine of mental discipline, which had, by the nineteenth century, formed an association, albeit an unnecessary one, with the liberal arts. Eliot argued, for example, that the student of the natural sciences "exercises his powers of observation and judgment [and] acquires the precious habit of observing appearances, transformations and processes of nature."[46] Yet, despite his attachment to mental discipline, Eliot's overall position can be seen mainly as an effort to open up the concept of the liberal arts to a new array of significant elements of the culture, including science.

The success of the effort to redefine the liberal arts is difficult to gauge in terms of school practice. During the period between 1871 and 1875, the Bureau of Education collected figures only on the three types of general curricula then in vogue—English, classical, and modern languages. The English curriculum actually was the most popular with enrollments roughly double that of the other two, but curriculum data on individual subjects are incomplete since only Latin, Greek, French, German, and English were tabulated in the period between 1876 and 1885-86. It was not until 1887-88 that data became available for mathematics, physics, chemistry, and other sciences.[47] Although the data are incomplete, they indicate a rather spotty performance on the part of the natural sciences. In 1890, for example, enrollments in physics as a percentage of total enrollments in grades nine through twelve was reported as 22.8 with a drop to 19.0 in 1900 and a further decline in 1910 to 14.6. By 1949 (the height of the "life adjustment" era), the percentage of enrollments in physics had declined sharply to 5.4, and that figure included not only advanced physics, but applied physics, fundamentals of electricity, radio and electronics, and fundamentals of machines. Although the initially reported percentages in such subjects as chemistry, geology, astronomy, and earth science were not nearly as high to begin with, they experienced similar declines in percentages of high school enrollments. The first figure reported for physical geography in 1900 was a healthy 23.4 percent, but by 1934, this had dropped to a minuscule 1.6 percent.

The reconstruction of the liberal arts through the inclusion of the so-called "moderns" into the American school curriculum as advocated by reformers such as Eliot apparently met with marked success in one sense, but only restricted success in another. Indeed, the sciences, for example, began to enjoy roughly equal status with the classical subjects with about 54 percent of secondary school students enrolled in any science course by the 1948-49 academic year, although it is noteworthy that that figure is somewhat below the 59 percent registered by the combination of business courses in the same year. (Of some significance also is the fact that in 1949, 72 percent of the total science enrollments were in general science and biology.) Likewise, modern foreign languages not only began to attain academic respectability, but eventually surpassed the classical languages in terms of enrollments. That success is tempered, however, by the fact that only 22 percent of students were enrolled in any kind of foreign language study in 1949.[48] This means, of course, that while the traditional liberal arts curriculum had indeed undergone something of a transformation during the first part of the twentieth century, the "modernized" form of the liberal arts was reaching only a select segment of the school population. (If anything, this tendency toward curriculum differentiation, by design or default, has become accelerated in the 1980s with the "shopping mall" becoming the most pervasive model of high school studies.[49]) In effect, there is no program of general education in the United States (defined as liberal arts or anything else); there is only a potpourri of hundreds of subjects from which students make sometimes considered and sometimes haphazard choices as to what subjects they will "buy." The laissez-faire doctrine advocated by Spencer and later by Sumner in social and economic relationships has somehow taken a firm hold in the curriculum of American schools.

Spencer's other vision of a curriculum governed by scientific principles also met with mixed success. The early leader in the American drive to create a program of studies governed by natural law was G. Stanley Hall. Like Spencer, Hall sought to extend evolutionary theory to mental life, even aspiring to become the "Darwin of the mind." As the acknowledged leader of the child-study movement in the late nineteenth century and founder of such influential journals as the *American Journal of Psychology* and *Pedagogical Seminary*, Hall attracted thousands of followers to his idea of an educational system controlled by scientific principles. Insofar as the curriculum was concerned, Hall, like Spencer, subscribed to the position that in their development individuals recapitulated the historical stages through which the human race had passed, and this principle guided many of his pronouncements as to how the course of study should be reformed. "The principle that the child and the early history of the human race are each keys to unlock the nature of the other," Hall affirmed, "applies to almost everything in feeling, will, and intellect. To understand either the child or the race we must constantly refer to the other."[50]

Based on the conclusions of his studies of the child in relation to the race, Hall became suspicious of the effort to develop the intellect particularly in the early years of schooling. Health became for him the all-controlling factor in directing educational policy, and he feared that early intellectual training might be detrimental to the health of children and even adolescents. Since natural laws were to govern the education of children, Hall felt that the safest course was to "strive first of all to keep out of nature's way."[51] As such, education according to nature began to take on an almost antiintellectual character and the development of the intellect began to lose its traditionally central place in educational debates. Although the specific doctrine that the developmental stages through which the child passed somehow recapitulated historical epochs began to lose its credibility, the more general idea that a science of education could redirect the purposes of education continued to have wide appeal and thus served to undermine to some extent the central role that the traditional liberal arts assigned to freeing the intellect.

The Triumph of a Spencerian Alternative to Liberal Studies

In addition to the predominant emphasis on science and the idea of a curriculum controlled by natural laws, the third implication of Spencer's educational reform was that the curriculum could be finely tuned to the *functions* that needed to be performed in order to survive in the modern world. This implication was revolutionary in its potential impact on the liberal arts ideal and it was substantially, although not altogether, realized as an alternative to the liberal arts as the foundation of general education. Like the other two reforms, this one was linked to science at least in the sense that it was alleged to be consistent with Darwinian theory as applied to society and, by extension, to education. Unlike the other two, however, its success was more visible and more enduring. Even though the victory of a curriculum reform that proposed to substitute the efficient performance of social functions for the ideal of a curriculum that embodied the main intellectual resources of our culture was anything but complete, that reform nevertheless stands today as a most potent enemy of the liberal arts.

Although the reconstruction of the modern American curriculum along directly functional lines was one of the principal motivations of educational reform in the twentieth century, its significance can probably best be illustrated through the work of one of its major exponents, David Snedden. Born in a tiny cabin and educated in a one-room schoolhouse in California in the late nineteenth century, Snedden eventually completed a classical course at St. Vincent's College in Los Angeles. As a young schoolteacher, he undertook to study the complete works of Spencer in his spare time; this experience led him to reject the standard curriculum of his time in favor of one that was directly tied to self-preservation.[52] To Snedden, this meant that a truly functional education could be derived scientifically from the analysis of human activity and translated into a socially efficient curriculum that, in effect, repudiated completely the ornamental trappings of the education that Spencer so much deplored. Later, as state commissioner of education in Massachusetts and a professor of educational sociology at Teachers College, Columbia University, he was in a position to reach a large and receptive audience for his ideas.

Although Snedden is sometimes particularly identified with vocational education, his influence was far more pervasive. In fact, he saw himself primarily as someone who was redefining general education in the twentieth century. Human functioning, according to Snedden, could be roughly classified into two major categories: production and consumption. Vocational education derived its legitimacy from its role in creating efficient producers, and liberal education would constitute that part of education that aimed at making human beings effective consumers or users. "The liberally educated man," he said, "utilizes the products and services of many producers; but because of his education he uses them well, both in the individual and social sense."[53] Together, vocational education for the producer and liberal education for the consumer would create the fully functioning human being. In this sense, liberal education would be as functional and as vital to human survival as vocational education.

Within a few years, Snedden's protege, Clarence Darwin Kingsley, translated that conception of general education into the famous seven aims of the Cardinal Principles report (1918).[54] Consciously or unconsciously, the seven "aims" of that report— health, command of fundamental processes, vocation, worthy use of leisure, worthy home membership, citizenship, and ethical character— followed in rough outline the conclusions of the effort of Spencer of more than a half century before to base the curriculum on categories of vital life activities (with the possible exception of the second of the aims). Kingsley stopped short, however, of actually recommending the abandonment of the traditional subjects of the curriculum; instead, the report recommended that those subjects be reorganized so that each might achieve at least one of those indispensable life functions. In other words, those subjects were no longer included in the curriculum because they represented the major intellectual resources of our culture; they now became *instruments* by which future adults would acquire the skills to function efficiently in their daily lives. So far had the idea of a directly functional education progressed by 1918, when the Cardinal Principles report was published, that its recommendations were considered by some educational reformers to be unduly moderate. By that time scientific curriculum makers such as Franklin Bobbitt and W. W. Charters, as well as Snedden, were calling for the substitution of functional categories for the subjects themselves. Snedden, in fact, declared Kingsley's report to be "almost hopelessly academic."[55]

In other words, the concept of general education was being fundamentally redefined by American educational leaders in the first quarter of the twentieth century. All education was to be specific and directed toward specific purposes. Even vocational education had very limited generality. Snedden declared in 1924, for example,

Two . . . delusions yet persist in much of our unanalyzed educational theory. One is that somehow there can be some general education that is valuable for any and all vocations. The other, a much more modern one, is that vocations or even a vocation can be so taught as to produce large amounts of culture or of civism.[56]

Even in the realm of vocational education, Snedden argued, we make the mistake of trying to prepare general farmers instead of poultry growers. He was critical, for example, of John Dewey's failure to articulate a program of vocational education suited to modern social needs. "The modern world," he said, "divides and again subdivides its vocations," and a modern educational system will reflect that great specificity. The same could be said of civic education, cultural education, moral education, and "educations in the uses of foreign languages." Each required its own specific form of preparation. "Only educational mystics or obscurantists or, shall we say, 'fools' can say otherwise," Snedden insisted.[57] Not only were there thousands of different kinds of education, "every distinguishable species of education and, of each species, each distinguishable degree is or should be designed 'to meet a need' " with each need to be met controlled by "foreseen ends."[58]

As if such specificity were not enough, Snedden argued further that each education had to be designed particularly to fit the characteristics of the person to be educated (what he liked to call the "educand"). A truly scientific education could not be designed until the curriculum was adapted to the traits of those who would be educated, particularly to the social functions that they would one day perform as adults. Since people performed different functions according to such attributes as gender, class, and occupation, the skills to perform those functions had to be anticipated and ultimately incorporated into a supremely differentiated curriculum. Under these conditions, the idea of a general education was, practically speaking, a self-contradiction.

To be sure, Snedden's vision of a minutely differentiated curriculum was never completely realized, but the general idea of different educations for different population groups, variously defined, has taken firm root in modern American education.[59] Moreover, the idea persists that education should be designed with very specific purposes in mind. (Hence, the continued emphasis on stating educational objectives in highly specific terms.) It is clear that despite the call to create a common curriculum endorsed by such influential contemporary groups as the Carnegie Foundation,[60] diversity and particularity reign supreme in terms of school practice.

It would be an obvious oversimplification to say that Snedden's curriculum ideology merely prevailed over the idea that an education should be common to all regardless of future destination. It is more likely that an educational ideology controlled by specific but differentiated social and individual purposes was more congenial to an industrial society itself highly specialized and differentiated. Snedden was probably articulating (albeit in an extreme form) basic twentieth-century values. And one should not overlook the very real obstacles that school officials would face in declaring one form of education to be suitable for all, a policy that would fly in the face of such sacred American values as autonomy and choice.

Conclusion

The idea of a liberal education as a basis for general education in American schools is alive—but barely. The incorporation of science and other "moderns" into a conception of the liberal arts was not, in itself, sufficient to maintain its place in general education. Even the "new" liberal arts competed rather unsuccessfully with a conception of a curriculum that was seen as directly tied to the real business of life. While the liberal arts curriculum maintained its status as an ideal suited to a social (or at least an intellectual) elite who had the leisure to pursue it, a general education tied to efficient performance of life's tasks predominated for the many. The ancient dichotomy between labor and leisure with its implications for strong class divisions was thus maintained. Secondly, the internal reconstruction of the elements of a liberal education proceeded only haphazardly. For liberal education to be successful in an era of mass public education, not simply the addition or substitution of subjects, but a massive reconstruction of what we mean by the arts, literature, history, political economy, and even science had to be accomplished. The liberal arts curriculum, after all, had its origins in the belief that it was an education only for that aristocratic few who had the leisure it required. What had to be created was a path which the masses could also follow to the kind of intellectual liberation that modern advocates of a liberal education such as Arnold and Huxley foresaw.

In place of such a reconstruction, educational leaders such as Snedden advocated a differentiated curriculum designed to fit people specifically for the tasks they needed to perform. Specificity is the great enemy of a liberal education. As Charles Bailey recently expressed it, "The first justification for engaging people in liberal general education . . . is that its very rejection of *specific* utility, and its espousal of intrinsically worthwhile ends, provides the maximum and most general utility."[61] In rejecting specificity, then, the liberal arts does not reject utility; it seeks a broader and grander utility than is represented by the specific and the immediate. It is a utility that lies, broadly speaking, in the development of rationality and the freedom that rationality provides to discover *why* I should believe and act as I do. Moreover, the espousal of intrinsically worthwhile ends should not be equated with education that has no purpose. Ends that are intrinsic to knowing literature, history, and science are ends that can be reasonably associated with their study. They are not external to them. Spencer's convictions to the contrary, knowing Newton's second law of thermodynamics is no more necessary for self-preservation than a knowledge of Homer's *Iliad*. Science is a vital element in a liberal education, not because we as individuals survive through our knowledge of it, but because it is an extension of our need to know about the natural world. It is on principles such as these that a modern conception of the liberal arts, and a general education based on the liberal arts, may be rebuilt.

Notes

1. See, for example, Ayers Bagley, *Study and Love: Aristotle's Fall* (Minneapolis, MN: Society of Professors of Education, 1986).

2. Herbert Spencer, "On the Genesis of Science," in *Essays on Education* (New York: E. P. Dutton, 1910), p. 296.

3. Herbert Spencer, *Education: Intellectual, Moral and Physical* (New York: D. Appleton and Co., 1860), p. 117.

4. Ibid., pp. 1-2.

5. Ibid., p. 4.

6. Ibid., p. 11.

7. Ibid., pp. 13-14.

8. Ibid., p. 15.

9. Ibid., pp. 19-20.

10. Ibid., p. 22.

11. Ibid., p. 23.

12. Ibid., p. 25.

13. Ibid., p. 36.

14. Ibid., p. 40.

15. Ibid., p. 62.

16. Ibid., p. 63.

17. Ibid., pp. 84-85.

18. Thomas Henry Huxley, "A Liberal Education; and Where to Find It," in *Science and Education: Essays* (New York: D. Appleton and Co., 1896), p. 77.

19. Ibid., p. 78.

20. Ibid., p. 70.

21. Ibid.

22. Ibid., p. 83.

23. Ibid., p. 79.

24. See, for example, Charles S. Blinderman, "Semantic Aspects of T. H. Huxley's Literary Style," *Journal of Communication* 12 (1962): 171-178; Walter E. Houghton, "The Rhetoric of T. H. Huxley," *University of Toronto Quarterly* 18 (1949): 159-175.

25. Thomas Henry Huxley, "Science and Culture," in *Science and Education* (New York: D. Appleton and Co., 1899), p. 137.

26. Matthew Arnold, *Culture and Anarchy* (Cambridge: Cambridge University Press, 1960; [1869]), p. 69.

27. Ibid., p. 70.

28. Ibid.

29. Huxley, "Science and Culture," p. 149.

30. Ibid., p. 152.

31. Matthew Arnold, "Literature and Science," in *Discourses in America* (London: Macmillan and Co., 1885), pp. 94-95.

32. Ibid., p. 99.

33. Ibid., p. 125.

34. Ibid., p. 127.

35. Richard Hofstadter, *Social Darwinism in American Thought* (Boston: Beacon Press, 1944, 1955), p. 32.

36. William Graham Sumner, "State Interference," in *Social Darwinism*, ed. Stow Persons (Englewood Cliffs, NJ: Prentice-Hall, 1963), pp. 105-106.

37. Ibid., p. 109.

38. William Graham Sumner, "The Concentration of Wealth: Its Economic Justification" in *Social Darwinism*, ed. Persons, p. 151.

39. Ibid., p. 156.

40. Ibid., p. 157.

41. National Education Association, *Report of the Committee on Secondary School Studies* (Washington, DC: Government Printing Office, 1893).

42. Charles William Eliot, "What Is a Liberal Education?" in *Educational Reform* (New York: Century Company, 1898), pp. 97-101.

43. Ibid., pp. 101-104.

44. Ibid., pp. 104-109.

45. Ibid., p. 110.

46. Ibid.

47. John Francis Latimer, *What's Happened to Our High Schools?* (Washington, DC: Public Affairs Press, 1958), pp. 12-15.

48. Ibid., pp. 21-57.

49. Arthur G. Powell, Eleanor Farrar, and David K. Cohen, *The Shopping Mall High School: Winners and Losers in the Educational Marketplace* (Boston: Houghton Mifflin, 1985).

50. G. Stanley Hall, "The Natural Activities of Children as Determining the Industries in Early Education, II," in National Education Association, *Journal of Proceedings and Addresses* 43 (1904): 443.

51. G. Stanley Hall, "The Ideal School as Based on Child Study," in National Education Association, *Journal of Proceedings and Addresses* 40 (1901): 475.

52. Walter H. Drost, *David Snedden and Education for Social Efficiency* (Madison, Wis.: University of Wisconsin Press, 1967), p. 5.

53. David Snedden, "The Practical Arts in Liberal Education," *Educational Review* 43 (1912): 379.

54. National Education Association, *Cardinal Principles of Secondary Education: A Report of the Commission on the Reorganization of Secondary Education* (Washington, DC: Government Printing Office, 1918).

55. David Snedden, "Cardinal Principles of Secondary Education," *School and Society* 9 (1919): 522.

56. David Snedden, "The Relation of General to Vocational Education," in National Education Association, *Journal of Proceedings and Addresses* 62 (1924): 1003-1004.

57. David Snedden, "Progress Towards Sociologically Based Civic Education," *Journal of Educational Sociology* 3 (1929): 483.

58. Ibid., p. 485-486.

59. See, for example, Jeannie Oakes, *Keeping Track: How Secondary Schools Structure Inequality* (New Haven, CT: Yale University Press, 1985).

60. See, for example, Ernest Boyer, *High School: A Report of the Carnegie Foundation for the Advancement of Teaching* (New York: Harper and Row, 1983).

61. Charles Bailey, *Beyond the Present and Particular: A Theory of Liberal Education* (London: Routledge and Kegan Paul, 1984), p. 35.

Introduction to Chapter II

The following chapter continues the discussion of the problem of reconciling the concept of individual differences with the concept of a common curriculum. This problem confronts teachers daily. It is also a matter of concern for those responsible for curriculum planning for the school.

In the Yearbook from which this chapter is taken, the various contributors address this problem, some of them from the standpoint of their respective special fields (mathematics, natural science, language and literature, aesthetics and fine arts, social studies). In the final chapter of that volume, John I. Goodlad summarizes aspects of individuality that call for the attention of teachers and workers in the field of curriculum. He makes a case for both diversity and commonality in schooling. Drawing upon data from his comprehensive study of schooling, Goodlad documents critical problems that arise as schools attempt to provide a reasonably common curriculum and simultaneously to accommodate individual differences. He makes recommendations for the percentage of a high school student's time that could be devoted to various parts of the "common curriculum" and still leave time for the pursuit of individual interests. He asserts, however, that "most provisions for individual differences should be in the organization of groups and in pedagogy."

John I. Goodlad is Professor Emeritus at the University of Washington. He is also President of the Institute for Educational Inquiry. The following chapter is reprinted from the Society's 82nd Yearbook, Part 1, Individual Differences and the Common Curriculum, *edited by Gary D Fenstermacher and John I. Goodlad.*

CHAPTER II

Individuality, Commonality, and Curricular Practice

JOHN I. GOODLAD

This chapter addresses four questions. First, what general characteristics of individual differences among learners appear to be particularly significant for curriculum planning? Second, what considerations appear to call for balance in accommodating individuality on one hand and providing some commonality in curricula on the other? Third, what appears to be the current state of practice in elementary and secondary schooling with respect to these dual concerns? Fourth, what are some promising directions for adjusting apparent deficiencies and imbalances?

Most of the central issues pertaining to commonality and differentiation were discussed in previous chapters of the 82nd Yearbook and the relevant literature cited. Consequently, I endeavor to refrain from elaborating on these issues and to choose references particularly relevant to the points I seek to make. However, revisiting some themes is virtually unavoidable.

Individual Differences

Three aspects of individuality in particular call for attention in curricular practice. The first of these is the developmental differences among learners of the same age. These are pronounced among five- and six-year-olds coming to school for the first time. Given equal time to learn school fare, children progress at markedly different rates. Indeed, even given more time, some children continue to lag far behind those who advance most easily and rapidly. By the time students enter the junior high school, differences in academic attainment are so great that many administrators and teachers see little promise or practicality in grouping them randomly for instruction. Consequently, a common practice is to accommodate these differences by separating students into high-, middle-, and low-track classes.

Second, boys and girls coming into elementary schools already demonstrate different modes or styles of learning. Some take readily to symbols such as letters and numbers. Others relate more naturally to building and manipulating. Conventional wisdom suggests that some people are more hand-oriented than head-oriented in how they learn and what they do. Some critics of schooling maintain that the teaching is overly head-oriented, disadvantaging those who might progress successfully in academics if given greater opportunity to learn them through emphasis on manual and kinesthetic activities. Individual differences are met best, they maintain, not through those organizational arrangements which essentially accept the inevitability of gross differences in achievement but through creative pedagogy designed to capitalize on different learning styles.

The third major aspect of individuality pertains to differences in interests, goals, and life styles. Some of these individual differences, too, are pronounced by the time children enter the formal educational system. Interests can be ignored as irrelevant to a predetermined school curriculum; they can be used as vehicles to get to this curriculum; or they can be cultivated as the roots of lifelong pursuits. Preoccupation with what stance to take regarding the recognition of students' interests has led to alternative, usually conflicting, ideologies regarding the curriculum.

Although arguments for or against a common curriculum often interweave these three aspects of individuality, it is possible to sort out the relationship between each one and the curricular debate flowing from it. Educators and others who extrapolate recommendations directly from observed differences in learning rate and accomplishment usually argue for a common curriculum in the early years and an increasingly differentiated one in the later years, the later years coming at least by the senior high school grades. They would accommodate these differences by means of achievement grouping or continuous progress plans such as nongrading in a common elementary school curriculum.[1] Many would carry these arrangements into the secondary school while recognizing the necessity for curricular differentiation. Conant, for example, based some of his recommendations for the comprehensive high school on the assumption that courses in the "hard" sciences and mathematics, beyond the introductory ones, would be taken only by the most able students.[2] Vocational education courses frequently are proposed as alternatives to the more advanced classes in the academic subjects.

Some people are unwilling, however, to accept differences in learning rates as irrevocable "givens." They do not regard curricular differentiation as inevitable and argue for more powerful, sometimes varied, pedagogical interventions. Carroll has provided a model of the components to be manipulated, all of which—even the way he defines ability and aptitude—imply a potential for modification through instruction.[3] The model is basic to Bloom's concept of mastery learning and the strategies he proposes for reducing the ratios of the difference in achievement among learners engaged in a common curriculum without slowing down those who initially take most readily to academic work.[4] There will come a time, he says, when we will not classify students as good, poor, fast, or slow learners. Bruner's heuristic, "We begin with the hypothesis that any subject can be taught effectively in some intellectually honest form to any child at any stage of development,"[5] would become more than a thesis; it would be a description of reality. The benefits of a common curriculum would become commonly attainable.

But, others argue, is not a commonly encountered set of learnings a denial of individual uniqueness? Schools are all too common in what they do. The result is a squeezing out of what does not conform to the ways of schooling, a denial of what does not fit the mold, and, all too often, alienation of those who come to see themselves as not conforming, sometimes to the point of perceiving themselves as having little worth. These critics maintain that individual interests and talents should be cultivated as ends and not merely exploited as means to achieve uniform goals for all. A society such as ours provides many opportunities for the utilization of this diversity.

The Case for Both Diversity and Commonality in Curricula

Except for some persons at the extreme edges of the debate, those who argue for a common curriculum and those who favor differentiation share some common ground—namely, that everyone must learn the fundamental processes of reading, writing, and figuring. During the past thirty years, criticism of the schools has fueled two distinct "back-to-basics" swings. Each has followed perceived overemphasis on individual differences, personal development, and the like. The swing back, in each instance, has been accompanied by little disagreement on the necessity of schools teaching the fundamentals.

The strip of shared ground diminishes in size, however, as agreement is sought regarding what is fundamental. During the 1970s, some legislatures sought to have the curriculum include what was sufficiently fundamental to support with state funds. Usually, they ended up with a broad set of goals encompassing most ways of knowing and all major domains of knowledge, including the arts. In a comprehensive inquiry entitled "A Study of Schooling," my colleagues and I analyzed goal statements in documents sent to us by all of the fifty chief state school officers.[6] We found explicit commitments in virtually all states to four broad goal areas: academic, social and civic, vocational, and personal. Nowhere did we find assertions that these were for some students or schools but not others. The implication is, rather, that the elementary and secondary schools of all states are to provide a broad, comprehensive program of studies for all students.

What these documents do not make explicit, however, is either the balance of attention to each subject to be experienced by each student or the variability of choice to be made available in seeking, for example, to develop individual talents. One would expect small schools to be sharply restricted in the choices available and that all schools would need to make decisions regarding what is most important to know and, therefore, to provide. The guiding criterion, presumably, if we take the state goals seriously, is that the things most worth learning are worth knowing by everyone. Optionality, to the degree provided, should not detract from commonality but extend beyond.

But this still leaves us with the issues of what and how much is to be encountered commonly and of how much of what is to be generally common is to be specifically common. One can argue persuasively that all citizens should understand something about the history of their country, but what is this "something" and must everyone encounter all of it? If "some" is enough, when does *just* some become not enough?

It begins to become obvious that the answers to these and related questions are relative; they never will be answered absolutely or finally. The best we can hope for is that the questions always will command our attention and that school programs are the result not of omission but of decisions of commission. It is my view that these questions have a relatively low place in decisions of educational policy and practice and that the answers are as much or more the product of omission than commission.

Rational processes of curricular decision making should be guided by a conception of why we have schools—of what schools are for. Schools should do what the rest of the society does not do well and what individuals and society very much need. Schwab reminds us that homes and families cultivate individuality: in language, values, goals, habits, level of self-esteem, and the like. The school, he argues, must be somewhat countervailing in assuring common awareness of the wider political and human community. The ideal to be sought is a kind of balanced tension between the centrifugal tendencies of homes (differing in ethnicity, national origin, religion, and social class) and the centripetal tendencies of schools (pressing toward greater homogeneity).[7] In the United States today, the growing diversity of homes, the increasing complexity of life, and the high entry levels of most vocations combine to raise the floor of what must be accomplished commonly in schools.

Simultaneously, our increased knowledge of individual differences and individuality demand more creative, sophisticated, professional approaches to engaging learners in common curricula extending beyond elementary education. If knowledge is to be increasingly democratized—that is, extended to larger percentages of the population for longer periods of time—then it simultaneously must be increasingly humanized—that is, rendered in such way as to be learnable. In effect, increasing the commonality of curricula calls for increasing the uncommonality or diversity of pedagogy.

A Review of Current Practice

There is growing evidence to suggest that practice in schools, especially at the secondary level, is virtually the opposite of what I am suggesting above as desirable. That is, pedagogy is quite uniform and becomes more so as curricular diversity increases at junior and senior high levels. In his chapter in the 82nd Yearbook, Kirst calls for state policies to control what he perceives to be a chaotic curriculum resulting from a relaxation in college and university entrance requirements and an elective system run rampant. The heads of several studies of high schools now underway have signaled their preliminary concern with curricular diversity.[8]

The findings of "A Study of Schooling" reveal both extraordinary lack of variety in pedagogy and persistent patterns of both commonality and uncommonality in the curricular encounters of students, this overall picture becoming more pronounced with progression upward from elementary to secondary grades. Based on observations in 887 secondary classes (with two to three complete observations in each), we conclude that the teachers used, on the average, only two different techniques and grouping configurations. The students were either listening to the teacher or working on assignments in large groups or as a total class.[9] These same procedures were very much in evidence, also, in the 129 elementary classes we observed (for two or three full days each), except that classes at the primary level almost consistently were divided into groups (usually three) for reading and mathematics. Primary and, to a lesser degree, upper-elementary teachers interspersed their talking or lecturing and monitoring of seatwork with two or three alternative procedures.

Lacking at all levels were the kinds of activities and teacher behaviors one tends to associate with awareness of and attention to individuals as persons and learners. Just under 2 percent of the instructional time spent by the secondary teachers in interacting with students involved corrective feedback (and only a fraction of this small percentage involved some guidance as to what to do about errors). At the elementary level, this average percentage increased to less than 3 percent. Teacher-student interaction, almost all of which was initiated by teachers, was overwhelmingly neutral in regard to affective tone. Students seldom were singled out for doing a good job, for contributing to class morale, or for scolding. We estimate that, overall, neutral (or flat and unemotional) affect characterized the classroom environment over 95 percent of the time.

Conspicuously absent from or at least grossly underrepresented in classes, especially above the primary level, were activities associated with students' own goal setting, problem solving, collaborative learning, autonomous thinking, creativity, and the like—behaviors identified over and over in the state documents previously mentioned. Only occasionally was there a class or group delving curiously into the characteristics of another culture or excitedly anticipating the outcomes of an experiment, conditions we so readily and idealistically attach to studies in the social and physical sciences. The methods in mathematics and the language arts were those most commonly displayed in the social studies and science classes. Indeed, the major differences were in the subject matter of the textbooks used, but not in the format and the kinds of questions to be answered at the end of the chapters or in teachers' quizzes.

It appears that, if there is anything about schooling that justifies the cliché "a school is a school is a school," it is the pedagogy commonly in use. If there is anything in common that students take away from their experience in schools, it is most likely to be a mental picture of how classrooms are conducted. Because the class-to-class variation in the techniques of instruction is so unvarying, it is likely that graduates carry away, too, an overlapping image of both what is and what should be. At any rate, students appeared passively content, generally reacting quite favorably to the "telling" mode of their teachers, a conclusion supported by our earlier study of the first four grades.[10] Also, data gathered in "A Study of Schooling" add up to the observation that teachers teach very much as they were taught through sixteen or more years of student life. Their professional education and subsequent experience appear not to jar them loose from equating the way teaching is with the way teaching should be.

There appeared to be a rather comfortable fit between certain pedagogical and curricular commonalities. We examined the contents of courses of study, textbooks, and teacher-prepared instructional materials used by our sample of 1,350 teachers. Three characteristics, in particular, caught our attention. First, the courses of study or curriculum guides tended not to sort out threads of common emphases, whether in the form of student behaviors or concepts and principles inherent in the subject fields, from topics likely to prove useful in developing these emphases. In other words, a concept such as interdependence was not differentiated from the topics one might choose from the social and natural sciences for purposes of teaching such a concept. There were not inferences to suggest that teaching interdependence might be something commonly expected of the schools, whereas choice of the topics for so doing might vary with location of the community and resources available.

Second, all types of curricular materials generally neglected or downplayed long-term curricular continuity. Topics followed topics by grades and shorter intervals but the threads connecting them—what curriculum specialists refer to as "organizing elements"—were obscured or missing. Compounding the first characteristic—namely, the confusion of ends and means or the nondifferentiation of examples and basic concepts, skills, and values—was a specification of topics to be covered. Implicitly, the nature of the courses of study and instructional materials encouraged the mode of teaching we found to dominate.

If the implication had been that students were to inquire into the nature of energy, for example, and might study magnets, batteries, air movement, or the actions of streams and waterfalls as alternative means to gain insight, we might have found teachers beginning with students' interests and past experiences instead of with the topics laid out for them. If students are required to learn about magnets, why pretend that they might exercise choice among alternative topics? And why not get the information across as quickly and directly as possible? Support of the assumptions imbedded in both questions gives credence to a theory of teaching and a set of teaching practices which dominate staff development programs today and go largely unchallenged.

The third characteristic of these curricular materials pertained to the clear fit between this topical specification and organization of what was to be taught, the exercises to be performed on concluding a topic or a segment of it, and teachers' quizzes. Rarely were students called upon to integrate information derived from many sources (in an essay, for example). Rarely were they called upon to read extensively beyond the textbook or for other than purposes of attaining specific information. The acquisition of rather easily tested information becomes a dominant "good," reinforced by teaching method, course of study, instructional material, and testing. Indeed, even the research on time on instruction and time on task and the relationship of these and other factors to student achievement tends to support and conform to this interlocking paradigm. The net impact appears to be a highly uniform set of expectations and activities for all students. But these tend not to be what primarily attract the attention of those persons seeking greater curricular variability, even though they are potentially powerful ammunition for their cause.

Variability sought in the name of providing for individual differences often pertains to curricular content, and here we found both considerable uncommonality and cause for alarm. There was substantial school-to-school variability in the use of time and distribution of the teaching staff to subject fields. And there was substantial within-school variability regarding the courses taken and content experienced by secondary-level students. Rather than assuaging my concerns about schools' provisions for individual differences among students, these curricular differentiations raised serious questions in my mind about the degree to which our schools assure equity regarding students' access to knowledge.

Curricular differences among elementary schools appeared to be a concomitant of efficient time utilization. We added up and averaged for each school the total time each class was in an instructional mode or setting for the various subject fields. (We recognize that classes vary in the degree to which this time is divided among handling routines, disciplining the class, or instruction and formal learning. But our intent here was simply to get an overall quantitative measure). School-to-school differences proved to be surprisingly great: from a low of 18.6 hours a week at Newport to a high of 27.5 at Dennison. The average number of hours for children to be in an instructional setting for our sample of elementary schools was 22.4.

It is clear from our data that all of these schools placed a high value on mathematics and language arts (reading, spelling, writing, and so forth). On the average, these subjects combined took up an average of 54 percent of class time. The remaining 46 percent was distributed among social studies, science, physical education, and the arts. Dennison, with 27.5 hours available, was able to give generous attention to social studies and science—about an hour to each daily. But Newport, with only 18.6 hours available each week, devoted less than two hours of this to social studies and just over an hour, or about 13 minutes daily, to science.

It appears that elementary school children could experience in common the entire array of subject fields implied by the goals cited previously. Even an average instructional week produced in our sample an average of 90 minutes in the language arts and 54 minutes in mathematics each day. Children did not necessarily experience less time in these subjects when the total work week was shorter but, obviously, something had to give. Equally obvious, when school and home cooperated to get the children to class on time and when school personnel stayed close to the amount of time scheduled for recess and lunch and kept clean-up time to a minimum, ample time for all subjects opened up. Curricular inequities resulted in part from school-to-school differences in the management of time. These inequities are evidence of a gap between practice and our rhetoric regarding the desirability of a reasonably common curriculum at the elementary school level.

At the secondary level, we examined the distribution of teachers to subjects as an indicator of curricular commonality or uncommonality. We added up the courses offered in each subject and, after adjusting for number and length of class periods, converted the total into full-time teacher equivalents (F.T.E.s). One could argue from the averaged results that the curricula of our schools were well balanced, except for a deficiency in the teaching of foreign languages. The percentages of F.T.E.s distributed to the several subjects at the junior high level were as follows: 22 percent to English, 17 percent to mathematics, 14 percent to social studies, 13 percent to science, 11 percent to vocational education, 11 percent to the arts, 10 percent to physical education, and 2 percent to foreign languages. The senior high average distribution was as follows: 24 percent to vocational education (a doubling over the junior high allocation), 18 percent to English, 13 percent to mathematics, 13 percent to social studies, 11 percent to science, 9 percent to physical education, 8 percent to the arts, and 4 percent to foreign languages.

We might quarrel with the marked gain for vocational education at the expense of all other subjects except foreign languages. But a greater concern arises when one looks at the data school by school. Let me use only the senior highs to illustrate. At Euclid, 41 percent of the teachers were in vocational education—just slightly less than the total for English, mathematics, science, social studies, and foreign languages. At Newport, teachers in these five fields totaled 62 percent of the teaching force, as contrasted to only 13 percent in vocational education. School-to-school differences in the distribution of teachers to each academic subject were not this extreme but they were substantial, with the percentage of teachers allocated to science, for example, at one school being double the percentage at another.

One would like to believe that marked school-to-school curricular differences resulting from the allocations of teachers were the product of careful, rational decisions. For example, one might expect an urban school serving a low socioeconomic community to stress vocational education, particularly in the senior high school years. Neither Fairfield nor Euclid, with 42 percent and 41 percent, respectively, of their teachers allocated to vocational education, is an urban school serving a low-income group. Rosemont High, with the lowest family income in our sample, is an urban school. Its vocational education program takes up 21 percent of the teaching force—slightly below average for the sample and half the Fairfield and Euclid allocations.

I failed to find in the schools visited either awareness of and concern about the vital issues of teacher allocation and its impact on the overall curriculum or a process of analyzing data regarding the curriculum of individual students. Principals, counselors, and teachers with whom I talked often were puzzled about my questions regarding school practices and arrangements which might make it difficult for some students to gain access to various curricular alternatives. This was the case even in schools where members of the staff expressed satisfaction and even pride over their interest and success in providing for individual differences. For example, I frequently encountered principals, counselors, and vocational education teachers who took pride in the preparation for and placement in jobs of students lacking an academic bent. "How long might students delay," I asked, "before beefing up vocationally oriented curricula with the academic courses generally required for college admission?" "Not later than the end of the sophomore year," I was told, unless the student was prepared to take time beyond the normal period required for graduation.

Do curricular adaptations of the kind I was inquiring into represent sound provision for individual differences or educational abandonment of individuals? The data we gathered on within-school curriculum variability suggest to me the latter conclusion.

Most of the secondary schools, both junior and senior high, made two major curricular adjustments to encompass or provide for student variability in academic attainment and assumed ability. The first was a separation into two broad divisions—one primarily academic and the other heavily vocational. The second was a division of courses into high, middle, and low tracks. Neither, usually, was the result of clearly articulated policy. Rather, both served as organizational, curricular, and pedagogical devices for accommodating substantial differences in the academic progress of the student body.

In most of the secondary schools we studied there was not an articulated policy or plan for assuring each student balanced exposure to the major curricular domains. Only rarely did I encounter the view (and commensurate practice) that all students should enroll in vocational education classes as part of their general education. Indeed, academically oriented students seeking such classes usually were blocked from them by schedules or because they lacked prerequisites for what often proved to be a sequence of courses in a job-training program (for example, cosmetology). Vocationally oriented students in turn frequently took their academic courses together, because of scheduling problems, track placement, or both. Various internal assumptions and arrangements conspired to segregate students according to academic accomplishments or career goals. There was, it turned out, a disproportionately large percentage of students from low-income families in job-oriented vocational programs, a disproportionately large proportion of whom were from minority groups in those schools made up of mixed racial populations.[11]

The secondary schools in our sample were predominantly tracked in the four basic subjects usually required for college admission: mathematics, English, social studies, and science. That is, students were assigned to high, middle, or low sections of the several subjects. It generally is assumed that this separation is designed to facilitate their differential rate of speed through the material. What is much less often assumed is that tracking creates other significantly differentiated provisions.

We analyzed hundreds of these tracked classes and ferreted out some of what went on in them. First, the differences in the content taught in high-track classes as compared with low-track classes in mathematics and English were such as to suggest virtually different subjects in the two tracks studied.[12] In English, high-track students read standard works of literature, engaged in expository writing, used grammar in language analyses, and prepared for the Scholastic Aptitude Test. They spent part of their learning time engaged in making judgments, drawing inferences, effecting syntheses, and using symbolism. Their teachers included in lists of what they were trying to teach such things as self-direction, creativity, and critical thinking.

Low-track classes in English were far more likely to be found practicing basic reading skills and the mechanics of language, writing simple narratives, and learning to fill out forms. They spent more time listening to their teachers than did students in the high tracks; there was a great deal more rote learning. Their teachers listed for them expectations of conforming: working quietly, being punctual, improving study habits, getting along with others, and obeying rules and regulations.

But these were not the only differences. Teaching practices upheld in the literature as most conducive to learning were observed most frequently in the upper tracks and least frequently in the lower; and practices associated negatively with student satisfaction and achievement were perceived most frequently in the lower tracks. Teachers in the upper tracks were clearer in their directions, more enthusiastic, more likely to give feedback with guidance, and perceived by students to be less punitive and more concerned about them as individuals. Students in high-track classes were more positive about their class experiences: they reported the highest levels of peer esteem and the lowest level of disruption and hostility among their classmates.

In several significant respects, then, students supposedly studying the same subjects were encountering different content, pedagogy, and class climate. The opportunities to gain access to knowledge were not at all the same or equal, the differences favoring students gaining greatest success in academic studies. And these upper-track students were disproportionately from the higher-income families and white.

It is worth noting that the heterogeneous classes (of randomly mixed student achievement and ability) in our sample more closely resembled the upper than the lower tracks in the several characteristics described. This is contrary to the conventional wisdom, which supports the belief that mixed classes tend to deteriorate in most respects to a lowest common denominator of expectations, pedagogy, and accomplishment, even though tracking has not been shown through research to be commonly beneficial. Increasingly, it appears, the burden of proof is on tracking, not mixed grouping.

I have provided in the foregoing only a sketchy account of data from "A Study of Schooling" that are relevant to this chapter. To the degree the schools studied are representative of schools generally, the data suggest several critical problem areas regarding the goal of providing a reasonably common curriculum and simultaneously accommodating individual differences among students. First, there is little consciousness among local school authorities and personnel regarding the need to provide a curriculum balanced among the goals of schooling and the domains of knowledge. Second, there is little in the guidelines and specifications of courses of study and textbooks to assure that the central elements of subject matter and ways of knowing will be commonly emphasized. Third, the commonly practiced ways of accommodating individual differences, clearly revealed in the tracking practices of secondary schools, appear more to sacrifice and penalize individuals than to cultivate their individuality. Fourth, the apparent between-school and within-school curricular and pedagogical differences create inequities, some of which are associated with low-income and minority status.

Some Directions for Improvement

Given the difficulties of considering in limited space ways of addressing all of these problem areas, I limit myself primarily to the goal of achieving for all students in elementary and secondary schools reasonably well-balanced access to the major domains of knowledge and knowing. In the process, I endeavor to suggest some degrees of freedom for accommodating differences in the three aspects of individuality discussed at the outset.

The Harvard Report, *General Education in a Free Society*, published in 1945, identified "five fingers" of human knowledge and organized experience: mathematics and science, literature and language, society and social studies, the arts, and the vocations.[13] I doubt that a similar committee appointed today would come up with a markedly different framework for a general, liberal program of studies. Inclusion of the vocations was forward-looking and gave Conant a dimension needed for the comprehensive high school he recommended in 1959.[14] There was substantial provision for vocational education in the junior high schools we studied and this field took up the largest number of teachers, on the average, among the senior highs. The rest of the curriculum at both levels was distributed among the other "fingers" plus physical education. But the gross variations among schools suggest the need for some guiding policies.

I resist the most commonly exercised guidelines—namely, college admission requirements—which constitute a meat-axe approach. The curricula of the high schools of California, for example, are being shoved about to meet the new admission requirements of the University of California, approved in 1982. Yet, only 4 percent of current secondary school enrollees, according to recent statistics, are likely to attend the University.

What is required as both a necessary confronting of first questions and some protection against the time-worn intrusions on sound curriculum planning is a definition of general education for children and youth. Some potentially useful definitions exist; there is no need to build them anew. The history of the emergence of four broad educational areas in goals for our schools—academic, social/civic, vocational, and personal—provides an initial consensus on breadth of commitment.[15] The Harvard Report and similar efforts, which differ only modestly in their outcomes, translate this commitment into substance. The rhetoric accompanying statements of state goals and most reports such as those of the Harvard Committee make clear that the domains are for all students—commonly and equally. Individual schools have no right to deny students access to some common learnings in these domains, to so emphasize one or two as to squeeze out the arts, or to train some students for jobs to the denial of vocational education for those who may not apply the learnings to a job but probably will use them as homemakers. How do we assure the implied access without the indiscriminate imposition of curricular requirements on all schools to satisfy the demands of special interest groups such as the faculty and trustees of tertiary institutions?

Let us specify, at the state level, percentages and degrees of freedom for each of the domains. I'll not quarrel over a few percentage points either way but here is my prescription for a four-year secondary curriculum (part of a reorganized continuum of early childhood, elementary, and secondary education which I describe elsewhere[16]): 18 percent of a student's program to literature and language (English and other); 18 percent to mathematics and science; 15 percent to each of the other three fingers; and 10 percent to physical education. This gives us a total of 91 percent of a student's total curricular time. The guidelines would permit a variation of up to 20 percent—which means that a student could take as much as 18 percent or as little as 12 percent in the arts, for example. Two students of quite different abilities and interests in mathematics, for instance, might take as much as 21 percent of their programs in mathematics and science, one taking an advanced course or two and the other seeking mastery in the common part of this domain. But neither student would be permitted either to opt out of the common portion or to stress one domain at the expense of any other. Simultaneously, teachers would be prevented from deciding to rule out the arts for a student for purposes of doing make-up work in English.

By adhering precisely to the recommended percentages or electing a downward variance of 20 percent in several domains, a student would leave free from 9 percent to 20 percent of his or her curriculum. This would be used for talent development in the arts, an academic subject such as mathematics, or sports. Students would be provided with vouchers for purposes of purchasing instruction in the public or private sector: college classes for advanced mathematics, a private tutor for instruction in singing, a professional trainer for swimming.

Bloom has effectively described and contrasted the unique differences between conditions promoting the development of talent and those employed to promote learning in schools.[17] The former emerges out of a fully supporting environment, modeled practice with immediate feedback, performance before an audience, and association with a like-minded peer group. Mastery and the development of personal style ultimately emerge. Surely the resulting satisfaction brings enrichment to the individual and, to a degree, carries one through the necessary demands of less preferred learnings. The potential for talent transcends socioeconomic level, ethnicity, and race. And so should provision for its development.

Beyond these curricular arrangements for both commonality and diversity, most provisions for individual differences should be in the organization of groups and in pedagogy. Our findings in "A Study of Schooling" revealed those schools that were in the top quartile for satisfaction and nearly all other characteristics to be almost invariably among the smallest in our sample; those in the bottom quartile on these same characteristics were among the largest. The studies of Barker and

Gump suggest the greater involvement of students in school affairs in small schools and their greater alienation in large ones.[18] A recent summary of research reports a falling off in curricular and economic advantages often assumed to be associated with larger schools, occurring in the 400 to 500 range in enrollment for elementary schools and the 600 to 800 range at the secondary level.[19] I often have feared that increased school size brought with it not only anonymity and alienation for teachers and students alike but also an invitation for electives to multiply with abandon. When Conant recommended a graduating class of 100 to assure the curriculum he wanted, surely he was not implying that bigger was necessarily better.

To secure for students a sense of identity, belonging, and closeness to teachers, I recommend that schools be kept small—below 400, 600, and 800 students at the three successive levels, respectively. Instead, we are closing our small schools! I recommend, further, that clusters of teachers and aides (up to four or five full-time equivalents in elementary schools and six or seven full-time equivalents in secondary schools), each including a head teacher, be associated with a group of from 100 to 150 students over the entire four-year span of a primary, elementary, or secondary phase of schooling. Each cluster would plan and provide the entire curriculum, except for the talent development sector. From twenty to thirty students would enter and a corresponding number would leave each of these largely self-contained units each year. Given the four years of association, teachers and students together would provide the support, analyses, and specific assistance required. The goal of assuring the learning of everyone else would parallel the goal of personal accomplishment in all domains except the sixth—the one reserved exclusively for developing the special interests and talents of individuals.

It is easy to envision in the environments proposed provision for attenuating the progress of gifted students and alleviating the deficiencies of those experiencing learning difficulties. Surely, administrators and teachers would not resort to the heavy-handedness of tracking. I hesitate to call for state-wide abolition of tracking, as has taken place in Sweden, simply because we resort too frequently to legislated solutions, whether or not well-advised.

I am seeking not either-or, familiar solutions to old and much argued issues but, rather, approaches that have at their heart the individual worth and welfare of persons engaged in the vital pursuit of education. Learning and doing common things commonly constitutes the essence of community, whether in school or out of it.

NOTES

1. An extreme position, reserved primarily for students disinterested in and ill-disposed to profiting from what schools have to offer—to the point of disrupting others who wish to learn—is to remove deviating individuals from school. See Robert L. Ebel, "What Are Schools For?" *Phi Delta Kappan* 54 (September 1972): 7.

2. James B. Conant, *The American High School Today* (New York: McGraw-Hill, 1959).

3. John B. Carroll, "A Model of School Learning," *Teachers College Record* 64 (May 1963): 723-33.

4. Benjamin S. Bloom, *All Our Children Learning* (New York: McGraw-Hill, 1981).

5. Jerome S. Bruner, *The Process of Education* (Cambridge, Mass.: Harvard University Press, 1960), p. 33.

6. Information from this study, providing probably the largest data bank on schools available to date, is drawn on extensively in this chapter. For a full report, see John I. Goodlad, *A Place Called School* (New York: McGraw-Hill, 1983).

7. Joseph J. Schwab, "Education and the State: Learning Community," in *The Great Ideas Today* (Chicago: Encyclopaedia Britannica, 1976), p. 235.

8. Educational Development Center, *American Schools Today and Tomorrow: A Summary of Eighteen Key Research Projects* (Newton, Mass.: The Center, 1981).

9. For a report on the findings, see Kenneth A. Sirotnik, *What You See Is What You Get: A Summary of Observations in Over 1000 Elementary and Secondary Classrooms*, Technical Report no. 29, A Study of Schooling (Los Angeles: Laboratory in School and Community Education, Graduate School of Education, University of California, 1981).

10. John I. Goodlad, M. Frances Klein, and Associates, *Looking Behind the Classroom Door* (Worthington, Ohio: Charles A. Jones Publishing Co., 1974).

11. Jeannie Oakes, *Limiting Opportunity: Student Race and Curricular Differences in Secondary Vocational Education*, Technical Report no. 28, A Study of Schooling (Los Angeles: Laboratory in School and Community Education, Graduate School of Education, University of California, 1981).

12. Jeannie Oakes, *A Question of Access: Tracking and Curriculum Differentiation in a National Sample of English and Mathematics Classes*, Technical Report no. 24, A Study of Schooling (Los Angeles: Laboratory in School and Community Education, Graduate School of Education, University of California, 1981).

13. Report of the Harvard Committee, *General Education in a Free Society* (Cambridge, Mass.: Harvard University Press, 1945), p. 102.

14. Conant, *The American High School Today.*

15. See John I. Goodlad, *What Schools Are For* (Bloomington, Ind.: Phi Delta Kappa Educational Foundation, 1979), pp. 46-52.

16. Goodlad, *A Place Called School.*

17. Benjamin S. Bloom and Lauren A. Sosniak, "Talent Development vs. Schooling," *Educational Leadership* 39 (November 1981): 86-94.

18. R. G. Barker and P. V. Gump, *Big School, Small School* (Stanford, Calif.: Stanford University Press, 1964).

19. John Ainley et al., *Resource Allocation in the Government Schools of Australia and New Zealand* (Melbourne, Australia: Australian Education Council, in press).

Introduction to Chapter III

The way teachers and curriculum specialists think about curriculum and about curriculum development has a significant influence on curricular decisions. This point is highlighted in the following chapter by Elizabeth Vallance, who identifies four alternative "systems of curriculum thought" and shows how each of these systems offers a different array of choices to the program planner. She then explores the implications for curriculum development of a quite different way of thinking about curriculum—one that is based on the concept of multiple ways of knowing.

We include this chapter because it deals with a way of thinking about curriculum that has attracted the interest of educators for whom the idea of multiple ways of knowing has a strong appeal. The chapter also provides an excellent example of how assumptions underlying various approaches to curriculum can be examined and how the consequences of making those assumptions can be assessed. This process of examining assumptions can be an instructive exercise for teachers and curriculum specialists, for it is a process that can help to make explicit the reasons for curricular decisions and thus make the act of teaching meaningful for both teachers and students.

Elizabeth Vallance is Director of Education at the St. Louis Art Museum. The following chapter is taken from the Society's 84th Yearbook, Part 2, Learning and Teaching the Ways of Knowing, *edited by Elliot Eisner.*

CHAPTER III

Ways of Knowing and Curricular Conceptions: Implications for Program Planning

ELIZABETH VALLANCE

Introduction: Useful and Ornamental Knowledge

A musician and a mathematics teacher, late one night after a rehearsal for a community theater production in which both are involved, have the following conversation. The musician speaks first.

> "Oho, I know what you are. You are an advocate of Useful Knowledge."
> "Certainly."
> "You say that a man's first job is to earn a living, and that the first task of education is to equip him for that job?"
> "Of course."
> "Well, allow me to introduce myself to you as an advocate of Ornamental Knowledge. You like the mind to be a neat machine, equipped to work efficiently, if narrowly, and with no extra bits or useless parts. I like the mind to be a dustbin of scraps of brilliant fabric, odd gems, worthless but fascinating curiosities, tinsel, quaint bits of carving, and a reasonable amount of healthy dirt. Shake the machine and it goes out of order; shake the dustbin and it adjusts beautifully to its new position" [1]

A distinction between Useful and Ornamental Knowledge is in many ways familiar to us. It parallels other dichotomies with which school people and the public struggle in setting priorities from the national to the individual school level. It echoes, for example, distinctions between required courses and electives, the basics and "frills," the core curriculum and its complements. These and other formulations attempt to make the necessary distinctions between what needs to be taught in school and what does not. But like most dichotomies imposed on complex subjects, a distinction between

Useful and Ornamental Knowledge is deceptively simple, and the dangers of using it as a basis of choice are many.

It will be helpful to bear in mind, in the course of this discussion, the situation of the two participants in the conversation reported above. The musician is a flamboyant character, church organist and choral director, a private teacher dedicated to music and active in community activities, including now the local production of *The Tempest*. The schoolteacher is passionately dedicated to mathematics and excels at teaching it. His encounter with the musician is, we gather, something of a first for him: his dedication to the useful knowledge of mathematics has been absolute. His role with the theater is that of an accountant.

But is mathematics *only* useful knowledge? And does it function best as an orderly machine? At first glance it would seem so; many in the educational community and among the public would agree. This chapter will turn on the curricular implications of several traditional distinctions available to curriculum planners. We shall see that the distinction between the useful and the ornamental is not a clear one, and that there are other choices than those between machines and dustbins. The rich variety of the ways of knowing would help both the musician and the mathematician to see their positions more clearly; certainly the lessons suggested by the multiple ways of knowing can help educators to refine the various distinctions by which they guide the choices they are able to make in planning educational programs.

The Uses of Conceptual Maps in Program Planning

It is customary to attack a curriculum-planning problem by first identifying the choices available within the prevailing conception of "curriculum" guiding the discussion. The conception of curriculum underlying a planning effort may simply be a given. This might be the case, for example, in developing the vocational skills program of a technical school where job placement in trades or industry is the accepted goal: the questions of which skills to teach and at what levels would presume consensus on the more basic questions of the dominant conception of curriculum held by the staff and community. Likewise, most basic questions may have been resolved long ago in a college-preparatory private school where the chief goal is to assure that its graduates are accepted into exclusive liberal arts colleges: the basic questions of the purposes of the school are not regularly open to debate.

Precisely because so much of the deliberation about the curriculum at practical levels can take certain decisions for granted, educators are not accustomed to clarifying the conceptual/philosophical lines along which their curriculum choices should be made. Few educators, after all, have the luxury of building a complete curriculum anew; that educators infrequently question the very bases of their enterprise is thus scarcely surprising. But the infrequency of the activity merely underscores the importance of being able to approach problems freshly when the opportunity does arise. It is in this activity of questioning the prevailing conceptions of curriculum that educators can come closest to making genuine changes in the educational system. For these reasons it is imperative that program planners have a firm and clear grasp both on a full array of choices and on the implications of each.

The choices available to educators are constrained by tradition, and the ways in which we define educational problems to begin with are constrained in the same way. Assumptions—or even conclusions reached after long debate—about what knowledge is of most worth have guided our curricular choices in one way or another for centuries, with school programs developed and reshaped continually along lines of subject matter and academic disciplines. Discussion of curriculum choices may well be colored by other principles (for example, by purposes of the economic betterment of immigrants or by conceptions of the mind as a machine to be refined), but by and large our program planning choices are shaped by an allegiance to the disciplines that was clarified during the Renaissance and has not been seriously challenged in the intervening centuries. The distinctions between college-preparatory and vocational curricula may be described in terms of which areas of knowledge are to be mastered. College "majors" follow strict departmental lines dividing the disciplines; even the exceptions to the strict rule tacitly accept it, offering "inter-disciplinary" majors or "general majors" acknowledged to cover a number of disciplines equally. Graduate and postgraduate studies continue the specialization on the disciplines as content—to be mastered, developed, applied, but always respected as knowledge *of* something. Our conceptions of knowledge, of the educated person, of expertise tend overwhelmingly to be phrased in terms of *what* is known.

Program planning choices phrased chiefly as choices among subject areas are necessary choices; selection from among the whole array of disciplines available within the western cultural tradition must indeed be defended on some grounds consistent with the school's overall purpose. The tradition of building curricula around the disciplines is one with which both educators and the general public are comfortable. Indeed most curriculum reforms refer to modifications of subject matter: adding sex education courses or modifying the subject matter to include creationist views of history are recent examples.

What may not be evident to educational planners is the extent to which an emphasis on content limits our conception of what education can be. Put a slightly different way, it is not always apparent to participants in program planning discussions just how small a subset of educational possibilities the traditional approach to curriculum structure is. Lacking any impetus to ask fundamental questions of purpose and direction, and therefore any immediate need for a conceptual system that might illustrate the broader context of our present choices, it is all too easy for educators to suppose that they are in fact addressing all the alternatives they need to consider. They may suppose that they have a map of an entire city, when in fact their map shows only a single street.

To the array of curricular choices now available, the expanded conception of the varieties of ways of knowing adds an invaluable and enriching new dimension. The extent to which the additional choices provided by this new perspective on knowledge will enhance educators' abilities to develop powerful and creative new programs is not yet known; much will depend on how broadly this conception of knowledge is accepted within the educational community. Much, too, will depend on the research it stimulates and the nature of the refinements of the general concepts offered here. If conceptions of knowledge outlined in other chapters of the 84th Yearbook survive the scrutiny of epistemologists, learning researchers, and practitioners and if experience with these ways of knowing demonstrates their power both as research tools in education and as guides to practice, then their implications for program planning could be substantial. The task of this chapter is to demonstrate the probable scope of possibilities admitted by a perspective on human knowing not previously accepted by educational practitioners.

Let us turn, first, to four systems of curriculum thought—four conceptual maps—currently available for program planning purposes and consider how the addition of a fifth one derived from this study of the ways of knowing changes the nature of the choices that can be made. The following discussion does not assume that the four systems of curriculum thought referred to here describe the full array of resources available to us. The systems outlined briefly here are selected chiefly because they approach the problems of practical choices in program planning from four quite different perspectives. As such, they illustrate quite clearly the innovative qualities of the system suggested by the varieties of ways of knowing addressed here.

Some Existing Systems of Curriculum Thought

Four systems of curriculum thought come to mind as models that have shaped the discussions about curriculum for the last decade or so. All four have not been equally useful to the curriculum profession, and it cannot be assumed that any one curriculum planner has systematically attempted to coalesce all four into a single meta-system such as will be suggested here. The point remains, however, that four systems at least are available and, in principle, could be applied in practical settings. The differences among these four systems, and the stunning practical implications of introducing a fifth system, will be the subject of the next few pages.

The chronologically first and surely the most directly influential of these four conceptual maps is Tyler's formulation of the procedures for specifying curriculum content.[2] The "Tyler rationale," enthusiastically embraced by a generation of reformists seeking to codify and streamline the program planning processes, identifies a series of sequenced steps in the curriculum development process. The steps are by now familiar to most educators: specifying of objectives, selecting learning experiences, organizing the experiences according to appropriate principles, and evaluating the extent to which objectives are met. The rationale provides a checklist in a logical progression, and its original complete formulation includes a thoughtful discussion of the issues to be addressed in making decisions at each step along the way.

The Tyler rationale may be treated simplistically and may be used to rationalize some quite superficial curriculum reforms; at its best, and used most responsibly, however, it offers a responsible guide to the procedures of constructing a curriculum. By specifying a cumulative sequence, the Tyler rationale attempts to ensure that each step in program planning is informed by appropriate decisions made at the preceding points.

Equally pervasive in curriculum thought, at least in the journals, is Schwab's conception of the "practical" concerns of curriculum planners and specifically his model of four "commonplaces" of the curriculum.[3] Not in themselves a guide to procedure, the commonplaces identify instead the points around which decisions can be made. Thus, curriculum decisions can be made concerning the subject matter of the curriculum, the teachers, the students, or the milieu in which all coexist; a decision about any one of these commonplaces will affect the other three. The commonplaces describe in general terms the features of any educational terrain, each more or less subject to manipulation by direct intervention; changes in any will color the quality of the others. Thus, for example, any change in subject matter must account for the educational preparation, capabilities, and interests of the students to whom it is addressed—and for teachers' capability of teaching it. Schwab specifies no order in which the commonplaces should be addressed; the model identifies points of change. Where Tyler's model attempts to describe *how* to construct a curriculum, Schwab's commonplaces identify *where* change can take place.

A third model of curriculum thought, commissioned over a decade ago by the National Society for the Study of Education and meeting with rather startling success, is found in *Conflicting Conceptions of Curriculum* edited by Eisner and Vallance.[4] The model addresses neither the procedures of curriculum change nor the points at which it can happen. Rather, it identifies five sets of general *concerns* that may drive a curriculum development effort and shape the decisions it must make. The "conflicting conceptions" are the differing and sometimes mutually exclusive themes underlying much discourse about the chief problems of curriculum work. Four of the conceptions refer to broad purposes of schooling. One body of curriculum writing sees the chief concern of the curriculum as the development of cognitive processes in children, providing cognitive skills that will enable them to attack problems and master material. Another line of thought envisions the school's chief task as that of facilitating the "self-actualization" of children, liberating children to achieve their full potential in intellectual and other realms. A third would use the school deliberately as an agency of social change, a basis for reconstructing society through a curriculum attuned to social problems and current conceptions of "relevance." The "academic rationalist" conception is concerned chiefly with passing on the established traditions of western culture, usually in the form of the established intellectual disciplines. The fifth conception, "curriculum as technology," is less concerned with the specific purposes of schooling than with their efficient management and reflects a line of thought where both the human mind and the educational system are construed in technical terms, subject to ever increasing efficiency and governed by logical application of means to ends. This fifth conception comes closest to the "machine" view that the musician decries in his mathematician colleague; the "academic rationalist" view is the only one offering consistent and specific recommendations on curriculum content. And although the five conceptions are not fully parallel (and are somewhat dated by now), they do identify alternative sets of fundamental concerns held by educators. Ultimately they map out alternative goals of education, distinguishing among sets of assumptions and lines of thought held by different participants in the educational dialogue. (It is interesting to ask where a test of the musician and the mathematician in these terms would take us. It seems evident that the mathematician, in his deification of the orderliness of mathematics, is an academic rationalist; the musician is more problematic, and may be a variant of a "self-actualization" proponent, arguing that the mind be liberated from the constraints of the technological conception.) The conflicting conceptions of curriculum offer, at base, alternative and competing purposes of education from which to select.

The fourth system of curriculum thought addressed here has had a quieter life, but has always struck me as especially helpful in assessing curricular questions. Huebner's essay on "Curricular Language and Classroom Meaning" offers five perspectives from which educational activity can be valued.[5] He calls these "rationales." They are: the *technical* (concerned with the efficient mobilization of resources to meet desired ends), the *political* (concerned with the power relationships developed within an educational system and community), the *scientific* (concerned with understanding educational phenomena), the *aesthetic* (concerned with the symbolic or aesthetic impact of educational phenomena on students), and the *ethical* (the value of the educational activity for the child, and the moral implications of the teacher's responsibility for it). American education, Huebner argues, has typically emphasized the first three to the exclusion of the latter two. For example, most educators and public participants in educational dialogues acknowledge the political content in some current school reform movements (creationism, or school prayer), are much concerned with effective schools and other distillations of the technical rationale, and orient most learning research to a scientific understanding of the educational process. The aesthetic and the ethical implications of curricular change often get lost in the shuffle. In any event, Huebner's five "rationales" provide a system of questions to ask in assessing the value of any educational enterprise; they provide filters through which to *understand* practical action.

What do these four systems of curriculum thought have in common? Each provides the program planner with a number of degrees of freedom in the program planning process. Each identifies the context within which the curriculum planner operates and by identifying a set of alternatives helps the program planner to broaden his or her thinking. Each, if responsibly used, attempts to guarantee that no curriculum choice is made simply by default, for lack of alternatives. Each constitutes a kind of map ensuring that the program planner realizes that the street he or she is walking down today is but one of many possibilities, and as such encourages him or her either to consider the other alternatives or to be prepared to defend the choice in their terms. The conceptual maps available broaden our perspective, stretch the limits of our vision, keep the alternatives alive.

By way of example, consider what some of these maps might reveal about a hypothetical college-preparatory high school curriculum that is organized according to subject-matter divisions and is heavily "academic" (English, science, mathematics), with each subject allotted roughly an hour per day in a schedule structured by bells and lessons guided by textbook chapters. The success of this curriculum will be measured by scores on standardized tests and by acceptance of its graduates by colleges. Applying only some categories from two of the four systems of curriculum thought outlined here, we might be able to say that this curriculum is structured along academic rationalist lines, is technologically efficient and therefore has a high political value in the community, but is aesthetically deadening to both students and teachers. In these terms, it may contrast sharply with another program that is also structured along academic rationalist subject-matter lines but is guided more by a "self-actualizing" concern for an aesthetically rewarding experience to children and, as an experimental program, is tolerated as politically neutral and unthreatening. Even this crude and hypothetical comparison gives an idea of the function of conceptual maps in providing a common language with which to discuss different curricula and a basis on which to compare them. Having even one such "map" or system of curriculum thought meets the need for a language of discourse; the addition of other complementary maps further expands our conception of what is possible in program planning.

These four systems of curriculum thought meet different needs for program planners. They provide different sets of concepts with which to approach a curriculum problem; not all will be appropriate or valuable in every dialogue, and there is a sense in which some are logically prior to others. The identification of which of the four commonplaces is most in need of reform (Schwab), for example, may well precede any considerations of the procedure by which new objectives should be developed (Tyler). An application of Huebner's five "rationales" could initiate a curriculum reform effort by identifying dimensions on which the present curriculum is weak, or the rationales might be brought to bear afterward, as a set of judgments to be made as part of the evaluation process. A consideration of the different "conflicting conceptions of curriculum" operating in a debate over curriculum priorities (Eisner and Vallance) may not be necessary if the participants hold a shared conception of the major concerns of the curriculum, but a taking-stock in terms of that model might be advisable midway through an application of Tyler's sequence for program development to resolve a dispute over content. Conceivably any given curriculum problem could be addressed using only one of the conceptual maps described here; a leisurely and well-staffed curriculum development project might have the luxury of considering all four in some appropriate order. In either case, the conceptual map serves the simple but important purpose of pinning down at least one set of possible choices and ensuring that the alternatives are available for consideration. A good conceptual map is liberating.

In short, conceptual maps or systems of curriculum thought, when applied by program planners in practical situations, expand the options for the curriculum by defining them in general terms. Any one system does this much by itself. The adoption of more than one enlarges the program planner's scope proportionately. The urgency of an immediate crisis, the pressures of time, or the lack of resources may dictate that the whole map cannot be explored and that the program must be developed quickly according to unexamined standard conceptions. Ideally, however, the curriculum planner can gradually acquire a repertoire of conceptual systems that can guide and shape curricular thinking in a variety of settings and contexts. The richest of these repertoires will stimulate the program planner to ask questions from as many different perspectives as possible before selecting the one that seems wisest.

Before examining the fifth conceptual map provided by a consideration of the multiple ways of knowing, let us risk a bit of meta-theorizing to identify the kinds of perspectives that the four fairly standard approaches to curriculum problems offer to the task of program planning. I will address this question only briefly, but the exercise will prove to be important for identifying gaps in our present lines of thinking about curriculum matters and, as such, will indicate the special contribution of this fifth conceptual map.

It is possible, for example, to argue that the four conceptual maps collectively offer two distinct kinds of assistance. One category includes those systems of curriculum thought that identify the areas to be addressed in the process of curriculum development. Schwab tells us to pay attention to subject-matter, teachers, students, and milieu, and Tyler provides a checklist of procedures to be addressed as we make changes in the curriculum (specify the objectives, identify learning experiences appropriate to them, arrange these appropriately, and evaluate the results). These two "process" maps function exactly as maps. They remind us of where we are and of what still needs to be considered before we can reach our final destination of a complete new curriculum. The contrasting category would embrace those systems of curriculum thought that themselves identify curricular options or provide criteria for assessing the appropriateness of curriculum content.

The perspectives charted by Eisner and Vallance identify some available biases in curriculum purpose and content (social reconstructionism, for example); Huebner's five "rationales" outline languages available to be used in arguing a curriculum to some public, and thereby provide bases on which to judge particular curricula. Thus, if we were to dichtomize the four conceptual maps sketched above, we would find a contrast between systems that somewhat abstractly identify things to think about in doing curriculum development (*process-oriented* systems) and those with *normative commitments* prescribing content areas and bases for evaluation. Collectively they help us to conceive of curriculum change and what it might include. None of the four, however, addresses curricular goals in terms not reducible to content mastery; none identifies or argues for a way of knowing that differs substantially from our traditional conception of knowledge as logical, linear, and scientifically guidable.

Alternatively, we can argue that the four curriculum maps serve three general purposes: (a) Huebner serves as a kind of critic and interpreter of the persuasive tools available to curriculum discourse, (b) the conceptions outlined by Eisner and Vallance themselves constitute schools of persuasion, arguments for curriculum content based on traditional conceptions of human knowledge or on critiques of social need, and (c) Tyler and Schwab both attempt to provide systems of curricular thought that are value-neutral techniques of curriculum development. The three basic approaches to understanding curriculum change—critique, persuasion, or technique—collectively ensure that our curriculum development is thorough, sensitive, methodical, and defensible against most critics. They ensure that our eyes remain open to the many kinds of questions appropriate to practical program planning. But the questions they illuminate still pertain chiefly to knowledge that is organized comfortably into subject-matter areas and taught with the assumption that sequential mastery of cognitive information is what education must be.

It is in this context, of course, that the notion of multiple ways of knowing assumes a special importance for curriculum planners. The notion that human knowing takes many forms introduces a fifth kind of curriculum map that cannot be understood in the same terms as the other four. It does not fit the deceptively neat dichotomy attempted above. For example, it neither prescribes areas of curriculum content nor provides procedures guaranteeing that the standard content options are considered. And it falls somewhere outside the three configurations argued above: it is not a system of critique, it is not a set of arguments attempting to persuade about specific curriculum content, and it is surely not a value-neutral technical system of rules. Like the system created by Eisner and Vallance, it attempts to identify some of the options available to the practitioner, but unlike that system the curricular implications of any one of the options are not clear: while "social reconstructionism" may have clear implications for the role of social studies in the school curriculum, it is hard to see what specific curricular implications arise from the concept of formal modes of knowing, or even scientific or aesthetic modes. The modes of knowing are not tied to conventional subject-matter divisions. As such, their relevance for program planning takes a new form.

The notion of multiple ways of knowing introduces a fifth perspective on practical curriculum questions. The remainder of this chapter shows how this is so and suggests the unique kinds of questions that this perspective poses for practical program planning work.

The Ways of Knowing as a System of Curriculum Thought

To acknowledge that there is a variety of kinds of human intelligence, and that the various ways of knowing may all be equally valuable to the development of human potential, is to accept an entirely new realm of possible curricular choices. In effect, the variety of ways of knowing constitutes a new system of curriculum thought. A diligent curriculum planner attempting to integrate all four of the systems outlined above might adopt the multifaceted conception of human intelligence as a fifth system, a fifth set of questions to ask in attacking a curriculum development problem. More important, however, is that a multifaceted conception of the modes of knowing introduces questions quite unlike any others that are traditionally asked in educational planning. Thus, the practical implications of this new conception for program planning purposes will be evident on two levels: it complements the curriculum maps already available to both theorists and practitioners, but more basically it challenges the assumptions on which all other systems of curriculum thought are based. At the very least, it demands that the questions we ask in coming to curricular decisions be enlarged; at the extreme it demands that they be reformulated.

Thus, on one level we already know that we can address at least four questions in the process of program planning: what can be changed, what are our major purposes in working toward educational change, how do we go about it, and in what terms can we best understand the implications of what we have wrought? (Schwab, Eisner and Vallance, Tyler, and Huebner, respectively). To these four questions we can now add a fifth: in which mode(s) of knowing have our children been educated up to now, and which should the curriculum foster? The notion that there are many ways of knowing and that schooling has traditionally excluded whole realms of intellectual development is immensely disturbing. It is also disturbing that our conceptions of curriculum thought have deliberately fostered this omission by being themselves based on a single limited conception of knowledge. Given that the ways of knowing outlined here are an appropriate demarcation of the vast realm of human intelligence, the relevance of these insights for program planning is clear in several areas.

Without examining the impact of this new perspective on every item within each of the four curriculum models mentioned here, some examples may suffice to illustrate how a multifaceted conception of knowledge can modify the questions each model may raise in program planning. Consider, for example, the academic rationalist perspective in the Eisner and Vallance model. Typically the academic rationalist approach to curriculum development is to weigh systematically areas of knowledge against the prevailing culture to identify "what knowledge is of most worth." The question of "worth" may be considered in its own terms; that is, a discipline may be valued and included in the curriculum because it is and always has been central to the progression of the western intellectual tradition. Therefore some form of mathematics is required in all school systems in the country. Mathematics is valued for its own sake as an established discipline; it is also valued these days as a necessary skill. In the conversation reported at the beginning of this chapter the musician and the mathematics teacher agree that it is Useful Knowledge, practical and orderly. In fact, the teacher uses it in his theater work. But if we admit that there may be many ways of knowing, we are forced to ask either of two questions about mathematics: (a) Which of the many ways of knowing are embodied in mathematics (and which of them can a mathematics teacher reasonably be expected to "teach")? or (b) Given the modes of knowing that we wish to foster in our curriculum, what will be the role of mathematics? The two questions are quite different. The first allows us to retain a subject-matter division of the curriculum and challenges us to identify new qualities within it; the premise of the second defines ways of knowing as the guiding concern, with mathematics admitted as a possible medium for teaching them. The ways-of-knowing paradigm therefore allows new rationales for traditional subjects while also admitting the possibility that traditional subjects might be modified to accommodate educational goals defined in a wholly new way.

The impact of the ways of knowing on Schwab's commonplaces also forces us to ask additional questions about each of the four commonplaces. For example, in considering changes in teachers, a program planner must be sensitive not only to the teacher's influence on the subject matter, students, and milieu but also to the teacher's capacity for accommodating a broader perspective on human cognition. What must a teacher know in order to address responsibly the development of aesthetic knowing in the course of teaching a standard literature survey course? How can Hector, the mathematics teacher, incorporate his spiritual knowledge of his subject matter in a mathematics lesson so that that knowledge is accessible to students (and should he)? What does a teacher need to know in order to address formal modes of knowing in an art class? Or, looking at the commonplace of "milieu," can an aesthetic way of knowing really be fostered in a milieu characterized by rigid hourly schedules, loud bells, a curriculum chopped into subject matters arbitrarily arranged?

An admission of multiple ways of knowing also enriches the questions that can be asked in any of Huebner's five rationales. From the point of view of the ethical value of a curriculum, for example, can we be sure of the ethical coherence of a curriculum that ignores *any* of the many ways of knowing and deprives any child of the power of intelligence? What political messages are conveyed by a curriculum that limits some children to a single cognitive mode, providing access to multiple modes only to children deemed "gifted"? How does the development of interpersonal or intuitive modes of knowing enhance the ethical values of a curriculum?

The concept of multiple modes of knowing forces us to ask of Tyler's orderly sequence of curriculum development whether the formal and practical knowledge applied in that process is appropriate for developing programs where the goal is to foster intuitive or aesthetic knowing. Is the Tyler rationale itself so fully a product of one or two specific modes of knowing that it must retire, or be greatly changed, in order to be responsive to the curricular demands of this new perspective?

The questions that a multifaceted conception of cognition raises for the curriculum maps now available to us are many more than those examples cited above, and it is not our purpose here to address them in detail. It is our intention, however, to argue that one of the most important implications of this new perspective for program planning is precisely that it changes the nature of the questions we fruitfully can ask. It does add a fifth system of curriculum thought to at least the four cited here. But more than simply adding another set of categories to consider, it changes the quality of the categories which we have traditionally used in making our curricular choices. It fundamentally alters the way curriculum problems are understood.

This change is critical. Both theorists and practitioners have traditionally been bound by the strong subject-matter bias that has colored western educational thought for centuries. More or less directly, and with more or less attention to its limitations, educators have embraced the notion that building a curriculum is chiefly a question of building a responsible structure of lessons to enable students to master content. Indeed, even those educators concerned less directly with content areas and more with the generalized skills of values clarification, discovery, or other processes have tacitly accepted the predominance of formal cognitive ways of knowing. The conceptual maps heretofore available to educators have not made alternative approaches to curriculum planning possible. It is feasible now at least to conceive of a curriculum organized not by subject-matter divisions at all, for example, but according to the various modes of knowing deemed important to the culture. Taking this notion to an absurd extreme for the sake of illustration, students might move from "Formal Reasoning" in first period to "Aesthetic Modes of Knowing" just before lunch, and so on, with each period integrating content from various disciplines; college majors eventually would be identified not by subject-matter department but by the mode of knowing in which students choose to specialize. While this quick example roundly violates the subtlety that this fifth perspective argues eloquently for, it does illustrate the jolt of change that the perspective might encourage. To acknowledge that human knowing takes many forms must also be to acknowledge that the organization of the curricula by which we hope to teach children may be subject to substantial change. That change cannot come about, however, unless curriculum planners are able to change their own approaches to the questions of what is knowable and how knowing can be taught.

It remains to venture some suggestions as to what specific questions we might ask of schooling, or of any given curriculum, under this revised perspective on the varieties of modes of knowing. Quite aside from how this perspective will influence the questions asked under each of several existing systems of curriculum thought, the issue suggests some larger questions that may be independent of any particular conception of the curriculum. Granting that the nature of the general questions is at present still conjectural, as we know little about how directly this line of thought will actually affect practitioners, it is nonetheless intriguing to wonder what sets of questions might ultimately displace the question of "What knowledge is of most worth?" Some possibilities come readily to mind:

1. Given that there are at least seven ways of knowing, which of them are appropriately to be addressed by schooling and which can be left to other realms of socialization? Should the curriculum attempt to account for all the ways of knowing available to us?

2. For those modes of knowing that can or should be addressed in the school curriculum, is there a hierarchy of importance? Are some to be considered "required" and others not? Would the verdict be the same for all students?

3. Do the different ways of knowing develop best at different times in a person's life? If so, how should the sequence of the curriculum accommodate these stages in order to maximize each student's access to the full array of modes of knowing?

4. Do some traditional subject areas provide better access to some modes of knowing than to others? If so, how can this knowledge guide

our selection of curriculum content? (Example: We assume that aesthetic modes of knowing may be taught through art, but *is* art the best channel to aesthetic knowing? And might art classes also teach formal modes of knowing quite well?)

5. Might the modes of knowing themselves be an appropriate basis on which to structure the curriculum, gradually coming to replace the traditional divisions along subject-matter lines?

6. In what terms are the goals of schooling most usefully phrased? Should mastery of a variety of ways of knowing be an explicit goal of a curriculum, or can this end remain tacit, secondary to other more measurable goals?

7. At what point in a student's career should he or she be encouraged to specialize in one or more ways of knowing, and what would be the curriculum-content implications of the decision?

8. What background do teachers, curriculum developers, and educational administrators need in order to foster a curriculum that encourages mastery of a wide variety of ways of knowing?

9. By what signs or indicators will educators know that a curriculum has been successful in teaching the various modes of knowing?

10. What curriculum materials and experiences are best suited to fostering a command of a wide variety of modes of knowing? Do textbooks by definition favor one mode over others? Do some modes of knowing demand more active involvement in creating, solving problems, or analysis than others?

Many such questions must be addressed before the full range of implications of multiple modes of knowing can be understood. Clearly the most fundamental implication is simply that the prevailing conceptions of the major issues facing program developers must shift if a variety of modes of knowing is to be accommodated. The questions that have prevailed in the curriculum area for the last three decades are predicated largely on an academic-rationalist and technological conception of the curriculum, on a sensitivity to the technical, scientific, and political implications of educational change, and on a logical, linear conception of knowledge. Curricular decisions to intervene in any of the commonplaces with any systematic approach to change have largely left those assumptions intact. The varieties of modes of knowing familiar to philosophers, historians of science, aestheticians, and others have not heretofore reached educators in a practical or meaningful way. But the possibilities for reorienting our ways of thinking about curriculum problems are vastly expanded with this exciting new perspective. It remains for further research to aid educators in understanding exactly what the responsible moves might be, and for practitioners to begin examining the alternatives in the new light that this "fifth" system of curriculum thought now allows.

Is the distinction between useful knowledge and ornamental knowledge a valid one? Perhaps, but the traditional tendency to divide knowledge into dichotomies is questionable, and what has typically been considered merely ornamental may have a value much greater than that label might suggest. Conceivably what is useful to one person may be merely ornamental to another, and vice versa, and it may be that in some fundamental sense *no* human knowledge is strictly ornamental. That possibility is a humbling one, for it demands of program planners that they discover some means of abolishing many standard dichotomies and of ensuring, through all the political and ethical messages a curriculum may convey to its public, that no student by virtue of his or her program of study is becoming more "useful" than any other. If the multiple perspectives on ways of knowing teach us nothing more as educators, they should teach us that the values and priorities and biases created by the modes of knowing that have shaped the education profession itself are now open to reexamination.

As to the distinction between the machine and the dustbin, through all this it still remains a compelling metaphor. Ultimately it is not the same as the distinction between useful and ornamental knowledge, as the musician suggests, for the latter refers chiefly to kinds of knowledge rather than to its uses. We may grant that a distinction between knowledge that is useful and knowledge that is not may one day disappear. It is less likely that the distinction between the machine and the dustbin will become irrelevant, for we must assume that there will always be plodders and dreamers, those comfortable with the straight and narrow path of predictability and those adventurers tantalized by the unexpected bits of glitter and disorder. Yet if educators do not seek to shape children into predictable "neat machines," neither do they aim for the uncontrolled disorder of "worthless but fascinating curiosities." Some mixtures of the two may be necessary. What will be important to remember is that mathematics is not only a machine: Hector finds it beautiful and even spiritual. And surely art, the area most often associated with the development of creativity and more likely to foster a delight in "odd gems," can be as mechanical and devoid of aesthetic knowlege as any subject. The distinction between the neat machine and the dustbin, then, may serve as a reminder and as a hope: a reminder that knowledge is more varied and more diverse than that, and a hope that knowing the variety of ways of knowing may help the education profession to find the points along a continuum between the two.

Notes

1. Robertson Davies, *Tempest-Tost* (New York: Penguin Books, 1980), p. 182.

2. Ralph W. Tyler, *Basic Principles of Curriculum and Instruction* (Chicago: University of Chicago Press, 1950).

3. Joseph Schwab, "The Practical: A Language for Curriculum," *School Review* 78 (November 1969): 1-23.

4. Elliot Eisner and Elizabeth Vallance, eds., *Conflicting Conceptions of Curriculum* (Berkeley, Calif.: McCutchan Publishing Corp., 1974).

5. Dwayne Huebner, "Curricular Language and Classroom Meaning," in *Language and Meaning*, ed. James B. Macdonald and Robert S. Leeper (Washington, D.C.: Association for Supervision and Curriculum Development, 1966).

Introduction to Chapter IV

On the first page of the chapter that follows, George Madaus asserts that "it is testing, not the 'official' stated curriculum, that is increasingly determining what is taught, how it is taught, what is learned and how it is learned." In his well-documented report, Madaus shows how this situation has come about. He enunciates seven "principles" relating to the influence of testing on the curriculum. He concludes by calling for "counterstrategies that have curriculum and instruction driving testing rather than testing driving instruction."

This chapter originally appeared in a 1988 NSSE Yearbook. There is ample reason to believe that the points that Madaus made then are equally relevant today. Calls for reforms that relate to curriculum and instruction still typically rely on test results to judge the effectiveness of the reforms. Teaching to the test still occurs. High stakes tests are no less common today than they were a decade ago.

We include this chapter because we believe it deserves to be read and reread by teachers, administrators, and curriculum planners. The historical background provided by Madaus and the identification of points at which testing clearly shapes the curriculum are examples of basic knowledge needed by educators who are involved in decision making related to curriculum.

George F. Madaus is Professor of Education at Boston College and Director of the Center for the Study of Testing. The chapter reprinted here originally appeared in the 87th NSSE Yearbook, Part 1, Critical Issues in Curriculum, edited by Laurel N. Tanner.

CHAPTER IV

The Influence of Testing
on the Curriculum

GEORGE F. MADAUS

For years, students of the senior class were required to read ["Phileopolis"] and answer questions about its meaning, etc. Teachers were not required to do so, but simply marked according to the correct answers supplied by Miss Quist, including: (1) To extend the benefits of civilization and religion to all peoples, (2) No, (3) Plato, and (4) A wilderness cannot satisfy the hunger for beauty and learning, once awakened. The test was the same from year to year, and once the seniors found the answers and passed them to the juniors, nobody read "Phileopolis" anymore.

GARRISON KEILLOR
Lake Wobegon Days

Garrison Keillor's amusing vignette from *Lake Wobegon Days* illustrates what this chapter is about. It is about the effects of testing on the curriculum, teaching, and learning. Its thesis is that testing is fast usurping the role of the curriculum as the mechanism of defining what schooling is about in this country. In recent years, it seems that the aims of education, the business of our schools, and the goals of educational reform are addressed not so much in terms of curriculum—the courses of study that are followed—as they are in terms of standardized tests. It is testing, not the "official" stated curriculum, that is increasingly determining what is taught, how it is taught, what is learned, and how it is learned.

I thank my generous colleagues, Walter Haney, Joseph Pedulla, Martin Rafferty CM, and James Bernauer SJ, for their help, ideas, and reactions. I also thank Rita Comtois and Amelia Kreitzer for their reactions, editorial assistance, and attention to detail.

Recently, as a means of documenting the increasing attention to testing, and the concurrent decreasing attention to curriculum concerns, Haney plotted the amount of space devoted over the last fifty years in *Education Index* to citations concerned with testing and curriculum. And while column inches in *Education Index* is admittedly a fairly crude way of charting what is happening in the world of education, his data certainly suggest that standardized testing seems more and more to be the coin of the educational realm. His results reveal that the average annual number of column inches devoted to citations concerning curriculum has increased only modestly over the last half-century: from 50 to 100 inches per year in the 1930s and 1940s, to 100 to 150 inches in recent years. In contrast, attention devoted to testing has increased ten-fold in the last fifty years, rising from only 10 to 30 column inches in the 1930s and 1940s to well over 300 inches in the 1980s.[1]

Proponents of testing argue that the power of testing to influence what is taught, how it is taught, what is learned, and how it is learned is a very beneficial attribute. This view of testing and curriculum is sometimes referred to as measurement-driven instruction. Its advocates hold that if the skills are well chosen, and if the tests truly measure them, then the goals of instruction are explicit; teacher and student efforts are focused on well-defined targets; standards are clear and uniform; accountability at all levels is easier and more objective; and the public has concrete information on how well the schools are doing.

Can measurement really drive instruction and influence the curriculum? How does a test come to exercise power over curriculum and instruction? What is the nature of that power? This chapter explores these issues. However, to anticipate, the lesson of history is clear. Tests can be, have been, and in some places are the engines that drive teaching and learning. Is this a good thing? The answer depends on one's philosophy of instruction, curriculum, education, and testing. There are profound implications in this driving metaphor about the nature of instruction, curriculum, education, teaching, and testing.

At the outset, let me make explicit my bias *against* measurement-driven instruction. It is nothing more than psychometric imperialism. Testing programs should, in my view, be seen as an ancillary tool of curriculum and instruction—albeit, a very necessary, useful, and important one—and nothing else. The long-term negative effects on curriculum, teaching, and learning of using measurement as the engine, or primary motivating power of the educational process, outweigh those positive benefits attributed to it. The tests can become the ferocious master of the educational process, not the compliant servant they should be. Measurement-driven instruction invariably leads to cramming; narrows the curriculum; concentrates attention on those skills most amenable to testing (and today this means skills amenable to the multiple-choice format); constrains the creativity and spontaneity of teachers and students; and finally demeans the professional judgment of teachers.

I shall begin by setting forth some basic definitions and distinctions regarding testing. Second, I shall describe seven principles concerned with the impact of standardized testing on education. Third, the effects of school system testing programs are outlined. Fourth, I examine the effects of state-mandated testing programs. Fifth, the recommendations of the various reform reports regarding testing and the possible consequences of implementing them are discussed. Finally, I examine the implications of the policy use of tests for curriculum development.

Types of Tests and Testing Programs

While standardized tests can be differentiated in a number of ways[2] I shall concentrate on the following four: (a) the variables measured, (b) the referent of the test score, (c) the source of testing, and (d) the influence of rewards or sanctions being associated with test results.

VARIABLES TESTED

A wide range of variables has been the subject of measurement, though the main emphasis has been on the measurement of cognitive rather than affective characteristics. The cognitive variables which have attracted most educational and commercial attention are "intelligence" and achievement in basic skill areas of the curriculum (reading, arithmetic). (This chapter focuses on the impact of standardized *achievement* tests only.)

As one proceeds up the educational ladder into secondary schools, where instruction is organized around subject matter areas rather than around specific skills, commercially available test batteries become less specific and less related to what is taught. High school test batteries closely resemble elementary school batteries in that they are more oriented to the basic skills of numeracy and literacy than to what is taught in specific subject fields like mathmematics, physics, history, and English literature. As a result such test scores are less relevant to the work of the high school teacher.[3] However, as we shall see, some of the recent reform reports call for the development of exams for each of the secondary school curricula areas. This has profound implications for curriculum and instruction at that level, an issue we shall explore later in the chapter.

SCORE REFERENT

The main distinction here is between norm-referenced tests, on which performance is assessed by reference to the performance of other students, and criterion-referenced tests, on which performance is assessed by reference to the mastery of specific content domains. It should be noted that norm-referenced information can also be structured to provide criterion-referenced interpretations and vice versa. While criterion-referenced tests are increasingly hailed as superior to norm-referenced ones in terms of information provided to teachers, norm-referenced information is valuable for comparative purposes. Further, the specificity of criterion-referenced information from commercially available tests, relative to what is actually taught at the local level, can often be dubious.

INTERNAL VS. EXTERNAL TESTING PROGRAMS

An important distinction relates to the source of, and/or control over, the testing program. Is it an *internal* or *external* testing program? An internal testing program is one which is carried out within a school at the initiative and under the control of the school superintendent, principal, or teacher. This category includes the traditional norm-referenced standardized achievement testing programs used by school systems since the 1920s, as well as the newer commercially available criterion-referenced achievement tests. Internal testing programs are not limited to the use of off-the-shelf commercial tests; in larger systems they can be built by school system personnel or customized for the system by a contractor. Internal testing programs also include traditional teacher-made tests which we will not treat in this chapter.

External testing programs are those controlled and/or mandated by an external authority, such as a state department of education, the state legislature or a private agency such as the College Entrance Examination Board (CEEB). While it can be a semivoluntary test like the Scholastic Aptitude Test (SAT), more commonly it is a test which the state mandates if students, teachers, or school districts are to fulfill certain requirements. State minimum competency exams linked to graduation decisions, the English 'O' and 'A' Levels, the Irish Leaving Certificate Examinations, and the old New York State Regents Examinations are all examples of the latter. External testing programs can use norm- or criterion-referenced tests, off-the-shelf commercially available instruments, tests built by the agency, or those delegated to a contractor.

External tests have long been a part of European educational systems. Until the advent of minimum competency testing, most educational testing in the United States had been internal in origin and control. External testing programs were relatively rare, the New York Regents Examinations and the CEEB examinations being notable exceptions. However, as we shall see, external testing is being mandated increasingly by state boards or legislatures as part of their efforts at educational reform.

HIGH-STAKES VS. LOW-STAKES TESTING PROGRAMS

High-stakes tests are those whose results are seen—rightly or wrongly—by students, teachers, administrators, parents, or the general public, as being used to make important decisions that immediately and directly affect them.[4] High-stakes student tests can be norm- or criterion-referenced, internal or external in origin. Examples include tests directly linked to such important decisions as: (a) graduation, promotion, or placement of students; (b) the evaluation or rewarding of teachers or administrators; (c) the allocation of resources to schools or school districts; and (d) school or school system certification. In all of these examples, the perception of people that test results are linked to a high-stakes decision is in fact accurate. Policymakers have mandated that the results be used *automatically* to make such decisions.

However, there are other uses of test results that do not always immediately and directly affect students but nonetheless are generally perceived by people as involving high stakes. For example, SAT results are of secondary importance in admission decisions for those colleges trying to fill vacant seats in the face of adverse demographics. Nonetheless, individuals and school systems act on the perception that these college admissions tests are of crucial and singular importance. Thus, we find that high schools are increasingly offering courses to prepare students to take these tests, and commercial coaching schools are doing a land-office business.

The Kentucky Essential Skills Test (KEST) is an example of a testing program which unintentionally evolved into a high-stakes situation. The KEST is a well-designed, state-mandated testing program covering grades K-12. It has no important rewards or sanctions linked directly and automatically to test performance. However, the state's newspapers rank the districts on the basis of the yearly KEST results. A recent evaluation found that this ranking was seen by many Kentucky educators as pernicious, misleading, detrimental to morale, and fostering an unhealthy competition between districts and schools within districts. Further, and more important, many educators felt that the ranking of districts caused the test to drive the curriculum and teaching in decidedly unhealthy ways.[5] The important point is that it was the media, not any direct mandate of the state legislature, that endowed KEST with such considerable significance.

In contrast to a high-stakes test, a low-stakes test is one which is perceived as not having important rewards or sanctions tied directly to test performance. An example would be traditional school district standardized and norm-referenced testing programs where results are reported to teachers, but there is no immediate, automatic decision linked to performance. In such programs teachers are free to ignore any results which they feel are discrepant. Further, the results are not perceived by them as being used to evaluate their teaching. This does not mean that results from such programs do not affect teachers' perception of students, nor that student placement decisions are not sometimes related to test performance. The important distinction is that teachers, students, and parents do not perceive test performance as a *direct* or *automatic* vehicle of reward or sanction.

The Impact of Tests: General Principles

Perhaps the most convenient way to summarize the considerable literature on the power of testing to influence the curriculum, teaching, and learning, is to list the major conclusions in the form of rules or principles.

Principle 1. *The power of tests and examinations to affect individuals, institutions, curriculum, or instruction is a perceptual phenomenon: if students, teachers, or administrators believe that the results of an examination are important, it matters very little whether this is really true or false—the effect is produced by what individuals perceive to be the case.*

Bloom coined this first principle.[6] Its importance lies in the fact that when people perceive a phenomenon to be true, their actions are guided by the importance perceived to be associated with it. The greater the stakes perceived to be linked to test results, the greater the impact on instruction and learning.

Further, Principle 1 encapsulates the symbolic power of tests in the minds of policymakers and the general public. The numerical scores from high-stakes tests have an objective, scientific, almost magical persuasiveness about them that the general public and policymakers are quick to accept. Test results become a synecdoche for standards. Policymakers are well aware of the high symbolic value tests and test results can have in creating an image of progress or reform. By mandating a test, policymakers are seen to be addressing critical reform issues forcefully, in a way the public understands. Thus, a high-stakes testing program is all too often a symbolic solution to real educational problems. It offers the appearance of a solution, and is believed by policymakers and the public to be a true solution. As test scores rise over time, policymakers point to the wisdom of their action and the general public's confidence in the schools is restored. However, the real possibility that the testing program may not be a cure for the underlying problem, and the reality of the power of such programs to distort the educational process must eventually be faced.

Principle 2. *The more any quantitative social indicator is used for social decision making, the more likely it will be to distort and corrupt the social processes it is intended to monitor.*

This principle comes directly from Campbell's work on social indicators.[7] It also reiterates the power paradox discussed above. Its effects are not limited to testing per se; they are much more general in scope, extending to any social indicator that is used to describe, make decisions about, or influence an important social process. Principle 2 is a social version of Heisenberg's uncertainty principle: you cannot measure either an electron's position or velocity without distorting one or the other. Any measurement of the status of an educational institution, no matter how well designed and well intentioned, inevitably changes its status.

This principle reminds us that while testing is historically seen as a relatively objective and impartial means of correcting abuses in the system, the negative effects eventually outweigh the early benefits. When test results are used for important social decisions, the changes in the system brought about by such a use tend to be both substantial and corrupting. How this comes to pass is described in the five remaining principles.

Principle 3. *If important decisions are presumed to be related to test results, then teachers will teach to the test.*

This accommodation to the power of a high-stakes test can be a double-edged sword. High-stakes tests can focus instruction, giving students and teachers specific goals to attain. If the test is measuring basic skills, preparing students for the skills measured by the test could, proponents argue, serve as a powerful lever to improve basic skills.[8] Unfortunately, the only evidence to support this position is that the scores on tests of basic skills rise, not that the skill necessarily improves. People fail to distinguish between the skill or trait itself and a secondary, fallible indicator or sign of them.

If the test is specific to a more specialized curriculum area where higher-level cognitive outcomes are the goal (for example, college preparatory physics), then the examination will eventually narrow instruction and learning, focusing only on those things measured by the tests.[9] Indeed, this narrowing of the curriculum has been one of the enduring complaints leveled at external certification examinations used for the important functions of certifying the successful completion of elementary or secondary education, and admission to third-level education or to certain jobs.

A review of the effects of such exams on the curriculum over many years and in several countries indicates that, faced with a choice between objectives which are explicit in the curriculum or course outline and a different set of objectives that are implicit in the certifying examination, students and teachers generally choose to focus on the latter. In 1938, Spaulding reported that teachers in New York disregarded the objectives in local curriculum guides in favor of those tested in the Regents examinations.[10] Morris found the rigidity of the exams was the principal reason that the chemistry curriculum in Australia remained almost unchanged from 1891 to 1959. He concluded that the proportion of instructional time spent on various aspects of the syllabus was "seldom higher than the predictive likelihood of its occurrence on the examination paper."[11] Similar observations about the influence of the exams on the curriculum have been made in India,[12] Japan,[13] Ireland,[14] and in England.[15] Turner sums up the English experience: "One only has to look at the timetable of the typical comprehensive school to see that the curriculum consists almost entirely of subjects which can be taken in public examinations."[16]

George Orwell illustrated this principle well when, recalling his own school days, he observed:

Subjects which lacked examination value, such as geography, were almost completely neglected, mathematics was also neglected if you were a "classical," science was not taught in any form . . . and even the books you were encouraged to read in your spare time were chosen with one eye on the English paper.[17]

Orwell's reminiscence is by no means unique. The testimony of many writers powerfully confirms the reality of cramming for external certification exams. Fiction, biography, poetry, drama, even the lowly detective novel, contain a large corpus of information directly from authors who have been through an external examination system and have been eminently successful in later life. The theme of cramming in English and Irish literature is pervasive, reaching even to the images evoked by the language. These images include: the student driven over the hurdles in a steeple chase; a goose stuffed for slaughter; a soldier engaged in cold-blooded warfare. The examination is a grinding machine and success is a form of divine election, with Oxbridge as the heavenly Jerusalem. The exam is often the common enemy and any strategy used by teachers or students to cope with it is justified. The stakes are too high to worry about the niceties of a well-rounded education. A related theme that also emerges is the frank admission of the sheer irrelevance of what was first memorized, then regurgitated on the exam, and quickly forgotten.[18]

Why does this happen? First, there is tremendous social pressure on teachers to see that their students acquit themselves well on the certifying examinations. Second, the results of the examination are so important to students, teachers, and parents that their own self-interest dictates that instructional time focus on test preparation. Bloom once recounted to me an experience that vividly illustrates the kind of pressure teachers in India can experience. He visited the classroom of a former student. To show his professor that he was keeping abreast of new developments the teacher departed from his prepared lecture notes. Almost immediately his students drowned him out with the chant: NOE! NOE! NOE! They forcefully reminded him that the material was *Not On the Exams*, and hence irrelevant.

Writing in 1888 about tests used at that time in the midwest for grade-to-grade promotion, the superintendent of the Cincinnati public schools described the twin pressures exerted on teachers by society and their own self-interests:

In the very nature of things, the coming examination with such consequences must largely determine the character of prior teaching and study. Few teachers can resist such an influence, and in spite of it teach according to their better knowledge and judgment. They cannot feel free, if they would. They shut their eyes to the needs of the pupils and put their strength into what will "count" in examinations.[19]

It is not necessary to use nineteenth-century educators, literary figures, or anecdotes from far away India to describe the effects of Principle 3. On a more contemporary note, Gregory Anrig, the former commissioner of education in Massachusetts, after taking office as the new president of the Educational Testing Service, described the dilemma of teachers with regard to Principle 3:

I don't know of any good teacher who wants to narrow what he or she does in order to ensure success on a specific test. No test is worth teaching to. But if you place too many conditions on the testing program, if you place too much importance on it, you could end up with teaching to the test. If you connect the test scores with such decisions as pupil promotion, teacher evaluation, or the distribution of financial aid, you will accomplish the kinds of pressures that narrow the public school curriculum. I'm not supportive of that.[20]

But, as I have mentioned already, there is a positive aspect associated with Principle 3. A high-stakes test can lever new curricular material. New curricula in physics, chemistry, and mathematics made an immediate impact in Irish schools when in the early 1960s they were prescribed and examined for the Leaving Certificate Examination.[21] Primary teachers in Belgium accepted curricular reforms only when, in 1936, the external exams given at the end of primary school were modified to incorporate the ideas of the new curriculum.[22] In New York State, curriculum specialists from the State Department of Education had little success in moving the emphasis in modern language teaching from grammar and translation to conversation and reading skills until the corresponding changes had been incorporated in the content of the Regents examination.[23] Revisions of the College Entrance Examination Board (CEEB) mathematics achievement tests to include modern mathematics played an important part in the radical revision of mathematics curricula in the 1960s.[24]

However, a paradox still remains. Despite the ability of the examination to introduce new material, the weight of examination precedent soon takes over and the way in which the new material eventually comes to be taught and learned is determined by the examination. Generally, if one looks at passing rates, the percentage drops sharply with the introduction of new exam material; then, each year for the next several, the passing curve rises until it eventually reaches and stabilizes at the original level. The question that educators must ask themselves is whether the positive aspects associated with Principle 3 outweigh the disadvantages that also flow from it. The answer is a value judgment and depends on one's view of education, the learner, teaching, curriculum development, and testing. My view is that in the long term, the narrowing of instruction and learning associated with this principle far outweighs any advantages.

Principle 4. *In every setting where a high-stakes test operates, a tradition of past exams develops, which eventually de facto defines the curriculum.*

Given Principle 3, the question remains: "How do teachers cope with the pressure of the examination?" The answer is relatively simple. Teachers see the kind of intellectual activity required by previous test questions and prepare the students to meet these demands. Some have argued strongly that if the skills are well chosen, and if the tests truly measure them, then coaching is perfectly acceptable.[25] This argument sounds reasonable, and in the short term, it may even work.[26] However, it ignores a fundamental fact of life: When the teacher's professional worth is estimated in terms of exam success, teachers will corrupt the skills measured by reducing them to the level of strategies in which the examinee is drilled. Further, the expectations and deep-seated primary agenda of students and their parents for exam success will put further pressure on teachers to corrupt the educational process. The view that we can coach for the skills apart from the tradition of test questions, embodies a staggeringly optimistic view of human nature that ignores the powerful pull of self-interest. It simply does not consider the long-term effects of the examination sanctions.

Principle 4 is beautifully illustrated in George Orwell's recollection of his history studies for the scholarship exam: "Did you know for example, that the initial letters of 'a black negress was my aunt; here's her house behind the barn' were also the initial letters of battles in the Wars of the Roses?"[27] Figure 1 offers an Irish example of the same phenomenon. A retired school inspector provided me with samples of student essays taken from the Primary Leaving Certificate examination of 1946-48.[28] Figure 1 shows how variations of the set theme are handed from one generation of examinees to the next through the memorization of stock responses that can be adapted to almost any prompt. Thus, a high score on the exam may not have indicated well-developed writing skills at all, but instead, simply the ability to use memorized material with whatever the theme for that year. The test-taking strategies mastered by students to meet the tradition of past tests vitiate the validity of the inferences about the students' ability to write.

A bicycle ride (1946)

I awakened early, jumped out of bed and had a quick breakfast. My friend, Mary Quant, was coming to our house at nine o'clock as we were going for a long bicycle ride together.

It was a lovely morning. White fleecy clouds floated in the clear blue sky and the sun was shining. As we cycled over Castlemore bridge we could hear the babble of the clear stream beneath us. Away to our right we could see the brilliant flowers in Mrs. Casey's garden. Early summer roses grew all over the pergola which stood in the middle of the garden.

A day in the bog (1947)

I awakened early and jumped out of bed. I wanted to be ready at nine o'clock when my friend, Sadie, was coming to our house. Daddy said he would take us with him to the bog if the day was good.

It was a lovely morning. The sun was shining and white fleecy clouds floated in the clear blue sky. As we were going over Castlemore bridge in the horse and cart we could hear the babble of the clear stream beneath us. Away to our right we could see the brilliant flowers in Mrs. Casey's garden. Early summer roses grew all over the pergola which stood in the middle of the green.

A bus tour (1948)

I awakened early and sprang out of bed. I wanted to be ready in good time for our bus tour from the school. My friend, Nora Greene, was going to call for me at half-past eight as the tour was starting at nine.

It was a lovely morning. The sun was shining and white fleecy clouds floated in the clear blue sky. As we drove over Castlemore bridge we could hear the babble of the clear stream beneath us. From the bus window we could see Mrs. Casey's garden. Early summer roses grew all over the pergola which stood in the middle of the garden.

Figure 1. Examples of compositions from the Irish Primary Certificate Examinations, 1946-1948.

An interesting result of Principle 4 is that if the examination is perceived as important enough, a commercial industry develops to prepare students for it. In the United States this phenomenon can be seen in the rise of commercial firms in virtually every major city, selling coaching services to students in preparation for the College Entrance Examination Boards (CEEB). Haney noted that one sign of the growing importance of commercial coaching schools in the United

States is that the phrase "test taking skills" first appeared as a separate indexing category in volume 33 of the *Education Index*, covering the period from July 1982 to July 1983. Many of the articles referenced under this new category dealt with improving admissions test scores through coaching provided either by commercial firms or computer tutorial soft-ware.[29] In Japan it is common for parents to enroll their children in special extra-study schools known as *juku*.[30] Beginning in the nineteenth century a whole industry of private coaching schools called "crammers" developed in Europe to prepare students for a fee for the tradition of important examinations. In the 1950s tutorial programs geared to the British 11+ examination were common, more so among parents of higher educational levels than among those of lower levels.[31] The important point about these coaching schools is not whether they are successful in preparing students for the exam; it is instead that the public perceives them as helpful and is willing to pay for their services.

Wilfred Sheed's description of one such crammer offers an amusing insight into the power of past examinations to affect preparation for a forthcoming exam. A student was sent to the Jenkins Tutorial Establishment in London which

offered . . . successful examination results as it might a forged passport . . . [bypassing] education altogether. Their only texts were examination papers— all the relevant ones set in the last fifty years, with odds of repetition calculated and noted as in the *Racing Form*. . . . Within six months, I was able to pass London matriculation without knowing any of the subjects involved; and by applying Jenkins' method later, to pass every exam that ever came my way afterwards. Hence I remain a profoundly uneducated man.[32]

The danger associated with Principle 4 is precisely the fact that while pupils may become proficient at passing tests by mastering the tradition of past exams, they may, as Sheed puts it, remain profoundly uneducated.

Principle 5. *Teachers pay particular attention to the form of the questions on a high-stakes test (for example, short answer, essay, multiple-choice) and adjust their instruction accordingly.*

The problem here is that the form of the test question can narrow instruction, study, and learning to the detriment of other skills. Rentz recounts a negative effect associated with Principle 5 which occurred as a result of the Georgia Regents Testing Program, a program designed to assess minimum competencies in reading and writing on the part of college students in that state. The head of an English department lamented:

Because we now are devoting our best efforts to getting the largest number of students past the essay exam . . ., we are teaching to the exam, with an entire course, English III, given over to developing one type of essay writing, the writing of a five-paragraph argumentative essay written under a time limit on a topic about which the author may or may not have knowledge, ideas, or personal opinions. Teaching this one useful writing skill has the beneficial effect of bringing large numbers of weak students to a minimal level of literacy, but at the same time, it devastates the content of the composition program that should be offering the better students challenges to produce writing of high quality. Because the Regents Test is primarily designed to establish a minimal level of literacy, our teaching to this test, which its importance forces us to do, tends to make the minimal acceptable competency the goal of our institution, a circumstance that guarantees mediocrity.[33]

Principle 5 has profound implications for the curriculum specialists. Given our free enterprise system, publishers have begun to look at state-mandated minimum competency tests, or basic skills tests, in order to design materials to better train pupils to take them. Children are apt, therefore, to find themselves spending more and more time filling out dittoed answer sheets or work books. Deborah Meier, a successful principal of a public school in Manhattan, testified at the 1981 NIE-sponsored hearings on Minimum Competency Testing (MCT) that in New York City reading instruction has come to resemble closely the practice of taking reading tests. In reading class, students, using commercial materials, read dozens of little paragraphs about which they then answer multiple-choice questions. Meier described the materials as evolving to resemble more and more the tests students take in the spring. She went on to point out that when synonyms and antonyms were dropped from the test of word meaning, teachers promptly dropped commercial material that stressed them.[34] A Connecticut superintendent recently told me that when that state adopted a cloze-type reading test his district immediately discarded materials they had used to prepare students for the more traditional multiple-choice state reading test in favor of drill material incorporating the cloze format. Someone must begin to challenge a practice whereby the method of measuring reading determines the materials and type of practice used to develop the skill. Along these same lines it is also interesting to note that in 1983 sales of ditto paper were way up nationally while sales of lined theme paper were down.[35]

Principle 6. *When test results are the sole or even partial arbiter of future educational or life choices, society tends to treat test results as the major goal of schooling rather than as a useful but fallible indicator of achievement.*

Of all of the effects attributed to tests those embodied in this principle may well be the most damaging. It is best summed up by the following observation from a nineteenth-century British school inspector who saw first-hand the negative effects of linking teacher salaries to pupil examination results:

Whenever the outward standard of reality (examination results) has established itself at the expense of the inward, the ease with which worth (or what passes for such) can be measured is ever tending to become in itself the chief, if not sole, measure of worth. And in proportion as we tend to value the results of education for their measurableness, so we tend to undervalue and at last to ignore those results which are too intrinsically valuable to be measured.[36]

Sixty years later, Ralph Tyler echoed the same message, warning readers that society conspires to treat marks in certifying examinations as the major end of secondary schooling, rather than as a useful but not infallible indicator of student achievement.[37]

We see the importance society places on test scores to the exclusion of other indicators in such things as: the media attention to declines in SAT scores; reports that our schools score lower than those of other countries on tests of mathematics and science; the Education Department's Wall Chart that ranks states by their performance on the SAT or the American College Test (ACT); newspapers ranking school districts and/or schools within districts by their performance on standardized tests; the use of test results by real estate agents in selling homes; and the money spent by parents on coaching schools for the SATs. The list could go on and on.

Principle 7. *A high-stakes test transfers control over the curriculum to the agency which sets or controls the exam.*

The agency responsible for a high-stakes test assumes a great deal of power or control over what is taught, how it is taught, what is learned, and how it is learned. This principle is well understood in Europe where a system of external certification examinations, controlled by the central government, or by independent examination boards, operates at the secondary level. And while this shift in power is also understood in this country by policymakers who are mandating graduation and promotion tests, the implications of the shift from the local educational authority (LEA) to the state department of education have not received sufficient attention and discussion.

Nor have the ideological differences between the educational values and bureaucratic values inherent in such a shift received sufficient attention. Further, since the tests for most state-level programs are developed and validated for the state department by outside contractors, it is important to realize that the state may be effectively delegating this very real power over education to a commercial company whose interest is primarily financial and only secondarily educational.[38]

The Effects of Internal Testing Programs

In the United States, unlike Europe, our system of education evolved based on local rather than state control. Circumstances of the time, the size of the nation, difficulties in communication and transportation helped to build a uniquely democratic system of education in a network of local units. With the exception of the New York State Regents examinations there generally were no state syllabi or state-mandated examinations. These are much more recent phenomena.

Thus, when commercial testing, based on an individual differences model, emerged after World War I, there was a ready market for tests that could be used for local rather than state purposes. These tests were designed not to certify individuals or make interdistrict comparisons, but to predict and select; to help make intradistrict and interschool comparisons; to diagnose individual learning needs; to group children and to compare local district performance to a national norm. By 1960, almost all districts, aided by the National Defense Education Act, purchased a standardized, norm-referenced test along with scoring services from one of the big five test publishers.

Recently, policymakers at the local level have discovered the accountability potential, and the power to influence teacher and student behavior inherent in attaching rewards and sanctions to standardized, multiple-choice, test performance. This section, therefore, deals first with the effects associated with traditional school system testing programs, and then with effects associated with the newer policy-related use of such tests by LEAs.

School-level effects. A consideration of the possible effects at the school level of using standardized tests suggests that one might expect effects on school organization and in a number of school practices. However, there has been relatively little systematic research on the impact on school districts, or on schools within districts, of using standardized tests in traditional ways. The assumption is often made that certain decisions and actions, such as the tracking of pupils and the allocation of slow learners to remedial classes, are taken on the basis of standardized test information. For example, Kirkland considers evidence relating to the effect of ability grouping on student achievement; however, she provides no evidence that the grouping was carried out in the first place on the basis of test information.[39] A variety of decisions relating to school organization and student placement can be and are made in the absence of test information. Evidence concerning the exact role of standardized test information in making such decisions is far from clear.

Sproull and Zubrow, after an intensive small-scale study in Pennsylvania, concluded that test results from traditional school district testing programs were not very important to central office administrators, and that administrators are not major users of test information.[40] Similarly, an experimental study of the effects of introducing traditional standardized testing in the schools of the Republic of Ireland found that school principals, when questioned about various aspects of school organization and practice, indicated that the overall impact of the standardized testing program at the administrative and institutional levels was slight.[41]

Teacher-level effects. The large-scale research that is available on teacher-level effects of traditional standardized testing is based on surveys of teachers. Surveys by Goslin[42] and by Beck and Stetz,[43] although a decade apart, present quite similar pictures of teacher perceptions about the usefulness of standardized testing for pupil-centered purposes; teachers tended to perceive such testing as useful for assessing individual and group status, for reporting to parents, and for planning instruction. However, Beck and Stetz also found that teachers were less positive about the use of tests in the context of school or teacher accountability. These latter negative attitudes about test use came at a time when the accountability movement was just beginning to gather momentum, but before the impact of state legislation linking test results to major sanctions (for example, pupil graduation or promotion, school or district accreditation, merit pay) could be felt.

In the 1980s two additional studies shed light on teacher attitudes and perceptions about standardized testing. Leslie Salmon-Cox[44] found that standardized test information was not used much by teachers, did not shape the curriculum, and did not lead to increased within-class grouping. Kellaghan, Madaus, and Airasian found that the opinions of Irish teachers remarkably resembled those of the teachers surveyed by Goslin, by Beck and Stetz, and by Salmon-Cox.[45]

How does one explain the rather consistent finding that standardized tests, while viewed favorably by teachers, were not of great relevance in their work? Salmon-Cox claims that the lack of relevance was due to the narrow range of outcomes the tests measured, that is, only certain aspects of the teachers' cognitive goals for pupils and almost none of their affective goals. Another possible explanation for the gap between teachers' attitudes toward tests and their reported use of them may be a function of the isolation experienced by teachers in their work. Perhaps tests are highly regarded because they basically confirm teachers' own judgments. In a profession in which there is relatively little professional interaction among practitioners, or between practitioners and other professionals, this confirmation may be of considerable significance for the teacher. The Irish data lend some support to this latter explanation and suggest an additional one. To the extent that test results are perceived as providing accurate information about pupils—though not as accurate as teachers' own perceptions—it is likely that the availability of test results will not be seen as having great relevance, and consequently will not exert great influence.[46]

For teachers, traditional standardized test scores can only be what Husserl has termed "occasional expressions."[47] They constitute data which cannot be interpreted by the teacher without recourse to additional information about the student—his or her home background, personal characteristics, or the circumstances under which the test was taken.[48] Further, the test data are always interpreted in light of the teacher's "hidden knowledge" of the pupil: knowledge gained from countless and constant daily evaluations made by the teacher in his or her everyday work.[49] Quite often, the test information simply confirms this "hidden knowledge."

It may well be that when the test results carry with them important consequences for the pupil, teacher, or school, as is the case with many externally imposed testing programs, then the perception of their relevance might be quite different. In a high-stakes testing program teachers cannot ignore results or treat them as occasional experiences, or interpret them in light of their hidden knowledge. The results leave no room for teacher input into the decision. Thus, teacher perceptions of test relevance might be quite different in such situations. We simply do not know.

Kellaghan, Madaus, and Airasian found that teachers in fact do make more use of test results than they are consciously aware of. Teachers' perceptions of pupils are affected by test information, perhaps to a greater extent than they realize. Furthermore, test information is somehow mediated to students and may affect their scholastic performance. This does not happen in the case of all students, or even most students, but it happens to a greater extent than one would predict from a consideration of teachers' reported uses of test information.[50] While these findings indicate that test information does play a role in influencing teachers' expectancies regarding pupils, perhaps even more significantly they underscore the influence of teachers' expectancies on pupils' scholastic performance in a more general way. Whether or not traditional standardized test information is available, teachers form expectancies for pupils which can affect how they perform scholastically.

Whether the influence of tests in altering teachers' perceptions of pupils is beneficial or not is difficult to assess. For some pupils, standardized test information can provide the teacher with a discrepant view of the pupil which leads the teacher to revise his or her expectations. Certainly, we know that teachers' ratings of pupils are more often raised than lowered when they have access to test information.[51] If higher ratings lead to higher expectations and ultimately to superior scholastic performance, then standardized test information would appear to be beneficial more often than it is not.

Student-level effects. It seems reasonable to assume that standardized test score information has its most serious impact on the student. Thus, it is not surprising to find that most research on the effects of standardized testing has been concerned with possible effects on pupils.

Bloom has argued that if the standardized test information is understood and utilized properly by students and teachers, it can do much to enhance a student's learning as well as his or her self-concept.[52] On the other hand, it is not inconceivable that learning the results from a test might adversely affect an individual's self-concept, level of aspiration, or educational plans. However, empirical evidence relating to the impact of providing students with test information in noncognitive areas is surprisingly scant. Part of the reason that research in this area is so sparse is the complexity of investigating the issue. Important distinctions have to be made between the pupil's level of education (test results often are not directly communicated to young pupils but are to secondary students); the kind or amount of information provided (norm- or criterion-referenced information, achievement or ability information); and the type of testing program involved (external test with important sanctions associated with the results or traditional school-based testing programs). The measurement of the students' self-concept is also no easy task, since it is not a unitary trait.

In considering findings on the effects of traditional standardized test information on pupils, a number of investigators have reiterated a point made by Flowers that traditional test information is of itself insufficient to overcome the effects of other variables such as differences in the communities, in the composition of school populations, in school assignments, in teacher types, and in other considerations.[53] As we discussed, the impact of traditional standardized test information on teachers is merely a part, and probably a relatively small part, of the pressure exerted on them by the educational environment. Even if expectancy processes operate in the classroom, standardized test information is only one factor in the network that creates such expectancies, and it is in such a context that any possible role it may have to play in affecting students has to be considered.[54]

INTERNAL HIGH-STAKES TESTING PROGRAMS

The research findings to date on the effects of traditional standardized test information, despite what many critics have said, indicate that the role is not a very major one. These findings cited above speak *only* to the effects of information from traditional school district testing programs. They were carried out before the advent of state-mandated testing programs aimed at reforming education, and before recent efforts by superintendents to use test information for accountability, to drive instruction, or to monitor student achievement continuously.

The most common use of high-stakes tests by LEAs is for purposes of student promotion from grade to grade, often referred to as "gates" testing, and for teacher accountability and in merit pay schemes. To date there have been few systematic evaluations of these uses of test information by LEAs. However, there is increasing anecdotal testimony that the seven principles enunciated above apply to such programs. We have already discussed the Meier testimony on the impact on instruction and curriculum material of gates testing in New York City. In 1974, when some New York City teachers perceived that the standardized tests used in grades two to nine might be used to evaluate them, someone leaked copies. An investigation determined that in a few schools the actual booklets had been used for coaching purposes. As a result the entire testing program had to be reconstructed with heavy emphasis on test security.[55]

In 1983-84 a National Board of Inquiry, formed by the National Coalition of Advocates for Students (NCAS) and chaired by Harold Howe II, assessed barriers to excellence in American education. One of their conclusions based on extensive testimony of teachers and administrators was that these newer uses of test information by LEAs were fast becoming a barrier to excellence, and were being used as exclusionary devices impacting heavily on low-income, minority, and handicapped children.[56] More recently, NCAS has found mounting evidence that some teachers are finding ingenious ways of removing low-scoring students from the test pool because of fear that they will lose their jobs if they do not keep test scores up.[57] Teachers quickly adopt strategies to deal with this type of accountability. There is historical precedent for this last finding. For example, a time-series analysis of promotion rates during the period when the Irish Primary Certificate exam was in effect showed an overall decrease. The data indicate that pupils who were not likely to pass the examination were prevented from failing by not being allowed to take it. The teacher quickly realized that if a weak student was retained twice during the primary grades, then he or she would have attained the school leaving age at or before exam time and would leave school without taking the exam. Thus, by weeding out weak students through retention in grade, schools achieved relatively high pass rates for pupils who did take the exam.

There is a need to evaluate systematically LEA sponsored high-stakes testing programs, to measure the positive and negative aspects of the program in order to arrive at a cost-benefit analysis of their effects. For example, will the various "gates" programs which use test results for grade-to-grade promotion improve student learning, or will they eventually increase the dropout rate? However, the difficulty with proposing such evaluations is that the policymakers who implement programs have a vested interest in them. They see their use of tests as a mechanism of power by which they can reform the system. Consequently, there is an understandable reluctance on their part to spend money to question the wisdom of their mandate.

One other growing use of test information by LEAs is in programs of continuous monitoring of student achievement (CAM).

CONTINUOUS ACHIEVEMENT MONITORING

The effectiveness of CAM programs, as well as that of measurement-driven instruction, has to date been assessed primarily by looking for improvement in pupil performance on the tests developed for the program itself, as well as on traditional commercially available standardized norm- or criterion-referenced tests. However, the impact on the administrative practices of district and school level administrators, and the impact on school organization, scheduling, or other areas of the curriculum not included in such programs, have not yet been systematically evaluated.

LeMahieu's evaluation of a CAM program in the Pittsburgh Public Schools is a rare exception and sheds some light on how these measurement-driven instructional programs work. His results indicated that the program had generally positive effects on students' achievement as measured by test scores.[58] The CAM program clearly focused the attention of students and teachers on the skills to be measured, and this largely accounted for the improvement in achievement.

However, LeMahieu also found this focusing phenomenon raises the following issues related to the seven principles: (a) the routinization of instruction by some teachers who may adopt the objectives of the monitoring program as the sole content of instruction in that domain; (b) a loss of residual learning outside of the CAM content; (c) competition for an extremely important and limited resource—instructional time—may increase as additional areas of the curriculum are added to the CAM program. In fact, Pittsburgh teachers reported that they took the time for supplemental instruction in mathematics (the area covered by CAM) away from other subjects. LeMahieu suggests that these difficulties can be overcome by careful planning and wise management but that these dangers are real and ever present.

Support for LeMahieu's first concern about the routinization of instruction comes in testimony to the NCAS Board of Inquiry regarding the Chicago Mastery Learning Reading (CMLR) program. A sequence of 273 separate reading "subskills" had to be mastered, one at a time, and then tested before the student could move on. Grade-to-grade promotion was based largely on success in the program. A teacher described how her teaching was affected:

Because CMLR is mandatory and accountability is emphasized with charts and reports about how many students have passed 80 percent of their tests, and because in many schools basal readers and other books are in short supply, or even nonexistent, CMLR becomes the central part of the reading instruction, and children never get a chance to read real books. CMLR crowds out real reading.[59]

The teacher's testimony speaks forcefully to the validity of the seven principles.

The Effects of External Testing Programs

During the last five years, efforts to reform education, particularly at the state level, have increasingly employed tests and test results in various ways. And this use of external tests in the policy sphere is a growing trend. For example, a fifty-state survey of reform measures conducted by *Education Week* found that: twenty-nine states required competency tests for students, and ten other states had such a requirement under consideration; fifteen states required an exit test for graduation, four additional states had such a measure under consideration; eight states employed a promotional "gates" test, while three others were considering such a mandate; finally, thirty-seven states had some sort of state assessment program, and six additional states had such a program under consideration.[60] This growing use of tests in the policy sphere by agencies external to the LEAs cannot help but affect what is taught, how it is taught, what is learned, and how it is learned.

The discussion of effects is organized around two principal policy uses. The first is the use of test information to *inform* policymakers about the current state of education. The second is the use of tests as *administrative devices* in the implementation of policy. In the former case, test results are used exclusively to describe the present state of education or some aspect of it, or in lobbying efforts for new programs or for reform proposals. The effects of this informational, descriptive use of test results on the educational process are indirect. This is in sharp contrast to the administrative use of test results whereby results automatically trigger a direct reward or sanction being applied to an individual or to an institution.

THE USE OF TEST RESULTS TO INFORM POLICY

The 1867 Act establishing the Department of Education recognized the need for gathering descriptive information about "the condition and progress of education in the several states and territories." Of course, at that time testing as we now know it did not exist. From the 1920s to the 1960s, standardized tests had little or nothing to do with state or federal policy. It was not until the early 1960s with the establishment of the National Assessment of Educational Progress (NAEP), that the Department began to gather test data systematically as part of its original mandate. Further, state departments of education have only recently begun to collect test data systematically to describe the status of education at the state level.

There were several reasons for this recent shift at the state level. First, the concept of equality of educational opportunity evolved from a concern about equality of inputs, resources, and access to programs into a preoccupation with achieving equality of outcomes. As a result, test scores began to be used as a primary indicator of educational outcomes. Second, advocates for minority groups began to point to the large discrepancies between the test scores of middle-class students, and their constituents began to lobby successfully for compensatory funds for programs to reduce these disparities. Third, the large expenditures in the 1950s and 1960s for curriculum development and compensatory programs led policymakers to ask for student test data as an indicator of the effectiveness of these programs. Fourth, as noted above, NAEP was designed as a basis for public discussion about, and a broader understanding of, educational progress and problems.

More recently, the numerous educational reform reports have used test results, including SAT and NAEP data for two purposes: first, to alert the country to what they conclude to be the mediocre state of American education, and second, to lobby for improvement programs to redress these weaknesses. Clearly, test data form an important basis for the current negative descriptions of the status of American education; this in turn has helped policymakers to pass reform legislation that might otherwise not have been instituted. While much of the reform legislation is clearly welcomed and needed, the question remains as to the validity of the inferences about the status of our schools made from available test data. Is the academic performance of our students as poor as it is painted in the various reports? While there are weak spots, particularly at the secondary level with higher-order skills, one could look at the same data and conclude that our schools are doing a quite creditable job and declines and weak spots may be due in large part to nonschool factors.

An illuminating example of how these indicators are actually used to inform such reports is provided by the Twentieth Century Fund Report. It opens with the following gloomy assertion: "The nation's public schools are in trouble. By almost every measure the performance of our schools falls far short of expectations."[61] However, in a commissioned background paper, published as an appendix to the Report itself, Peterson examines all of the available indicators, including test scores, and concludes that "nothing in these data permits the conclusion that educational institutions have deteriorated badly."[62] It would seem that the Task Force did not take cognizance of its own commissioned paper.

Stedman and Smith in their excellent review of these reform proposals point out that they are quintessential political documents. Testing evidence was used selectively to buttress arguments and ignore evidence that might lessen the impact of the message. They examined critically the way test score indicators were interpreted and concluded not only that it was sloppy, but also that we have little in the way of valid, longitudinal national indicators of the academic performance of students. NAEP is the single exception to the latter indictment.[63] The reform reports are excellent illustrations of the pitfalls associated with using test data in the policy arena where careful analyses, contradictory inferences, and caveats about the limitations of the data are at best not understood, or at worst not welcome.

THE USE OF EXTERNAL TESTS AS ADMINISTRATIVE MECHANISMS IN POLICY

During the 1960s state boards and legislatures began to use external tests as a mechanism of power. They began to attach rewards or sanctions to student performance on mandated tests. The test results in effect became a triggering device to make things happen automatically to individuals, schools, or districts. Tests quickly became a principal weapon in the arsenal of policymakers interested in school reform. It was felt that the fear of diploma denial because of a low score on a state test would motivate a target population of lazy or recalcitrant students. Further, the test was viewed as a strong and useful weapon in the armament of the school when they had to tell parents that their child was not ready for promotion or graduation. The weapon metaphor used by advocates to describe this use of tests is very revealing.

Impact on administrative practices and school organization. There has been little research evidence on the impact of using external test results as an administrative mechanism on school organization or administrative practices at the local level. However, certain aspects of these mandated testing programs directly affect pupil placement and therefore should, it seems, affect school organizational practices and the allocation of resources. For example, some minimum competency testing programs mandate that districts must provide students falling below the cut-score with remediation; whether this is done as part of the regular class or on a "pull-out" basis, it involves decisions about instructional organization and the allocation of resources. Other state-level programs require that once a predetermined number of pupils fall below the cut-score the district, or a school within the district, must submit an improvement plan to the state education agency. The development of such a plan requires a series of actions on the part of school administrators. In short, linking important rewards or sanctions to performance on an externally mandated test *should* begin to affect what district and school administrators do regarding resource allocation and their organizational and curricular decisions.

In conjunction with its testing program some states have allocated money for programs to remediate anticipated failures. However, to date, the nature and effectiveness of these efforts have not been adequately evaluated. There is some evidence that remediation becomes equated with test preparation. For example, in Florida a State Task Force on Educational Assessment studying that state's Functional Literacy Test reported that "in all cases observed, spot remediation was being practiced. That is, students were being coached on the specific skills represented by questions they missed on the 1977 test."[64] In testimony to the Florida State Board of Education, a history teacher reported that students were absent from history class for two periods and on return were declared remediated. He concluded that "what really counts here is successful passing of the functional literacy test."[65] New Jersey teachers testifying at the NIE-sponsored 1981 Clarification Hearings on Minimum Competency Testing, reported a similar phenomenon. More recently, the NCAS Board of Inquiry found that, despite the fact that the tests were justified on the basis of ensuring remedial help, there was "no guarantee that such help will be forthcoming; nor do schools take precautions to protect students who do not meet test standards from being stigmatized as 'failures'."[66] The power of the exam and the type of questions posed seem in many instances to dictate the type of remediation offered students.

Impact on teachers. There has been an absence of systematic data concerning the impact of external state testing programs on teachers. What data there are indicate that the tests are narrowing instruction as the first seven principles become operative. For example, the NCAS Board of Inquiry reported that many teachers and parents saw tests as the real curriculum, affecting the daily practice of teaching. They reported that the tests narrowed the curriculum and fostered teaching to the test.[67] In Florida, the State Task Force concluded that "time for remediation [on the basic skills measured by the test] is obtained by having students drop one or more of their regular subjects to spend less time in them." Further it was found that accompanying remediation was a tendency "to reduce investment in elective areas, such as art and music, but key academic programs were affected as well."[68] In New Jersey, the Department of Education admitted that teachers teach to that state's basic skills test, and even provided districts with copies of previous tests that some teachers used for extensive drill work weeks or even months before the exam.[69]

Impact on students. While there are no hard data available, there was considerable anecdotal evidence presented at NIE-sponsored hearings on minimum competency testing that many students who failed a graduation test the first time dropped out of school and never took the test again. These students came to be referred to as "ghosts." Whether or not their decision to drop out is directly or indirectly related to failing the graduation test is unknown. However, as we noted above, NCAS found that high-stakes tests, whatever their origin, were being used as exclusionary devices, and were impacting most adversely on the poor, minority, and handicapped students. There is a great need to study seriously the extent to which state-level high-stakes tests may be influencing the dropout situation. Again there are serious political problems in attempting such a study because of the vested interests of some policymakers in the success of the program.

Richman, Brown, and Clark have examined how personality dimensions of high school students change after the students learned of their success or failure on a state minimum competency test (MCT) linked to the receipt of their high school diploma. Students who were at high risk to fail the MCT, and subsequently did fail, showed

marked increases in neuroticism and apprehension with a corresponding decrease in general self-esteem, responsibility, assertiveness,
warmheartedness, and leadership potential. This is the only study we
know of that examined the direct effects on noncognitive traits of
providing external test information to students.[70]

Popham, Cruse, Rankin, Sandifer, and Williams report that
student test scores have risen dramatically in Texas, Detroit, South
Carolina, and Maryland.[71] In all of these locations, measurement was
perceived as a catalyst to improve instruction. In addition, a number of
people have pointed to a sharp decrease in the numbers of students
failing minimum competency graduation tests as evidence of the
program's success.[72] This phenomenon of pointing to increases in
passing rates is not unusual. For example, in 1881 Sir Patrick Keenan
justified a system of paying teachers on the basis of student
examination results in Ireland by reporting that over the ten-year
period the percentage passing in reading had increased from 70.5
percent to 91.4 percent; in writing from 55.7 percent to 93.8 percent;
and in arithmetic from 54.4 percent to 74.8 percent.[73] However,
alternative explanations for these gains have never been sufficiently
explored. They may be due solely to teaching to the test, which was
certainly the case in the payment-by-results example. They may not
generalize to other measures of the same construct and in fact may
change the original construct the test was designed to measure.[74] A
recent Congressional Budget Office (CBO) study sheds some light on
such claims. It concluded that the end of the achievement score decline
began about 1968-69, before the advent of external state testing
programs. Further, the data suggest that declines in basic skills might
generally have been less severe than those associated with higher-
order skills.[75]

In short, once again there is a need for carefully designed studies of
the impact of high-stakes state-level achievement tests on schools,
teachers, and students. We would predict that effects associated with
the seven principles would eventually begin to assert themselves.

Testing and the Reform Reports

Several of the recent national educational reform reports have
called for a system of national, but not federal, examinations at major
transition points administered by an agency external to the local
school district. Some have dubbed these exams maximum competency
tests to distinguish them from present minimum competency

certification tests. Consider, for example, this recommendation in *A Nation at Risk*:

Standardized tests of achievement (not to be confused with aptitude tests) should be administered at major transition points from one level of schooling to another and particularly from high school to college or work. The purposes of these tests would be to: (a) certify the student's credentials; (b) identify the need for remedial intervention; and (c) identify the opportunity for advanced or accelerated work. The tests should be administered as part of a nationwide (but not Federal) system of State and local standardized tests.[76]

This proposition, and a similar one in the Carnegie Commission Report,[77] are in essence very similar to the English examination system leading to the General Certificate of Education (GCE), Ordinary (O) level and Advanced (A) level. English students, depending on their career plans, take a number of individual exams in various content areas such as physics, chemistry, mathematics, English literature, and French. These exams are quite different from basic skills competency tests used in some of our states for certification, which are skill oriented, not subject matter or program specific. There are five troubling issues associated with proposals to transplant an analogous system here. To date these issues have not received sufficient attention.

First, there is the tension that runs through these reports between the perceived desirability of maintaining a decentralized system of education controlled by individual communities on the one hand, and the call for a national external examination program used for certification on the other. The administrative mechanism used to insure that standards are met (an external test) in effect greatly diminishes cherished local control over what is taught as well as over how it is taught and learned. European secondary schools, while more independent than their American counterparts in some ways, have no control over the curriculum. When you buy into an external certification test, you accept ipso facto the straightjacket of constraints on your syllabus and instruction. This particular dilemma did not receive attention in any reports.

Second, assuming that we are willing to diminish further local control by mandating a new type of national external testing program, we have no independent boards that could exercise such a role. In England, on the other hand, there are eight respected examinations boards ranging from the prestigious Oxford and Cambridge School Examinations Board and the University of London Board to lesser known regional boards such as the Welsh Joint Education Committee, all under the coordinating aegis of the National Council for Examinations. Our present solution at the state level would probably be to issue a request for proposals and contract to construct and score the tests. But this is a state-by-state solution; it would not result in the nationwide examination system called for in some of the reports. The Carnegie study of American high schools recommended that the College Entrance Examination Board (CEEB) build what they labeled a new Student Achievement and Advisement Test.[78] It seems unlikely that the fifty states would agree on common syllabi, or approve of the transfer of such enormous power over the curriculum to any outside body.

However, even if it were possible to set up acceptable, independent boards and turn over to them the management of a national certification examination system, they would most likely be conservative, narrow, and rigidly stereotyped. H. G. Wells remarked of such boards, "They must never do the unexpected because that might be unfair."[79] In Tom Sharpe's *Vintage Stuff*, the fictional headmaster, Dr. Hardbolt, humorously explains this inherent conservatism of examination boards thus:

Now where most teachers go wrong is in failing to apply the methods used in animal training to their pupils. If a seal can be taught to balance a ball on his nose, a boy can be taught to pass exams. "But the questions are surely different every year," said Mr. Clyde-Browne. Dr. Hardbolt shook his head. "They can't be. If they were, no one could possibly teach the answers. Those are the rules of the game."[80]

This conservatism was also true of our own homegrown version of external certification exams—the New York State Regents. In 1938, Spaulding reported that exam questions were rejected on the ground that:

"They will not be expecting that," or "They have never had a question like that." The result is that the examinations, instead of leading the way toward better teaching, have often tended merely to perpetuate the kind of teaching to which a majority of teachers had become accustomed.[81]

Spaulding's observation about perpetuating a certain cozy, predictable, conservative style of teaching brings us to the third issue about which we need much more discussion, that is, the long-term negative effects of teaching for the examination flowing out of the seven principles. Inevitably, both the behavior and content of exams become institutionalized. There is a passage from Lewis Carroll which describes beautifully the corrupting process of an established examination tradition.

[The] pupils' got it all by heart; and, when Examination time came, they wrote it down; and the Examiner said Beautiful! (What depth!). They became teachers in their turn, and they said all these things over again; and their pupils wrote it down; and the Examiner accepted it; and nobody had the ghost of an idea what it all meant.[82]

The fourth issue related to proposals for the establishment of maximum competency testing is the tendency for such a system to become elitist. There is bound to be university bias to such GCE-type exams which equate scholastic and academic skills with merit. What about the needs of the nonacademic student? Perhaps we will end up with a double system of external exams like England. There, in addition to the GCE, there is also a Certificate of Secondary Education (CSE) which is based on curricula that are more general and practical. What are the implications of a dichotomized diploma which depends on the type of exams taken? Will such a system slam the doors to higher education for those taking the less prestigious nonacademic exams? It happens in Europe.

The danger in imposing a similar external exam system here is that it may, in fact, close doors to the poor and to minorities. We have been quite successful in this country in steadily raising the final attainment level of students. A very high proportion of our students get their high school diploma. Green warns us that if we now replace indices of attainment, that is, the last level or grade reached, with those of achievement, that is, test scores, we can expect that this will work in opposition to further marginal gains in attainment.[83]

If achievement levels are tightened or raised through external certification exams, and these exams expel failures from the system, then we need to consider this cost in personal and national terms. The Board of Inquiry of NCAS found that tests were already becoming an exclusionary device, affecting the poor, minorities, and the handicapped. Further, as mentioned above, no one has examined whether minimum competency tests—never mind maximum competency tests—have affected the dropout rate. Green also reminds us that having the high school diploma is no big deal today, but not having it is a disaster. We need considerably more discussion and thought concerning the potential of a system of certification tests to create such a disaster for certain vulnerable populations.

Finally, in all the reports there is a tension between the recommendations to upgrade the professional status of teachers and those related to certification testing. Certification testing essentially takes promotion or graduation decisions out of teachers' hands. It seems that the public and policymakers have come to mistrust teachers' judgments and want to replace them with external examinations. They point to the number of students they see passed on from one grade to the next solely on the basis of seat time, as evidence that teachers can not or will not make the tough calls. The simple solution seems to be to hand over critical decisions to a surrogate teacher—a multiple-choice test.

Teachers could use external test results to inform their decisions, but they are diminished as professionals if they, in the final analysis, do not make such decisions. While European secondary teachers may be content to delegate this function to an anonymous external agency, American teachers have traditionally accepted the role of final arbiter as part of their professional responsibilities. As a North Carolina teacher testifying at the NIE Clarification Hearing put it:

Allowing an [external minimum competency test] to make the decision for us, I think, is a copout. Instead as educators we need to accept full responsibility for these difficult decisions. We must look at teacher observations, a child's academic, physical, social, and emotional growth, a child's performance on classroom tests and criterion-referenced tests to fairly evaluate any child.[84]

Those interested in curriculum development, instruction, teaching, and testing need to think through the implications inherent in these proposals for a new type of certification test. Do we want a national curriculum in secondary school subjects that would follow from a national test? There is need for considerably more public debate around these issues than has taken place to date. Ultimately, the decision will be based on the prevailing philosophy of education of those in power and how they view the external tests as a mechanism of power. Historically, the dangers of embarking on this road are clear.

Implications for Curriculum Development and Instruction

Can curriculum recapture its rightful role in defining the goals for our schools? What counterstrategies are available to minimize the potentially corrupting influences of high-stakes tests on the curriculum, teaching, and learning? Given the present political mood of the country—educational reform is currently good politics—there are no easy answers. Policymakers will not readily abandon the use of high-stakes tests to drive instruction and learning.

Consequently, people from various educational disciplines must begin to frame and justify attractive counterstrategies to the use of high-stakes tests. Further, any counterstrategies must include the use of test information. That is, if a counterstrategy is to be taken seriously, it must acknowledge the fact that standardized testing has a legitimate role to play in curriculum and instruction. The late French philosopher-historian Michel Foucault, during a visit to America, made the following observation: "Its cost, importance, the care that one takes in administering it, the justification that one tries to give for it seem to indicate that it possesses positive functions."[85] He was describing Attica prison, not examinations, but the statement easily encompasses the place of examinations in education. The point is that an institution or mechanism of discipline and control cannot be reduced to its negative functions. And, while I have chosen to concentrate on what I regard as the long-term negative consequences of using high-stakes tests as a mechanism of power to drive instruction and learning, formal testing programs can provide valuable descriptive information about achievement.

To begin with, I feel that those concerned with curriculum and instruction need to lobby for a lowering of the stakes associated with test performance per se. Currently test results in most high-stakes situations *automatically* trigger an action without regard for other, possibly contradictory information that might contraindicate the mandated course of action. It is this automatic disposition that gives those who control the test their power over the actions of others. Those concerned with curriculum, teaching, and learning must make the case that test information be *one* piece of information used alongside other indicators, when a person(s), rather than a test score, authorizes a critical decision about pupils, teachers, programs, schools, or school systems.

There is also a need to make the case against the overreliance on the administratively convenient multiple-choice format as the principal indicator of educational outcomes. Frederiksen correctly points out that the economies associated with the multiple-choice format have "nearly driven out other testing procedures that might be used in school evaluation."[86] Further he reminds us of the fact known at least since the Tyler-Wood controversy of the early 1930s, multiple-choice tests tend not to measure more complex abilities.

One counterstrategy offering an alternative that might lessen some of the negative effects associated with present high-stakes testing can be found in the *Paideia Proposal*. Paideia recognizes the need for testing, but of a kind essentially different from that recommended in other reform reports. First, testing is squarely in the hands of the LEAs; in fact, tests would be designed and administered by teachers. Second, Paideia calls for examinations which do not merely involve the regurgitation of textbook or course material, the ever present danger associated with the external exams proposed in other reports. Paideia envisions examinations in the fuller sense of the term: direct, supply-type indicators of student outcomes quite different from the usual multiple-choice, selection format.[87]

Sizer suggests that a good way to operationalize a Paideia curriculum is to have teachers work out examinations—in the fuller sense of the term—which would be used at "key checkpoints." Such an exercise focuses curricular and instructional issues for teachers, and sharpens their priorities.[88] His discussion and the testing philosophy it embodies closely resemble Ralph Tyler's work in the Eight Year Study and later, when he was University Examiner at the University of Chicago.[89] Essentially, in both instances Tyler worked with classroom teachers to help them crystallize their course objectives; teachers had to make explicit the evidence they would accept that their objectives had been realized. The examination flowed out of this interaction. Direct measures were always used until such time as there was evidence that indirect techniques yielded essentially the same results; direct measures were the criterion for the validation of any indirect measure of an objective.

A problem with implementing a Paideia-type testing program is that it lacks the administrative simplicity and low cost of the other reform proposals. To work, it also needs measurement people skilled in the Tyler approach to cooperate closely with teachers—a resource in short supply in many LEAs, particularly in small to medium size and poorer districts. Alternatively we would need teachers much better trained in Tyler's approach to student evaluation than is presently the case. Further, the experience of the University Examiners' Office shows that this approach is expensive. There, the exam became available in the bookstore after each administration, which was both costly and sometimes demoralizing for the

Examiner's staff, which had to begin to build a new exam from scratch. Nonetheless, Paideia advocates could read Tyler with profit, for what they are advocating is certainly nothing new.

Despite problems, Paideia offers a possible way to restore the balance between curriculum, teaching, learning, and testing. But, Paideia is not the only nor necessarily the best solution to restoring the balance between testing, curriculum, and instruction. What is needed at this juncture in American education is more discussion of creative counterstrategies that have curriculum and instruction driving testing rather than testing driving curriculum and instruction— counterstrategies in which testing is the servant not the master of curriculum, instruction, and learning.

Notes

1. Walter Haney, "College Admissions Testing and High School Curriculum: Uncertain Connection and Future Directions," in *Measures in the College Admissions Process*, ed. Renee Gernand (New York: College Board, in press).

2. For a full discussion of the ways in which tests can be differentiated, see Thomas Kelleghan, George F. Madaus, and Peter W. Airasian, *The Effects of Standardized Testing* (Boston: Kluwer-Nijhoff Publishing, 1982).

3. For a full discussion of the sensitivity of commercially available tests to detect the effectiveness of instruction, see George F. Madaus, Peter W. Airasian, and Thomas Kelleghan, *School Effectiveness: A Reassessment of the Evidence* (New York: McGraw-Hill, 1980).

4. I first heard the term "high-stakes test" used by W. James Popham at a conference sponsored by the Connecticut Department of Education. I was struck by its appropriateness and adopted the term.

5. Center for the Study of Testing, Evaluation, and Educational Policy, "An Evaluation of the Kentucky Essential Skills Tests in Mathematics and Reading," (Chestnut Hill, MA: Boston College, 1986). Paper submitted to the Kentucky Department of Education.

6. Benjamin S. Bloom, "Some Theoretical Issues Relating to Educational Evaluation," in *Educational Evaluation: New Roles, New Means*, ed. Ralph W. Tyler, Sixty-eighth Yearbook of the National Society for the Study of Education, Part 2 (Chicago: University of Chicago Press, 1969).

7. Donald T. Campbell, "Assessing the Impact of Planned Social Change," in *Social Research and Public Policies: The Dartmouth/OECD Conference* (Hanover, NH: Public Affairs Center, Dartmouth College, 1975).

8. W. James Popham, "The Case for Minimum Competency Testing," *Phi Delta Kappan* 63 (October 1981): 89-92; W. James Popham, Keith L. Cruse, Stuart C. Rankin, Paul D. Sandifer, and Paul L. Williams, "Measurement-Driven Instruction: It's on the Road," *Phi Delta Kappan* 66 (May 1985): 628-635.

9. George F. Madaus, "Public Policy and the Testing Profession—You've Never Had It So Good?" *Educational Measurement* 4 (Winter 1985): 5-11.

10. Francis T. Spaulding, *High School and Life: The Regents' Inquiry into the Character and Cost of Public Education in the State of New York* (New York: McGraw-Hill, 1938).

11. G.C. Morris, "Educational Objectives of Higher Secondary School Science" (Doct. diss., University of Sydney, Australia, circa 1969).

12. S.N. Mukerji, *History of Education in India: Modern Period* (Baroda: Acharya Book Depot, 1966); J.T. Srinivasan, "Annual Terminal Examinations in the Jesuit High Schools of Madras, India" (Doct. diss., Boston College, 1971) and A.K. Gayen et al., *Measurement of Achievement in Mathematics: A Statistical Study of Effectiveness of Board and University Examinations in India*, Report I (New Delhi: Ministry of Education, 1961).

13. William K. Cummings, *Education and Equality in Japan* (Princeton, NJ: Princeton University Press, 1980).

14. George F. Madaus and John Macnamara, *Public Examinations: A Study of the Irish Leaving Certificate* (Dublin: Educational Research Centre, St. Patrick's College, 1970).

15. Patricia Broadfoot, ed., *Selection, Certification, and Control: Social Issues in Educational Assessment* (New York: Falmer Press, 1984). See also: J.D. Koerner, *Reform in Education: England and the United States* (New York: Delacorte Press, 1968); E.G.A. Holmes, *What Is and What Might Be: A Study of Education in General and Elementary in Particular* (London: Constable Press, 1911); Robert Bell and Nigel Grant, *A Mythology of British Education* (Frogmore, St. Albans, Herts, England: Panther Books, 1974); Peter Gordon and Dennis Lawton, *Curriculum Change in the 19th and 20th Centuries* (New York: Holmes and Meier, 1978); Norman Morris, "An Historian's View of Examinations," in *Examination and English Education*, ed. S. Wiseman (Manchester: Manchester University Press, 1961).

16. Glenn Turner, "Assessment in the Comprehensive School: What Criteria Count?" in *Selection, Certification, and Control*, ed. Broadfoot, p. 69.

17. George Orwell, "Such, Such Were the Joys," in *The Collected Essays, Journalism, and Letters of George Orwell, In Front of Your Nose, 1945-1950*, ed. S. Orwell and I. Angus (New York: Harcourt Brace Jovanovich, 1968), p. 336.

18. Martin Rafferty, "Examinations in Literature: Perceptions from Nontechnical Writers of England and Ireland from 1850 to 1984" (Doct. diss., Boston College, 1985).

19. Emerson E. White, "Examinations and Promotions," *Education* 8 (1888): 518.

20. Robert J. Braun, "Education Firm Chief Warns of Stress on Skills Tests," *Newark Star Ledger*, 11 October 1981, p. 80.

21. Madaus and Macnamara, *Public Examinations*.

22. F. Hotyat, "Evaluation in Education," in UNESCO, *Report on an International Meeting of Experts Held at the UNESCO Institute for Education* (Hamburg: UNESCO, 1958).

23. Ralph W. Tyler, "The Impact of External Testing Programs," in *The Impact and Improvement of School Testing Programs*, ed. Warren G. Findley, Sixty-second Yearbook of the National Society for the Study of Education, Part 2 (Chicago: University of Chicago Press, 1963), pp. 193-210.

24. Commission on Mathematics, *Program for College Preparatory Mathematics, U.S.A.* (New York: College Entrance Examination Board, 1959).

25. Popham, "The Case for Minimum Competency Testing"; Popham et al., "Measurement-Driven Instruction"; Jason Millman, "Protesting the Detesting of PRO Testing," *NCME Measurement in Education* 12 (Fall 1981): 1-6.

26. The following exchange between the Bishop of London and Matthew Arnold during the latter's testimony to the Royal Commission on Education against payment by results captures the view that if the skills are well chosen and measured correctly then measurement-driven instruction is proper and beneficial. Keep in mind that the

discussion assumes a supply-type rather than selection-type answer on the part of the student.

Bishop of London (BL): "Do you think there is any difference between doing a sum in an examination and doing it on the counter of a shop?"

Matthew Arnold (MA): "I think there is a difference between preparing them to do rightly the sort of sums that are set in an examination and preparing them to use their heads on matters of calculation."

BL: "Certainly, there is a very great difference. But that merely means that the sums are wrongly set, as it were, that the sums set at the examinations are not of the right character?"

MA: "Yes, I think so; that is what I mean."
Royal Commision on Education, *Minutes of Evidence*, Fifteenth Day, 7 April 1886, pp. 208-209.

27. Orwell, "Such, Such Were the Joys," p. 337.

28. For a full description of the Irish Primary Certificate, see George F. Madaus and Vincent Greaney, "The Irish Experience in Competency Testing: Implications for American Education," *American Journal of Education* 93 (February 1985): 268-294.

29. Haney, "College Admissions Testing."

30. Cummings, *Education and Equality in Japan.*

31. P.E. Vernon, ed., *Secondary School Selection: A British Psychological Society Inquiry* (London: Methuen, 1957).

32. Wilfred Sheed, *Transatlantic Blues* (New York: E.P. Dutton, 1982), p. 117.

33. L.B. Corse, as quoted in Robert Rentz, "Testing and the College Degree," in *Measurement and Educational Policy*, ed. William B. Schrader (San Francisco: Jossey-Bass, 1979), p. 76.

34. National Institute of Education, *Transcripts of the Minimum Competency Testing Clarification Hearings*, Washington, DC, July 8, 9, 10, 1981 (prepared by Alderson Reporting Co., Washington, DC, 1981).

35. David Grady, "The New #2 Pencil," *Computer Update* 6 (May/June 1983): pp. 65-67.

36. Holmes, *What Is and What Might Be*, p. 128.

37. Tyler, "The Impact of External Testing Programs."

38. Madaus, "Public Policy and the Testing Profession."

39. Marjorie C. Kirkland, "The Effects of Tests on Students and Schools," *Review of Educational Research* 41 (October 1971): 303-350.

40. Lee Sproull and David Zubrow, "Standardized Testing from the Administrative Perspective," *Phi Delta Kappan* 62 (May 1981): 628-630.

41. Kelleghan, Madaus, and Airasian, *The Effects of Standardized Testing.*

42. D.A. Goslin, *Teachers and Testing* (New York: Russell Sage Foundation, 1967).

43. M.D. Beck and Frank P. Stetz, "Teachers' Opinions of Standardized Test Use and Usefulness" (Paper presented at the Annual Meeting of the American Educational Research Association, San Francisco, April 1979).

44. Leslie Salmon-Cox, "Teachers and Standardized Achievement Tests: What's Really Happening?" *Phi Delta Kappan* 62 (May 1981): 631-633.

45. Kelleghan, Madaus, and Airasian, *The Effects of Standardized Testing.*

46. Ibid.

47. E. Husserl, *Formal and Transcendental Logic*, trans. Dorian Cairns (The Hague: Martinus Nijhoff, 1969).

48. K.C.W. Leiter, "Teachers' Use of Background Knowledge to Interpret Test Scores," *Sociology of Education* 49 (1976): 59-65.

49. Philip W. Jackson, *Life in Classrooms* (New York: Holt, Rinehart and Winston, 1968).

50. Kelleghan, Madaus, and Airasian, *The Effects of Standardized Testing*.

51. Ibid.

52. Bloom, "Some Theoretical Issues."

53. C.E. Flowers, "Effects of an Arbitrary Accelerated Group Placement on the Tested Academic Achievement of Educationally Disadvantaged Students" (Doct. diss., Teachers College, Columbia University. 1966).

54. Kelleghan, Madaus, and Airasian, *The Effects of Standardized Testing*.

55. Anthony J. Polemini, "Security in a Citywide Testing Program," *NCME Measurement in Education* 6 (Summer 1975): 1-5.

56. National Coalition of Advocates for Students, *Barriers to Excellence* (Boston: National Coalition of Advocates for Students, 1985).

57. Joan McCarty First and Jose Cardenas, "A Minority View on Testing," *Educational Measurement: Issues and Practice* 5 (Spring 1986): 6-11.

58. P.G. LeMahieu, "The Effects on Achievement and Instructional Content of a Program of Student Monitoring through Frequent Testing," *Educational Evalutation and Policy Analysis* 6 (Summer 1984): 175-187.

59. National Coalition of Advocates for Students, *Barriers to Excellence*, pp. 48-49.

60. *Education Week*, 6 February 1985.

61. Task Force on Federal Elementary and Secondary Education Policy, *Making the Grade* (New York: Twentieth Century Fund, 1983).

62. Ibid., p. 59.

63. L.C. Stedman and M.S. Smith, "Recent Reform Proposals for American Education," *Contemporary Education Review* 2 (1983): 85-104.

64. Task Force on Educational Assessment Programs, "Competency Testing in Florida: Report to the Florida Cabinet," Part I (Tallahassee, FL: Florida State Department of Education, 1979), p. 10.

65. State of Florida, "Recorded Minutes of the Cabinet Meeting, August 15, 1987" (Tallahassee, FL: Florida State Department of Education, 1979), p. 67.

66. National Coalition of Advocates for Students, *Barriers to Excellence*.

67. Ibid.

68. Task Force on Educational Assessment Programs, "Competency Testing in Florida," p. 11.

69. Robert Braun, "'Politicizing' Skills Test Scores Carries Great Risk for Students," *Newark Star Ledger*, 12 October 1981, p. 15.

70. C.L. Richman, K.P. Brown, and M. Clark, *Personality Changes as a Function of Minimum Competency Test Success/Failure*, NIMH Grant PHS 1R01 Mh 36491, n.d. Request for reprints may be made through C.L. Richman, Wake Forest University.

71. Popham et al., "Measurement-Driven Instruction."

72. Ralph D. Turlington, "Good News from Florida: Our Minimum Competency Program Is Working," *Phi Delta Kappan* 60 (May 1979): 649-651.

73. P.J. Keenan, *Address on Education to National Association for the Promotion of Social Science* (Dublin: Queen's Printing Office, 1881).

74. Robert Linn, George F. Madaus, and Joseph J. Pedulla, "Minimum Competency Testing: Cautions on the State of the Art," *American Journal of Education* 91 (November 1982): 1-35.

75. Congressional Budget Office of the Congress of the United States, *Trends in Educational Achievement*, April 1986, pp. 59-115.

76. National Commission on Excellence in Education, *A Nation at Risk: The Imperative for Educational Reform* (Washington, DC: U.S. Government Printing Office, 1983), p. 28.

77. E.L. Boyer, *High School: A Report on Secondary Education in America* (New York: Harper and Row, 1983).

78. Ibid.

79. H.G. Wells, *An Experiment in Biography* (New York: Macmillan, 1934), p. 280.

80. Thomas Sharpe, *Vintage Stuff* (London: Penguin Press, 1982), p. 47.

81. Spaulding, *High School and Life*, p. 198.

82. Lewis Carroll, *The Penguin Complete Lewis Carroll* (London: Penguin Press, 1939), p. 563.

83. Thomas F. Green, *Predicting the Behavior of the Educational System* (Syracuse, NY: Syracuse University Press, 1980).

84. National Institute of Education, *Transcripts of the Minimum Competency Testing Clarification Hearings*, p. 300.

85. Michel Foucault, in an interview with John Simon, "Michel Foucault on Attica," *Telos* 19 (1974): 156, cited by James Bernauer, S.J., "Foucault's Political Analysis," *International Philosophical Quarterly* 12 (March 1982): 89.

86. Norman Frederiksen, "The Real Test Bias," *American Psychologist* 39 (March 1984): 193-202.

87. Mortimer J. Adler, *The Paideia Proposal: An Educational Manifesto* (New York: Macmillan, 1982).

88. T.R. Sizer, Appendix III in *Paideia Problems and Possibilities: Consideration of Questions Raised by the Paideia Proposal by M.J. Adler* (New York: Macmillan, 1983).

89. For a description of the Eight Year Study, see Eugene Smith and Ralph W. Tyler, *Appraising and Recording Student Progress* (New York: Harper, 1942). For a description of the University of Chicago Examiner's Office, see Benjamin Bloom, *All Our Children Learning: A Primer for Parents, Teachers, and Other Educators* (New York: McGraw-Hill, 1981), pp. 245-266.

Introduction to Chapter V

The centrality of the textbook in American education is widely recognized. In the following chapter, Professor Daniel Tanner asks why this is the case. Given this broad consensus, it is hardly surprising that major proposals for curriculum reform require changes in textbooks to bring the books into alignment with the reforms proposed. As Tanner notes, the textbook was seen as the dominant vehicle for the national projects for curricular reform in the late 1950s and in the 1960s.

Textbooks have also been the center of controversy. The problem of censorship of texts (and of collateral reading materials as well) persists, often with stifling effects on the curriculum as texts are "watered down" to avoid controversy.

Tanner's recommendations for dealing with problems to which he refers in this chapter should be helpful to teachers, curriculum planners, and administrators.

The problems identified in this 1987 essay are still with us. Some of them again received attention in another NSSE publication—the 89th Yearbook, Part 1, Textbooks and Schooling in the United States, edited by David Elliot and Arthur Woodward.

Daniel Tanner is Professor of Education at Rutgers University. The chapter reprinted here originally appeared in the Society's 87th Yearbook, Part 1, Critical Issues in Curriculum, edited by Laurel N. Tanner.

CHAPTER V

The Textbook Controversies

DANIEL TANNER

"The significant position of textbooks in the program of American education is so generally recognized that the Society seems to be fully justified in sponsoring a yearbook on the theme 'The Textbook.' It is the textbook that in thousands of classrooms determines the content of instruction and as well as the teaching procedures."[1]

These were the opening words of the Thirtieth Yearbook, Part II, of the National Society for the Study of Education, published in 1931. More than half a century later, the textbook was still being described as "the predominant classroom resource," accounting for up to 80 percent of the subject matter in the course of study.[2]

Throughout the twentieth century textbooks have been variously criticized by progressive educators for determining the curriculum, whereas radical romanticists have favored the virtual elimination of textbooks and the preplanned curriculum,[3] while those on the far right have sought to censor textbooks so as to eliminate the treatment of unsettling ideas and issues. Then there are the futurists who became so enamored with the new electronic media during the 1960s and early 1970s that they predicted that print will play only a secondary role in the classroom of the future.[4] In a publication commemorating the centennial year of the U.S. Office of Education, a scenario of schooling was presented as a vision of the future (the year of 1997) in which textbooks and other books, and even teachers, would be replaced by the computer.[5] (Ironically, the futurists who predict the virtual demise of conventional print media for teaching and learning invariably use the book to convey their message to the education profession and the general public.)

Why is the textbook, along with other books in the classroom and school library, so dominant and durable? In an age of microelectronic-media technology, why is it that the textbook and other conventional print media continue to serve as the predominant classroom resource? Is the dominance of the textbook and other conventional print media largely attributable to the resistance of the school to change? Or are there unique attributes and functions indigenous to these conventional

115

print media which distinguish them from other media as a principal teaching-learning resource? These are some of the questions, along with related issues, to be addressed in this chapter.

Dominance and Durability of the Textbook

In *The Textbook Problem*, published in 1927, Ellwood P. Cubberley noted that because of the greater standardization of the curriculum in European schools, teachers there did not have access to the great variety of textbooks available in the United States; and with the greater standardization and uniformity of instruction and instructional tools in Europe, there was less reliance on the textbook. "In no country are there more teachers engaged in the work of textbook-making, and nowhere are textbooks in preparation subjected to such a severe trying-out process before publication. In no country, moreover, are the textbooks in use revised more frequently to keep them abreast of the progress of knowledge and the best educational thought," wrote Cubberley. He went on to point out that "nowhere does the experienced and capable teacher have so many supplementary texts to put into the hands of her pupils as do the teachers in the United States."[6] Nevertheless, a survey by William C. Bagley, reported in the Thirtieth Yearbook of the National Society for the Study of Education, found that modern educational theory in the preparation of teachers was bringing about less reliance on the " 'straight' recitation from the single textbook," and that this was "affecting elementary school practice in a fairly profound fashion, and it is apparently not without its influence upon the secondary school." Bagley also found that this transformation was in greater evidence among teachers who had participated to a greater extent in programs of teacher education. Moreover, the beginning teacher was more likely to depend upon formal textbook methods than teachers with several years of experience.[7]

More than half a century later, Goodlad reported in his study of schooling that there was evidence of the use of a wide range of textbooks and materials in classrooms, although heavy emphasis was being given to workbooks and worksheets in a mode not always distinguishable from testing. Goodlad also found that textbooks dominated the instruction in the sciences and mathematics, although workbooks and worksheets were commonplace in the latter subject.[8]

LOW COST, HIGH INFLUENCE

In the Thirtieth Yearbook of the NSSE (1931), Nelson B. Henry reported that books used in public elementary and secondary schools amounted to only 1.6 percent of the total school expenditures. Henry concluded that "textbooks are surprisingly inexpensive, especially when their importance in the education of the children of this country is considered."[9] A half century later, in the widely heralded report, *A Nation at Risk: The Imperative for Educational Reform*, issued by the National Commission on Excellence in Education, under the auspices of the U.S. Department of Education, the following finding was highlighted:

Expenditures for textbooks and other instructional materials have declined by 50 percent over the past 17 years. While some recommend a level of spending on texts of between 5 and 10 percent of the operating costs of schools, the budgets for basal texts and related materials have been dropping during the past decade and a half to only 0.7 percent today.[10]

Nevertheless, the textbook continues to serve as the predominant classroom resource in determining the content of instruction as well as the teaching procedures, and one must reach the same conclusion today as did Henry: "textbooks are surprisingly inexpensive." Yet to this day, in seeking to reduce the school budget, school boards and administrators tend to look first at reducing expenditures for textbooks and collateral curricular materials as students are made to work with shopworn books for yet another year.

The decline in expenditures for textbooks and other instructional materials by 50 percent over the past seventeen years, as noted in the report of the National Commission on Excellence in Education, appears to have been the result of the back-to-basics retrenchment of the 1970s and early 1980s. With most of the states embarking on minimum-competency testing, and with school districts seeking to hold the line on school budgets, teachers were focusing instruction on facts and skills in teaching-to-the-test while resorting to inexpensive workbooks, and photocopied materials.

THE NEED TO UPGRADE TEXTBOOKS AND COLLATERAL CURRICULAR MATERIALS

The report of the National Commission on Excellence in Education (1983) failed to attribute the decline in expenditures for textbooks and other instructional materials to the factors cited above, or to any other factors. Interestingly, in the section of its report on "Recommendations: Standards and Expectations," the Commission offered eight recommendations, of which five were focused on textbooks and related instructional materials. These recommendations called for the upgrading of textbooks and materials so as to assure (a) more rigorous content by enlisting "university scientists, scholars, and members of professional societies, in collaboration with master teachers . . . as they did in the post-Sputnik era"; (b) the systematic evaluation of textbooks through field trials and other means; and (c) the funding of textbook development in "thin-market" fields (for the disadvantaged, disabled, and gifted learner).[11] No mention was made as to why the unprecedented national curriculum reforms during the crisis of the cold war and post-Sputnik I era had failed to achieve what had been promised, nor how the misguided efforts of the past might be rectified.

Nevertheless, it was clear that the call to upgrade textbooks was a response to what was increasingly being perceived as the "dumbing down" of textbooks as a result of the back-to-basics retrenchment and of the objections that had been raised by various special-interest groups to the treatment of controversial ideas, problems, and issues in textbooks. Before returning to the problem of the "dumbing down" and censorship of textbooks and collateral curricular materials, a brief examination of the unprecedented national efforts to upgrade school textbooks and other instructional materials in the wake of the cold war and Sputnik I is in order.

Nationalizing Influences on the Textbook

"The National Science Foundation, which has recognized expertise in leading curriculum development, should again take the leadership role in promoting curriculum evaluation and development for mathematics, science, and technology."[12] So stated a report issued in 1983 for the National Science Board of the National Science Foundation. In making this recommendation, the report was referring to the national curriculum reform projects financed under the auspices of the National Science Foundation during the effort to mobilize our schools in the sciences and mathematics to meet the alleged crisis of the cold war and post-Sputnik I era.

The rationale undergirding this national curriculum reform effort in the wake of Sputnik I was explicated by Jerome Bruner in a report of a conference in 1959 called by the National Academy of Sciences.

In the opening paragraph of the report, Bruner linked the need for a national effort for curriculum reform with "what is almost certain to be a long-range crisis in national security."[13]

The final chapter of the report was devoted to the place of the newer instructional media in these national curriculum projects. In examining the potentials of programmed instructional materials and teaching machines, Bruner held that it was unlikely that such devices will dehumanize learning any more than books dehumanize learning. "A program for a teaching machine is as personal as a book," contended Bruner.[14] During the early stages of the leading national curriculum projects, it was indicated by some project leaders that explorations were being made into the possibility of developing programmed instructional materials. But none of these projects actually developed such materials. Clearly, with these projects claiming to embrace the inquiry-discovery mode, the convergent mode of programmed instruction was inimical to the presumably emergent inquiry-discovery approach.

Although the leading national curriculum reform projects of that era proceeded to develop multimedia approaches in their curriculum packages, the mainstay, nevertheless, was the textbook. Hence, in the preface to the early editions of the text *Physics* by the Physical Science Study Committee, James R. Killian, Jr., president of the Massachusetts Institute of Technology, described the textbook as "the heart of the PSSC course."[15] Soon, the magnitude of textbook sales was to become the criterion for gauging enrollments and determining the success of these projects; however, it was eventually revealed that the enrollments in the new science courses were being inflated by the project administrators by over 100 percent.[16] At the same time, the authors and publishers of competing texts were claiming that their textbooks were indeed embracing the main elements and currents of the "new" physics, biology, chemistry, mathematics, and so on. In effect, the national curriculum projects exerted a pervasive nationalizing influence on the textbook industry. But as it became apparent that the national curriculum reform projects were failing to measure up to the extravagant claims made for them, alternate approaches began to appear. However, the crisis of the cold war and space race was to become overshadowed by the crisis of student protest and disruption in the wake of the prolonged war in Vietnam, with the result that the role of the National Science Foundation in curriculum reform in elementary and secondary education went into a virtual eclipse.

The Textbook and Codified Knowledge

Why did the textbook serve as the dominant vehicle for the national curriculum reform projects led by university scholar-specialists during the late 1950s and the decade of the 1960s? In *The Structure of Scientific Revolutions*, Thomas Kuhn makes the case for textbooks as indispensable devices in science education in which they serve to "expound the body of accepted theory, illustrate many or all of its successful applications, and compare these applications with exemplary observations and experiments."[17] Kuhn holds that in the social sciences, history, and other fields, where the paradigms are relatively weak as compared with the sciences, textbooks are more likely to be accompanied by parallel readings than in the sciences because in these fields, the student "has constantly before him a number of competing and incommensurable solutions to . . . problems, solutions that he must ultimately evaluate for himself."[18]

With university scholar-specialists leading the national curriculum reforms during the 1950s and 1960s, discipline-centered knowledge became the focus of curriculum redevelopment, and the social scientists endeavored to imitate their colleagues in the natural sciences in seeking to demonstrate the "structure" of their disciplines. And with disciplinary knowledge being the focus of curriculum reform, it was inevitable that the textbook would serve as the principal vehicle for embodying the codified knowledge said to represent each discipline. Hence the school curriculum was to be comprised of separate disciplines or domains of codified knowledge.

By the late 1960s, it had become increasingly apparent that the discipline-centered basis for curriculum reform had neglected the nature of the learner and the need for interdisciplinary curricular structure to serve the function of general education in a free society. In other words, to meet the function of general education, the design of the school curriculum must take into account the nature of the learner and must reveal knowledge applications in the life of the learner and in the wider social life. In contradistinction, the national curriculum reforms had been focused on specialized, abstract, and puristic disciplinary knowledge representing the theoretical knowledge edifices of the university scholar-specialist.[19]

CODIFIED KNOWLEDGE AND CURRICULAR DISPUTATION

In seeking to study the problems connected with federal involvement in school curriculum development, especially in connection with the rise and fall of the national curriculum projects of the 1950s and 1960s, the National Institute of Education formed a Curriculum Development Task Force in 1975. In the introductory chapter of a book containing the papers commissioned for the Task Force, the chairman of the Task Force attributed the collapse of the federally supported curriculum projects largely to the forces of censorship, capped by a congressional attack on one of these projects in 1975.[20] Although the new biology textbooks had been attacked in some quarters by antievolutionists, the fact remains that most of the projects were not targets of censorship and were already in a state of decline by the late 1960s for reasons cited earlier.

Despite Kuhn's view that there is relatively little disputation in the natural sciences where the disciplinary paradigms are strongest, in contrast to other fields, school textbooks in biology, ecology, and general science have been subjected to enormous pressures of censorship and "dumbing down" to an extent no less portentous than in the social studies, history, and literature. One only has to cite the continued controversy over evolutionary theory in school science textbooks and the pressures by religious fundamentalists demanding that equal treatment be given in science textbooks to the doctrine of creationism as a viable alternative "theory." Or one can cite the opposition raised in some quarters to the study of human reproduction in biology textbooks.

Clearly, although the paradigms in the natural sciences are stronger than in other disciplines, the natural sciences are no less immune from disputation when the subject matter interfaces with philosophical ideas, personal and social views, and social applications. The censorship of ideas has reverberations throughout the school curriculum and cannot be confined to a given discipline or subject as long as that discipline or subject has relevance to the life of the learner and the wider social life. No discipline or subject matter is an island in the curriculum although, in the departmental knowledge edifices of the university, the disciplines or subject fields are often treated as independent, self-serving entities.

Textbook Censorship

At the opening of this chapter, the question was posed as to why the textbooks and collateral print media continue to serve as the predominant classroom resource during an age of microelectronic technology. A number of factors have been explored in this chapter, explaining the certain unique properties and functions of the textbook and conventional print media. Some of these properties become evident when addressing the following question: Why is it that efforts to censor ideas in the school curriculum tend to be centered on textbooks and other books used in the classroom and school library, and not on computer programs, programmed textbooks, or workbooks?

Apparently, beyond the more rudimentary levels of treatment of subject matter, and with the exception of technical subject matter and the subject of school mathematics, textbooks, along with other books used in the classroom and found in the school library, are of enormous potential use in exposing the learner to powerful ideas and unsettling issues that cannot be broached in any comparable way through the computer program, programmed textbook, or workbook. Whereas the computer program and other programmed instructional materials are geared predominantly to *established-convergent* learning situations, in which all action-relevant aspects of the system are specifiable and predictable, textbooks and library books can serve as pedagogical vehicles not only for *established* learning, but for *emergent* learning situations through which the student can explore problems and issues in open-ended ways.[21]

A PERSISTENT HISTORICAL PROBLEM

It is indeed baffling that the contributors to the Thirtieth Yearbook of the National Society for the Study of Education, *The Textbook in American Education*, examined so many ramifications of the textbook without addressing the problem of censorship. Not only had history and social studies textbooks undergone attack in the name of Americanism during the 1920s, but it was over the use of the textbook *Civic Biology*, authored by George Hunter, that John T. Scopes, a Tennessee high school teacher, was brought to trial in 1925 for having violated a state statute prohibiting the teaching of evolution. The case, which was called "the world's most famous court trial,"[22] came about when Scopes had commented to some friends that any teacher using the state-approved biology textbook could not help but violate the Tennessee statute against the teaching of evolution. With William Jennings Bryan on the side of the state and Clarence Darrow representing the defense, the case attracted great national and international notoriety, and eventually was dramatized in the theatre and as a motion picture. Scopes was convicted and fined $100. On appeal the state Supreme Court ruled the law constitutional, but reversed the lower court's decision on a technicality, thereby obviating the possibility of an appeal to the U.S. Supreme Court to test the constitutionality of the Tennessee law. The Tennessee law in question was eventually replaced by a statute prohibiting the use of any textbook containing subject matter on evolution without the qualifying statement that evolution is a theory and not a scientific fact.

In *Anti-intellectualism in American Life*, the late Richard Hofstadter concluded, "Today the evolution controversy seems as remote as the Homeric era to intellectuals in the East, and it is not uncommon to take a condescending view of both sides."[23] Hofstadter not only failed to recognize the growing national influence of Christian fundamentalism, but also that textbooks are used nationally and that any timidity or self-censorship by textbook authors and publishers has ramifications in schools in every sector of the nation. As discussed later, the problem of censoring and the "dumbing down" of schoolbooks so as to avoid controversial ideas was to reach a critical state in the mid-1980s.

Only three years following the publication of Hofstadter's book, and some forty years after the Scopes decision, a biology textbook used by a high school teacher in Little Rock was found in violation of an Arkansas statute against the teaching of evolution. Although the lower court decision was upheld by the state Supreme Court, the decision was reversed by the U.S. Supreme Court, which ruled the statute an establishment of religion in violation of the First Amendment.[24] The evolution-creationism textbook controversy has continued to this day, and in 1986 reached the U.S. Supreme Court once again.[25]

Aside from the very large number of court cases involving school textbooks as related directly to the curriculum, there is the continuing problem of censorship of textbooks and collateral reading materials. Before examining the contemporary situation, mention should be made of two notorious series of censorship incidents that occurred during the years toward the end of the Great Depression, and extended into the early cold-war period following World War II. By far the leading social studies textbook series for the junior and senior high schools during the decade of the 1930s and extending into the first years of the 1940s was *Man and His Changing Society* by Harold Rugg at Teachers College, Columbia University. The frame of reference for this textbook series was the evolution of modern American democracy with a focus on the pervasive problems and issues confronting our contemporary society. By the late 1930s, Rugg's textbooks came under full attack by the National Association of Manufacturers, the Advertising Federation of America, the Hearst press, the American Legion, and other ultra right-wing groups and individuals seeking to portray the Rugg textbooks as subversive of American ideals and institutions.[26] Although the American Historical Association's Commission on the Social Studies had come under similar attack during this same period by ultra rightists, the Rugg textbooks became the main target and, eventually, the casualty of the onslaught. Articles in *Time, Saturday Evening Post, Forbes, Nation's Business*, and other magazines were attacking progressive education and, more specifically, the Rugg textbooks. To no avail, noted authors, educators, and textbook publishers protested the removal of the Rugg textbooks from the schools and described the situation as a "state of panic" in which "prejudice and hatred are displacing reason and tolerance essential for the functioning of democratic institutions."[27] During the early 1940s the Rugg textbooks were undergoing full eclipse as school boards were urgently ordering their removal from the schools.

Considering the great notoriety of the Rugg textbook controversy and the stifling effect on the school curriculum and on the school textbook industry as a result of the censorship of the Rugg textbooks, it is puzzling that Hofstadter made no mention of this episode in his Pulitzer-prize winning work, *Anti-intellectualism in American Life*. Nor did Hofstadter mention the notorious episode of censoring the *Building America* series of social studies books which followed the Rugg episode. Curiously, Hofstadter chose to portray progressive education largely as an antiintellectual movement, as he failed to recognize the continuing and courageous battle on the part of leading progressive educators against the censorship of schoolbooks and in defense of academic freedom.[28]

Soon after the Rugg episode, during the cold-war years immediately following World War II, the *Building America* series of supplementary social studies texts came under the fire of the superpatriots and special-interest groups.[29] Created during the Great Depression by the Society for Curriculum Study (which later merged with the NEA Department of Supervision and Directors of Instruction, leading to the creation of the Association for Supervision and Curriculum Development), *Building America* was conceived to provide for the thoughtful examination of contemporary socioeconomic problems in the social studies curriculum in junior and senior high schools. The first editorial board of *Building America* (1934) included such figures as Paul R. Hanna, who created the series and served as chairman, Edgar Dale, Harold Hand, Jesse Newlon, Hollis L. Caswell, and James E. Mendenhall—young individuals who were to go on to make lasting contributions to American education. All of them contributed their own money to get the project under way. The first issue, "Housing" (1935), led to a grant from the General Education Board of the Rockefeller Foundation to cover the expenses of the project during its first year. Additional grants were made by the Foundation during the early years of publication. In 1940 the *Building America* series was being published by the Americana Corporation. By 1945, sales of the monthly paperback texts had reached more than a million copies per issue. The monthly texts were also published in hardbound annual editions. Over a period of thirteen years of publication (1935-1948), the widely acclaimed *Building America* series included ninety-one texts bearing such titles as "Food," "Power," "Health," "Youth Faces the World," "Our Constitution," "Social Security," "We Consumers," "Education," "War or Peace?," "Crime," "Civil Liberties," "Women," "Advertising," "Italian Americans," "Our Water Resources," and "Our Land Resources"—all focused on topical issues.

But 1945 was the year when attacks on the *Building America* series were to begin in earnest by the conservative press and ultra right-wing groups seeking to portray the texts as un-American. The locus of these attacks was mainly in California where the texts and the editorial board of *Building America* were targeted for scrutiny by the State Joint Legislative Fact-Finding Committee on Un-American Activities. Authors of the *Building America* texts and members of the editorial board were accused of being affiliated with communist-front organizations. When the charges were disproved, these individuals were attacked as having been "fooled" by communist-front organizations. As chairman of the editorial board, Paul R. Hanna, professor of education at Stanford University, took much of the brunt of the attacks. Pressures were being exerted to confine the curriculum to the fundamentals and to eliminate social studies and controversial ideas in favor of American history focused on factual subject matter and patriotic treatment.[30]

Although the *Building America* series had been approved by the California Board of Education upon the unanimously favorable recommendations of the California Curriculum Commission, the notoriety of the case led to a sharp decline in the sales of the texts and the withdrawal of Americana as publisher. The last issue in the *Building America* series appeared at the end of 1948 as school boards were having the texts removed from the schools.

The "Dumbing Down" of Schoolbooks

One only has to review the current issues of the American Library Association's *Newsletter on Intellectual Freedom* to realize that the censorship of schoolbooks is not only a continuing problem, but a heightened problem for American education. Virtually every issue of the *Newsletter* contains reports of incidents of the censorship of school library books or textbooks, along with related court decisions. Obviously, only a small fraction of the incidents of schoolbook censorship is reported, as most school administrators, teachers, and school librarians seek to avoid making a public issue over a local censorship incident. Then there is the common problem of self-censorship in which teachers avoid the use of collateral reading materials that might contain unsettling ideas.

WATERING DOWN THE CURRICULUM
TO AVOID CONTROVERSY

It is not only teachers who engage in self-censorship. Textbook authors and publishers also yield to real or imagined pressures as to what is acceptable or unacceptable to various constituencies. A notable example is the Human Sciences Program of the Biological Sciences Curriculum Study (BSCS), designed for students between ten and fourteen years of age. Although the BSCS leadership had been outspoken in defending academic freedom, the director of BSCS, William V. Mayer, acknowledged that a modular approach was taken in the Human Sciences Program so as to allow for the substitution (or elimination) of modules on topics that may be objectionable, such as the module on human reproduction and population. Mayer wrote:

We have, in the absence of data to the contrary, refrained from full explication of certain social matters that are still contentious within the population in order that students may not be disadvantaged by community refusals to use BSCS materials. We can and have rejected community pressures we regard as unfounded or motivated outside the scientific sphere, such as creationism in lieu of or parallel to evolution. But we cannot fight all battles in all communities simultaneously and effectively. . . . Our Board has given us directions in this regard.[31]

In the process of marketing the Human Sciences Program, BSCS proceeded to feature the modular organization of the materials and subject matter as "flexibility in packaging," allowing teachers and administrators to "modify the program to meet local needs by deleting activities either not germane or considered inappropriate for the local population." This was billed by BSCS as providing for "curriculum flexibility," rather than as serving to compromise the curriculum.[32]

The "watering down" of the curriculum is the inevitable consequence of externally imposed or self-imposed censorship, violations of the academic freedom of teachers, and curricular reductionism whereby the curriculum is confined mainly to basic skills and factual subject matter devoid of controversial ideas, problems, and issues. Essentialists typically take the position that academic freedom is the province of higher education, not elementary and secondary education. According to Raymond English, "academic freedom in its true sense has no place in precollege education" on the ground that "the schools and the teachers in them are servants of the community and of the families that make up the community."[33] Not only does such a view ignore the fact that education is a state function, but it relegates the majority of the rising generation who do not go on to college to the status of second-class citizens. Such a narrow view also assumes that the "community" is necessarily manifested in the form of the lowest common denominator of public enlightenment. It fails to recognize that "community" can also mean "cosmopolitan" in exemplifying the highest, widest, and wisest ideals and practices for public education. At the turn of the century, Dewey advised parents and educators that, "What the best and wisest parent wants for his own child, that must the community want for all of its children. Any other ideal is narrow and unlovely; acted upon, it destroys our democracy."[34]

Enlightened, well-educated parents want an enriched idea-oriented curriculum for their own children. When schools provide such a curriculum for the more advantaged children and youth while delimiting the disadvantaged to an error-oriented curriculum through the use of mechanical exercises in workbooks, ditto sheets, and programmed instructional materials, such differentiation militates against equality of educational opportunity.[35] There is a commonly held notion that higher-ability students prefer curricular materials and methods that are less directive and more discovery oriented, whereas lower-achieving students respond better to more directive and structured materials and methods. In reviewing the research on learning from media, Clark reports that the opposite seems to be the case:

Higher-ability students seem to like methods and media that they perceive as more structured and directive because they think they will have to invest less effort to achieve success. However, these more structured methods prevent the higher-ability students from employing their own considerable skills and yield less effort than the less directive methods and media. Lower-ability students seem to like less structured and more discovery-oriented methods and media.[36]

Those who hold the position that the school curriculum should properly be limited to subject matter concentrated on facts and fundamental skills have exerted a powerful influence on textbooks. Surprisingly, this position is shared by many in higher academe who see the school mainly as a "tooling up" for college. Hence Daniel Bell, a leading advocate of general education in college, proceeded to delimit the function of the secondary school as appropriately "concentrating on facts and skills," whereas he portrayed the college years, through general education, as "a broad intellectual adventure" and as an experience in "the testing of oneself and one's values."[37]

Not only does this view raise ominous consequences for a free society when the majority of youth who do not go on to higher education are denied the opportunity to engage in a "broad intellectual adventure" and the testing of their values in school, but it assumes that the engagement of intellectual curiosity and the formation and testing of values are inappropriate during the developing years of adolescence. To deny such experience is to deny adolescence as a critical period of human development and to place the adolescent in "no-man's-land." For most adolescents, the high school years are the last opportunity they will have to investigate controversial issues systematically in the formal educational setting.

In growing recognition that the forces for censoring schoolbooks and delimiting the school curriculum to established-convergent learning through facts and fundamental skills have great reverberations for higher education, the American Association of University Professors established in 1985 a Commission on Academic Freedom and Pre-College Education. The Commission's first report was focused on the problem of challenges to elementary and secondary school textbooks, library books, and other curricular materials. "The interest of higher education in threats to freedom in the schools is beyond doubt," declared the report as it went on to recommend ways through which universities can work with schools in combating censorship pressures.[38]

By the mid-1980s it was becoming increasingly apparent that the avoidance of controversial ideas in the curriculum, and more specifically in textbooks, was resulting in a watered-down curriculum. This was particularly disturbing to many educators in view of the mounting evidence revealing widespread deficiencies in higher-order thinking abilities on the part of students after years of back-to-basics retrenchment.[39]

Bettelheim and Zelan criticized reading texts for focusing on dull, repetitive drills, rote learning, and the failure to engage children in dealing with interesting ideas.[40] In this connection, there is a need to assess the extent to which the widespread use of readability formulas in the preparation of textbooks has resulted in the watering down of subject matter. Paradoxically, such formulas often serve to make the textbook less stimulating as interesting ideas are avoided in favor of more simplistic prose and mechanistic treatment.

A study commissioned by the Advisory Panel on the SAT Test Score Decline, sponsored by the College Board and the Educational Testing Service, found that the cognitive levels of textbooks in social studies, literature, grammar and composition had undergone a decline in level of cognitive maturity over a thirty-five-year period, and that the less challenging textbooks were associated with lower SAT scores by students using such texts. However, the researchers found that sixth-grade basal readers had become increasingly difficult since the late 1960s.[41]

In an address to school administrators in 1984, U.S. Secretary of Education Terrel H. Bell accused the publishers of "dumbing down" their textbooks, but Bell failed to acknowledge that the "dumbing down" of textbooks is the inevitable result of curricular reductionism through "back-to-basics" and censorship pressures.[42]

A STATE RESPONDS

In an ironic turn of events some forty years following the attacks on the *Building America* series in California, the California Board of Education in the fall of 1985, upon recommendation of the State Curriculum Development and Supplemental Materials Commission, unanimously rejected every science textbook submitted for use in seventh- and eighth-grade classes on the ground that the textbooks were "watered down" to avoid controversy. The Board and State Superintendent Bill Honig criticized the publishers for producing textbooks that avoid or fail to address adequately such controversial topics as evolution, human reproduction, and environmental problems. Within several months, the publishers produced revised editions of their textbooks. One publisher, who did not even list the topic of evolution in the textbook index, soon produced a revised edition with an entire chapter on evolution. Honig also announced that textbooks for all other subject areas would come under the same scrutiny as the science textbooks.[43]

Within a year following the action taken on the science textbooks, the California Board of Education voted to uphold the recommendation of the State Curriculum Development and Supplemental Materials Commission in rejecting every mathematics textbook for use in grades K-8. The Commission failed the textbooks for stressing "apparent mastery" of mechanical skills without engaging students in the understanding of concepts and in applying their mathematical knowledge, skills, and experience in problem-solving situations that are new or perplexing to them.[44] As in the case of its earlier report on science, the Commission based its recommendations on the evaluations of a panel of experts composed of university professors in the discipline and in education, curriculum directors and specialists from various school districts, and teachers. In conducting the evaluations, a framework of criteria was used, drawn from the research literature in mathematics and science education.[45]

The remarkable speed with which publishers proceeded to respond to these criticisms and recommendations by issuing revised textbooks can be appreciated when it is realized that if California were a nation, it would rank sixth among the nations of the world in the size of its economy.[46] "We now know that as a state representing 12 percent of the textbook market, we can stand up and be counted," stated Superintendent Honig. He went on to note that "publishers are willing to make changes based on quality criteria, if we ask them, and educators across the country have applauded our efforts."[47] However, as discussed earlier, publishers also respond to the narrow-minded influences of special-interest pressure groups when such influences are dominant.

The power of state adoption in the textbook marketplace as discussed in the recent incidents in California is, of course, a two-edged sword in that the practice of state adoption by a few "super states" can serve to shape the content of textbooks (and the curriculum) nationwide. Consequently, it is essential that the textbook selection committee be comprised of leading professional educators who have the expertise upon which the State Board of Education can rely. It is also essential that state-approved lists be sufficiently comprehensive so as to meet local needs. In these respects, the contemporary structure for textbook adoption in California, where the State Board of Education relies on the professional expertise of the Curriculum Development and Supplemental Materials Commission, and where the approved lists are comprehensive, serves to militate against the kinds of episodes that occurred in California and elsewhere during the 1940s in connection with the Rugg textbooks and the *Building America* series. Whereas the recent actions in California were based upon the best available professional knowledge, the actions of the 1940s were narrowly political, censorial, and contrary to the best available professional knowledge. Unfortunately, the historical record reveals that educators have been all too willing to abrogate their professional responsibilities as they readily yield to the dominant tide of the times, no matter how ill conceived and narrowly directed. The mark of a profession is that decisions are based upon the best available evidence, not on political opportunism or expediency.

Censorship and political interference and distortion of the curriculum can best be prevented at the local level when textbook evaluation and selection are based upon the best available professional knowledge. This requires a structural arrangement whereby textbook selection and evaluation are made by the professional staff of the school and school district in the form of a standing curriculum committee. The superintendent of schools must exercise considerable leadership acumen in educating the local board of education on their need to draw upon the expertise of the professional staff. There have been instances where school administrators have been censured by local boards of education for having censored textbooks and other curricular materials. Censorship is less apt to occur when the school board serves to represent the wider public interest, and not narrow individual or special interests. Obviously, this also applies to state boards of education.

Research on the Textbook

Content analysis has served as a useful device in gauging the extent of inclusion or exclusion of topics, ideas, and issues in textbooks and other curricular materials. Unfortunately, however, it has also been used for narrow political purposes to eliminate controversial ideas or to inject the biases of special-interest groups into the curriculum. For example, in its attacks on Rugg's textbooks during the early 1940s, the National Association of Manufacturers (NAM) engaged Ralph Robey, a professor of banking and economics at Columbia, to prepare "objective" abstracts of the material in the textbooks so as to ascertain the author's attitude toward our governmental and economic institutions. Despite the establishment of a committee of the American Historical Association to investigate the approach taken by Robey and the NAM in using the textbook abstracts, Robey and the NAM were successful in creating notoriety in connection with the Rugg textbooks and in using the abstracts to build their case against Rugg.[48]

In 1986, U.S. Secretary of Education William J. Bennett cited studies financed by the U.S. Department of Education to buttress his contention that school textbooks fail to give appropriate recognition to the contributions of religion to American culture. Bennett was quoted as citing these studies as evidence of "the assault of secularism on religion."[49] One of the studies was conducted by Paul C. Vitz, a psychology professor at New York University, who made a content analysis of the social studies textbooks for grades 1-6 from ten publishers. Vitz held that these textbooks "are representative of the nation as a whole." Among Vitz's reported findings were the following: "Serious Christian or Jewish religious motivation is featured nowhere. . . . Patriotism is close to nonexistent in the sample. Likewise, any appreciation of business success is seriously underrepresented. Traditional roles for both men and women receive virtually no support, while role-reversal feminist stories are common."[50]

Secretary Bennett was criticized by U.S. Senator Lowell P. Weicker, chairman of the Senate Education Appropriations Subcommittee, for subsequently approving Vitz for another grant for the content analysis of textbooks despite the low rating given to Vitz's research proposal in peer review. He also criticized Bennett for seeking to use the offices of the Department of Education for bringing his ideologies into school textbooks, when the law governing the department's organization prohibits it from exercising "direction, supervision, or control" over school textbooks.[51]

School textbooks and school library books have been subjected to the pressures of ideologies from the left as well as the right extremes of the political spectrum. Vocal minorities have influenced the treatment of material in textbooks ranging from basal readers to high school history and literature. Books have been removed from the curriculum and from school libraries because of pressures from vocal minorities as well as from right-wing groups.

Considering the great significance of the textbook in the curriculum, and the great disputations attaching to the content and uses of the textbook, it is surprising how little research has been conducted on how textbooks influence teaching and learning. "Textbooks command attention because they not only provide the basic source of school instruction but also transmit culture, reflect values, and serve as springboards for the intellectual development of individuals and the nation," commented Eloise Warming. She went on to note that "little, if any, research has been done on the effectiveness of learning from conventional textbooks."[52]

In the third edition of the *Handbook of Research on Teaching*, only one index entry is made for school textbooks, and the single entry is for the natural sciences. In this connection, the authors note that textbooks "receive far less attention in science education than many other instructional variables."[53]

In the first edition of the *Handbook of Research on Teaching*, Lumsdaine sought to explain the paucity of research on the textbook in these words:

The usual textbook does not control the behavior of the learner in a way which makes it highly predictable as a vehicle of instruction or amenable to experimental research. It does not in itself generate a describable and predictable process of learner behavior, and this may be the reason why there has been little experimental research on the textbook.[54]

Was Lumsdaine explaining the problem by explaining it away, or was he alluding to the special attributes of the textbook? Unlike convergent teaching-learning materials such as workbooks or programmed instructional materials, textbooks can be designed so as to provide for a great range and variety of emergent ideas and uses, or they can be limited mainly to established-convergent knowledge in the form of facts and skills. So limited, textbooks are no longer textbooks as Kuhn describes them. Instead, they become workbooks. Rather than being used to open up areas of inquiry to the learner, they become closed-ended.

Over many decades it has been recognized that effective teachers use textbooks in more emergent ways than less effective teachers and make use of a wide range of collateral reading materials and activities to supplement and enrich the textbook. Nevertheless, the potential for experimental research on the different uses of the textbook by teachers, and on student attitudes toward a subject as the result of having used alternative kinds of textbooks, remains an untapped mine.

Conclusions

Schools in a free society are distinguished from those in a totalitarian society through a commitment to using the best available evidence in examining ideas, problems, and issues in the curriculum. As emphasized throughout this chapter, the enormous disputation evoked by the textbook since the time of its inception is testimony to its unique power as a medium for teaching and learning.

The better school textbooks exemplify organized knowledge in provocative and emergent ways, rather than in established-convergent or closed-ended ways. Nevertheless, effective teachers have long recognized that the textbook should not determine the curriculum. A rich variety of penetrating resource materials and activities must be provided to relate the curriculum to the life of the learner and to the wider social life. Obviously, when textbooks and other curricular materials are used for emergent learning rather than merely for established-convergent learning, teachers and school administrators run the risk that special-interest groups and individuals in the local community will seek to restrict or eliminate the use of such books or materials.

The following conclusions and recommendations are offered in connection with the problems and issues raised in this chapter:

1. The selection of textbooks and other curricular materials should be based upon the best available professional evidence, rather than narrow political or special interests. Hence such selection should be the responsibility of the professional staff of the school and school

district. The superintendent of schools has the responsibility for "educating" his board on these matters. The same should apply at the state level where state approval of school textbooks is practiced.

2. The educational interests of the learner are ill served when the learner is denied the opportunity to investigate controversial ideas, problems, and issues of common concern in a free society. The professional staff of the school and the local school board should be knowledgeable about and committed to the policy statements on academic freedom as developed by the leading professional associations, such as the American Association of School Librarians, Association of Supervision and Curriculum Development, National Council for the Social Studies, National Council of Teachers of English, National Science Teachers Association.

3. A standing curriculum committee composed of faculty, supervisors, head school librarian, and the curriculum director should be responsible for handling complaints lodged against the use of any textbooks, school library books, or other curricular materials, and to protect individual teachers from censorship attacks. The complaints of individuals or special-interest groups should never be the basis for removing or restricting books or other curricular materials. The school administration and school board should rely on the recommendations of the curriculum committee.

4. The school curriculum committee should be able to call upon the expertise of university or college faculty whenever it is felt that assistance is needed in evaluating textbooks and other curricular materials for adoption, and in assisting the school in countering censorship pressures. University and college faculties should be available to assist their school colleagues in these matters.

5. The recent "back-to-basics" retrenchment of the curriculum has resulted in the watering down of textbooks and the excessive use of workbooks and mechanical exercises on ditto sheets. Emphasis has been given to error-oriented teaching at the expense of idea-oriented teaching. There is a growing recognition that such practices have resulted in the decline in higher-order thinking abilities. Textbooks and other curricular materials should be evaluated as to the extent to which they stimulate students to engage in emergent learning and not merely established-convergent learning.

6. A selling point of many publishers is that their school textbooks follow a strict control through readability formulas. The readability of texts is enhanced by interesting ideas. Texts should be

built on the richness of idea development or concept development rather than being regulated by "word count."

7. The proportion of the school budget allocated for textbooks and other curricular materials is negligible, especially considering that textbooks and collateral materials are so central to the content of instruction and instructional procedures. Consequently, budgetary allocations for textbooks, school library books, and other curricular materials can be increased markedly without effecting an appreciable increase in the total school budget.

8. The copyright date should not be the chief criterion for ascertaining whether a textbook should be replaced by an "up-to-date" book. A new copyright date does not signal that the book is necessarily updated in content and superior in quality. Textbooks need to be evaluated by the professional staff and by responsible scholars to ascertain the extent to which they meet qualitative criteria as determined by the best available evidence in the professional literature.

9. No textbook, no matter how excellent it may be, should serve as the sole source of the course of study or should determine the modes of instruction. Students need to learn to work with a wide range of resource materials, and teachers must draw upon a rich variety of resource materials to meet the comprehensive needs of their students. Curriculum guides and lesson plans should not be derived principally from textbooks. Unfortunately, this is the case in far too many schools where "curriculum development" is largely a matter of textbook adoption.

10. A principal criterion in the evaluation of a textbook, and other curricular material, is the extent to which it interfaces with other studies in the total school curriculum. Textbooks and other curricular materials should not be adopted and used as though the subjects in the school curriculum are isolated and independent knowledge compartments. At the secondary school level, the departments should not work in isolation in adopting textbooks and other curricular materials.

11. Aside from the illegality of the all too common practice of reproducing copyrighted material without the consent of publishers, is the matter of denying students the opportunity of using the source material in its original, unexpurgated form. This is indeed poor economy in view of the minute fraction of the school budget devoted to schoolbooks and other curricular materials. Such practices also

make it uneconomical for publishers to keep valuable materials in print.

12. Students should not only be allowed, but encouraged, to take their schoolbooks home.

13. Books and materials in the school media center should not be restricted. In far too many schools, controversial works of fiction and nonfiction are "closeted away" from students.

14. Homework assignments should extend beyond the textbook and beyond other conventional classroom materials by engaging students in the systematic use of reference resources in the school media center, the community library, and other educative community agencies. Homework assignments should stimulate student engagement in emergent learning.

15. Greater attention needs to be given in programs of preservice and in-service teacher education to the selection and uses of the textbook and other curricular materials, particularly in connection with the scope and sequence of the total school curriculum.

In too many instances, school boards, administrators, and teachers have allowed individuals and special-interest groups to determine what is and what is not appropriate in the school curriculum. Under such circumstances, school administrators and their faculties are abrogating their professional responsibility for ensuring that special interests are not served at the expense of the wider public interest.

The function of general education in a free society is to foster the development of a common universe of discourse, understanding, and competence for an enlightened citizenry. This cannot be accomplished when the curriculum is reduced to basic education or focused on specialized technical knowledge to the exclusion of pervading ideas, problems, and issues affecting the life of the learner and the life of society. Textbook adoption has proceeded as though each textbook defines a particular subject matter independent of all other subject matters in the curriculum. Indeed, too many textbooks are written in this vein. The consequence is that the vital interdependence of knowledge is neglected along with the crucial function of general education.

Censorship efforts tend to be centered on conventional textbooks and school library books, and not on computer programs, programmed texts, or workbooks. This is testimony to the power of the textbook and other schoolbooks as principal sources of ideas for emergent learning. The textbook also serves as the key vehicle for initiating the learner to various sources of codified knowledge. No other instrument has been able to challenge the textbook for its dominance and durability as a medium for systematized learning.

NOTES

1. J. B. Edmonson, "Introduction," in *The Textbook in American Education,* ed. Guy M. Whipple, Thirtieth Yearbook of the National Society for the Study of Education, Part II (Bloomington, Ill.: Public School Publishing Company, 1931), p. 1.

2. Eloise O. Warming, "Textbooks," in *Encyclopedia of Educational Research,* 5th ed. (New York: Free Press and Macmillan, 1982), pp. 1934, 1936.

3. Herbert R. Kohl, *The Open Classroom* (New York: Random House, 1969), pp. 14, 41.

4. Neil Postman and Charles Weingartner, *The School Book* (New York: Delacorte, 1973), pp. 88-89.

5. U.S. Office of Education, *OE 100: Highlighting the Progress of American Education* (Washington, D.C.: U.S. Government Printing Office, 1967).

6. Ellwood P. Cubberley, *The Textbook Problem* (Boston: Houghton Mifflin, 1927), p. 4.

7. William C. Bagley, "The Textbook and Methods of Teaching," in *The Textbook in American Education,* ed. Whipple, pp. 24-25.

8. John I. Goodlad, *A Place Called School* (New York: McGraw-Hill, 1984), pp. 205, 207, 209, 211, 215.

9. Nelson B. Henry, "The Cost of Textbooks," in *The Textbook in American Education,* ed. Whipple, pp. 223, 233.

10. National Commission on Excellence in Education, *A Nation at Risk: The Imperative for Educational Reform* (Washington, D.C.: U.S. Department of Education, April 1983), p. 21.

11. Ibid., p. 28.

12. National Science Board, *Educating Americans for the 21st Century* (Washington, D.C.: National Science Foundation, 1983), p. 46.

13. Jerome S. Bruner, *The Process of Education* (Cambridge, Mass.: Harvard University Press, 1960), p. 1.

14. Ibid., p. 84.

15. James R. Killian, Jr., "Preface to the First Edition," in Physical Sciences Study Committee, *Physics,* 2nd ed. (Boston: D.C. Heath, 1965), p. vi.

16. Wayne W. Welch, "The Impact of National Curriculum Projects: The Need for Accurate Assessment," *School Science and Mathematics* 68 (March 1968): 225-234.

17. Thomas S. Kuhn, *The Structure of Scientific Revolutions,* 2d ed. (Chicago: University of Chicago Press, 1970), p. 10.

18. Ibid., p. 165.

19. See Daniel Tanner and Laurel N. Tanner, *Curriculum Development: Theory Into Practice,* 2d ed. (New York: Macmillan, 1980), chaps. 11, 12; Alvin M. Weinberg, *Reflections on Big Science* (Cambridge, Mass.: M.I.T. Press, 1967).

20. Jon Schaffarzick, "Federal Curriculum Reform: A Crucible for Value Conflict," in *Value Conflicts and Curriculum Issues,* ed. Jon Schaffarzick and Gary Sykes (Berkeley, CA: McCutchan Publishing Corp., 1979).

21. Daniel Tanner and Laurel N. Tanner, *Supervision in Education: Problems and Practices* (New York: Macmillan, 1987), pp. 124-127; Robert Boguslaw, *The New Utopians: A Study of Systems Design and Social Change* (Englewood Cliffs, N.J.: Prentice-Hall, 1965), pp. 7-9, 21.

22. *The World's Most Famous Court Trial, Complete Stenographic Report* (Cincinnati: National Book, 1925).

23. Richard Hofstadter, *Anti-intellectualism in American Life* (New York: Alfred A. Knopf, 1970), p. 129.

24. *Everson v. Arkansas*, 393 U.S. 97 (1968).

25. *Edwards v. Aguillard*, No. 85-1513 (1987).

26. Donald W. Robinson, "Patriotism and Economic Control: The Censure of Harold Rugg" (Doct. diss., Rutgers University, 1983).

27. "Publishers Protest Removal of Rugg Textbooks," *Publishers Weekly*, 22 June 1940, p. 2345.

28. Hofstadter, *Anti-intellectualism in American Life*, pp. 305, 323-390.

29. Robert E. Newman, Jr., "History of a Civic Education Project Implementing the Social-Problems Technique of Instruction" (Doct. diss., Stanford University, 1960).

30. California Senate Committee on Education, "Proceedings in the Matter of Investigation in Regard to Textbooks and Educational Practices in the Public Schools" (April 17, 1947).

31. William V. Mayer, "The BSCS Past," *BSCS Journal* 1 (November 1978): 9.

32. "The Human Sciences Program," *BSCS Journal* 3 (April 1980): 1-2, 4.

33. Raymond English, "The Politics of Textbook Adoption," *Phi Delta Kappan* 62 (December 1980): 278.

34. John Dewey, *The School and Society* (Chicago: University of Chicago Press, 1899), p. 7.

35. Goodlad, *A Place Called School*, p. 298.

36. Richard E. Clark, "Reconsidering Research on Learning from Media," *Review of Educational Research* 53 (Winter 1983): 455.

37. Daniel Bell, *The Reforming of General Education* (New York: Columbia University Press, 1966), p. 181.

38. Committee on Academic Freedom and Pre-College Education, American Association of University Professors, "Liberty and Learning in the Schools: Higher Education's Concerns," *Academe* 72 (September-October 1986): 31a.

39. Arthur N. Applebee, Judith A. Langer, and Ina V. S. Mullis, *The Writing Report Card: Writing Achievement in American Schools* (Princeton, N.J.: National Assessment of Educational Progress, 1986), p. 11.

40. Bruno Bettelheim and Karen Zelan, *On Learning to Read: The Child's Fascination with Meaning* (New York: Alfred A. Knopf, 1982).

41. Jeanne S. Chall, Sue S. Conard, and Susan Harris, *An Analysis of Textbooks in Relation to Declining SAT Scores* (New York: College Entrance Examination Board, 1977).

42. Cited in Edward B. Fiske, "Are They "Dumbing Down" the Textbooks?" *Principal* 64 (November 1984): 44.

43. California State Department of Education, *News Release*, 10 December 1985, p. 3.

44. Curriculum Development and Supplemental Materials Commission, State of California, *Report on Mathematics Instructional Materials* (Sacramento: California State Department of Education, 1986).

45. Science Curriculum Framework and Criteria Committee, *Science Framework Addendum* (Sacramento: California State Department of Education, 1984).

46. *New York Times*, 21 September 1986, p. 40.

47. California State Department of Education, *News Release*, 10 December 1985, p. 2.

48. Robinson, "Patriotism and Economic Control: The Censure of Harold Rugg", pp. 384-393.

49. *New York Times*, 3 June 1986, p. C1.

50. Paul C. Vitz, "Religion and Traditional Values in Public School Textbooks," *Public Interest* 84 (Summer 1986): 90.

51. *Chronicle of Higher Education*, 16 April 1986, pp. 13, 24.

52. Warming, "Textbooks," p. 1933.

53. Richard T. White and Richard P. Tisher, "Research on Natural Sciences," in *Handbook of Research on Teaching*, 3d ed., ed. Merlin C. Wittrock (New York: Macmillan, 1986), p. 880.

54. A. A. Lumsdaine, "Instruments and Media of Instruction," in *Handbook of Research on Teaching*, ed. N. L. Gage (Chicago: Rand McNally, 1963), p. 586.

Introduction to Chapter VI

A common complaint from critics of education is that instruction in elementary schools is dominated by textbooks. In the following chapter, Susan Stodolsky asks if teaching is really by the book.

The question is important, for an affirmative answer suggests that important curricular decisions about what is to be taught, when, and in what manner are made by textbook publishers rather than by teachers.

Stodolsky reviews research on this topic, including her own studies of teachers' use of textbooks in elementary mathematics and social studies. She finds great variety in the ways teachers use textbooks and in the extent to which they use them. She identifies and clarifies various meanings that can be attached to the idea of "teaching by the book" and concludes that the "popular vision of slavish adherence to texts does not seem supportable."

Stodolsky's report shows that an apparently simple question cannot be addressed fully without recognizing the complexities that surround it. She points out, for example, that studies of textbook use need to take into account the nature of the textbooks themselves—the topics included in them, the material contained in the text on those topics, the activities suggested for students in the teacher's edition of the text. Variations in the use of texts "seem to result from teachers' own convictions and preferences, the nature of the materials they use, the school context in which they teach, the particular students in their class, and the subject matter and grade level . . ."

Susan Stodolsky is Professor of Education and Psychology at the University of Chicago. Her chapter is reprinted from the Society's 88th Yearbook, Part 1, From Socrates to Software: The Teacher as Text and the Text as Teacher, *edited by Philip W. Jackson.*

CHAPTER VI

Is Teaching Really by the Book?

SUSAN S. STODOLSKY

There is a widely held belief that classroom instruction in elementary school is dominated by textbooks. Indeed, there is little doubt that textbooks are present in most classrooms most of the time.[1] But the assumption that textbooks drive instruction because they are ubiquitous may not be tenable. Exactly what the presence of textbooks signals about their use has not been adequately studied or analyzed. In this essay I shall review the limited research literature on this topic, raise some questions that need answers, and present some preliminary findings about textbook use in actual classrooms.

What Does It Mean to Teach by the Textbook?

At first glance, this question seems to have an obvious answer. As Freeman suggests, "a prevailing image is of a teacher who begins instruction on the first page of the book on day one and proceeds page by page through the entire text over the course of the academic year."[2] The phrase "teaching by the book" conjures an image of close (if not slavish) adherence to textbook content, order, and suggested activities, and implies that the textbook is the central, if not the only, material used during instruction.

Teaching by the book might be exemplified by a reading group working through a basal reader lesson by lesson.[3] Another example is a social studies class following a common routine in which students take turns reading orally from the textbook and then answer the book's questions.[4] Math students who are regularly assigned problem sets from their textbook might also be seen as taught by the book.

A definition of textbook-driven instruction derived from these presumably straightforward examples is more ambiguous than might

The support of the Benton Center for Curriculum and Instruction at the University of Chicago for the research reported in this chapter is gratefully acknowledged. Yu Amin Cheng provided valuable research assistance.

be expected. To what extent and in what ways ought one adhere to textbook content and suggestions in order to be teaching by the book? If a teacher selects content from a given lesson, phrases her own questions to the class, conducts a lesson suggested for small groups with the whole class, or uses a worksheet prepared by another publisher, is she teaching by the book? If the order of lessons is changed or certain sections of text are deleted, is instruction still textbook-driven? Does teaching by the book mean exclusive use of the book?

Teaching by the book has often been taken as synonymous with teacher-centered lessons. There has been a facile and unwarranted equating of teacher-directed instructional techniques with textbook-driven instruction. Particularly in subjects other than the basics, a variety of instructional arrangements are called for in various curricular programs. An image of teacher-led lessons, frequent recitations, and seatwork is invoked to describe the textbook-driven classroom. But all books do not call for these arrangements. The existence of a teacher-centered program does not necessarily mean that the textbook is being followed. Conversely, the creation of a student-centered environment does not necessarily signal departure from a textbook program. Some books and curricula require establishment of peer work groups, games, laboratory exercises, or computer-aided instruction. To study teachers' use of textbooks one should not merely examine teachers' classroom practices. Rather, comparisons must be made of their practices with the requirements, recommendations, and content of their textbooks. The particular nature of a textbook or curriculum package must be considered more systematically in determining its impact on instructional processes.

There are a number of components or aspects of textbook use to distinguish in order to consider fully the ways in which we can say textbooks dominate or influence classroom instruction. While superficially a simple idea, "teaching by the book" is actually open to many interpretations. In fact, different grounds are adopted by individuals when they assert that teaching is textbook driven. The various meanings attached to the idea of teaching by the book will be clarified in this chapter.

For analytic purposes, it is essential to separate various aspects of textbook use, although it sometimes may be difficult to separate them in actual classroom practice. Such conceptual clarification is needed because clear distinctions have not been consistently present in the literature on the role of textbooks in instruction. Researchers who have studied the use and influence of textbooks on teacher planning and instruction have approached the issue with different criteria in mind.

There are at least three major areas in which textbook use and influence should be defined and analyzed: topics, actual material contained on the pages in the books, and activities suggested in the teacher's editions that accompany student texts. These three components of textbooks constitute potential sources of influence on teaching and teacher planning, although these sources of influence are not fully interdependent or mutually exclusive. Thus, a teacher can plan instruction around topics in the textbook but depart from the actual book materials. Similarly, suggested activities in teacher's editions can be used in conjunction with text materials or independently. On the other hand, if the materials on the pages of the book are actually used it follows that book topics are being covered.

In considering textbook use the particular characteristics of a book must be determined. Too little attention has been given to the nature of books in relation to their use. Textbooks and teacher's editions are structured differently according to the subject matter and grade level they serve[5]—a fact ignored in most discussions of text use. It is likely that aspects of textbook use vary in different subject areas and for pupils of different ages.

When texts are written, different principles of instructional design are frequently followed. Books also adhere to different philosophical and pedagogical positions. Among other characteristics, textbooks vary in their degree of specificity and prescriptiveness. Different series seek different educational goals. To determine accurately if a teacher is following a book, the composition of the book, its instructional recommendations, and its topical content need to be considered systematically in conjunction with classroom procedures.

Noting the idiosyncratic nature of textbooks and curriculum materials places the study of textbook use squarely in the arena of curriculum and program implementation. To assess the fidelity of an instructional program, first the defining characteristics of the program must be specified. The same principle must be followed in studying the relation between teachers' classroom practices and textbooks or curricular materials.

Research in Textbook Use

TOPICS

The major influence textbooks are presumed to have on

instruction is in specifying topics and content to be covered. Content determination is a central educational decision with profound consequences for student learning. Some studies of textbook use have investigated the match between textbook topics and instructional topics. These studies essentially ask, Is the topical coverage in the textbook isomorphic with topics actually taught by teachers in whose classes the books are found?

Grave concern about the role of textbooks in determining content stems from criticism of their actual content, as well as the way in which the books are structured. A frequent complaint is of superficial coverage in which topics receive a "mention," particularly in social studies and history books.[6] In other fields, such as mathematics, critics decry a lack of richness in content and a slow pace that puts American students behind their Asian and European counterparts. DeSilva reports that inaccuracies and errors are present in many books used in the social sciences and sciences.[7] Sex, race, and class biases have also been documented.[8]

The quality of writing and text organization has often been found wanting, particularly as publishers have attempted to conform to readability formulas.[9] Chall showed that the reading material in literature, reading, and history textbooks generally became simpler in terms of language structure, readability, and challenge over two decades, coincident with declines in average student performance on the SAT.[10] Using schema theory, Armbruster and Anderson described text in elementary social studies and science books as "inconsiderate" because it is structured with insufficient coherence and information.[11] The nature of the questions asked in reading series and textbooks in other school subjects has also been analyzed and criticized by Armbruster and Ostertag and by Nicely, among others.[12]

Studies in the field of reading provide the most convincing evidence for a strong influence of textbooks on topical content. A number of investigators have confirmed that the content of basal reading series is used rather consistently, particularly in the primary grades.[13] A teacher's pace in introducing new vocabulary, for example, can be determined by examining the basal textbook in conjunction with time allocation to its pages.[14] These studies leave open the question of whether teachers follow suggestions for specific instructional practices in the teacher's guides—a point to which I return later.

Researchers at the Institute for Research on Teaching at Michigan State University delineated a number of decisions teachers make about their instruction. The decisions are: "(1) how much time to allocate to a subject, (2) what topics to cover, (3) with which students, (4) when and in what order, and (5) to what standards of achievement."[15] They have used a variety of methods in their research program on mathematics instruction in upper-elementary and junior high school.

Freeman et al. defined a three-dimensional taxonomy of topics found in math textbooks and standardized tests at the fourth-grade level: "The three dimensions of the taxonomy describe the general intent of the item (e.g., conceptual understanding or application), the nature of material presented to students (e.g., measurement or decimals), and the operation the student must perform (e.g., estimate or multiply)."[16] They also determined the extent to which a given topic was emphasized in a textbook by counting the number of student exercises devoted to it. Using the topics derived from the intersection of the taxonomy dimensions, the researchers assessed the match between texts, instruction, and tests in a series of studies.

Freeman and Porter investigated the influence of a variety of factors, including textbooks and teacher's manuals, on teachers' plans and instructional actions.[17] In the case of math teaching, they found that textbooks had the most influence in the realm of topics and sequence and made little contribution to decisions about time allocation, defining standards, and determining which students should receive particular types of instruction.

Nevertheless, in detailed case studies of math instruction in classes of seven elementary teachers in three school districts, Freeman and Porter gathered information that challenges the notion that most teachers teach by the book.[18] In the study, teachers kept logs of their instructional practices and were interviewed periodically. In the interviews, the investigators suggested three styles of textbook use and found teachers who fit into each of them. One style included strict adherence to both content and order of the book ("start with the first lesson of the book at the beginning of the year and work straight through the book lesson by lesson"). In the second style the order of topics in the text was preserved, but the teacher skipped certain portions. The third style was characterized by changing the order in which chapters or topics were presented—this type of teacher was seen as skipping around in the book.

More specifically, Freeman found that the teachers used an average of 35.2 percent of the lessons in their math textbooks.[19] When they examined the extent of coverage of specific topics in the texts, as defined with their taxonomy, individual variation was also found. Considering only topics that were emphasized in the textbooks (i.e., at least twenty student exercises dealt with the topic), teachers ranged from 64 percent to 90 percent coverage of those topics in their classes. On the other hand, between 20 percent and 77 percent of the topics that received little emphasis in the texts (i.e., less than five student exercises on the topic) were presented.

The case studies did show that textbooks have an influence on instructional topics in elementary math classes. Over 80 percent of instructional time in the observed classes was devoted to topics that were covered in teachers' primary textbooks. However, teachers were selective in their topical coverage and also supplemented instruction with other materials. The overlap in topics among math textbooks at this grade level is such that a certain similarity in topics occurs regardless of the book used.

These researchers believe the extent of teachers' adherence to textbook topics is a function of the degree to which teachers see the textbook "as a legitimate content authority" and of their own convictions about the content they think their students should master. While teachers vary in the way in which they use textbooks, they also vary in their beliefs.[20]

An issue in the study of topics is how broadly or narrowly they are to be defined. The breadth or specificity of topic definition can influence the likelihood of finding a close correspondence between instructional topics and those in text or curricular materials. If topics are defined very generally and broadly (e.g., operations with fractions, the Revolutionary War), it is more likely that a match can be found between text topics and those that occur as a focus of instruction. On the other hand, defining topics very narrowly is more likely to result in some discrepancy between classroom practice and text-prescribed topics.

A similar but more limited effort to analyze textbook and test content was conducted by Armbruster et al. at the Center for the Study of Reading at the University of Illinois in connection with three third-grade reading curricula and two standardized reading tests.[21] Sixteen reading comprehension skills, such as following directions, identifying the main idea, and recalling details, were identified in the curricular materials and tests. Individual reading curricula had distinctive skill emphases and the tests did not tap many of the skills addressed in the textbooks. When topical analyses are done in some detail in both math and reading, variation is found from textbook to textbook, suggesting that the selection of a particular book could indeed be consequential in terms of the resulting content of an instructional program. Unfortunately, Armbruster and her colleagues did not directly address the actual classroom use of the reading textbooks they coded for comprehension skills.

The studies at the Center for the Study of Reading and the Institute for Research on Teaching stand as exceptions with regard to the systematic classification of instructional topics in textbooks. Publishers specify scope and sequence in most textbooks—certainly in reading and mathematics—and Flanders has made use of that information to determine how much new content is introduced in math texts from first grade through algebra.[22] Nevertheless, systematic analyses of content coverage in a broad range of subjects and texts are not readily available. Closer to our central concern, in only a few instances has the match between textbook topics and classroom instruction been studied through direct observation, the use of teacher logs, or other reliable means.

There are other reports in which investigators have concluded that instruction is dominated by textbooks. Some of the work used questionnaire responses of teachers, while other investigators directly observed or interviewed teachers. In their case studies of science and mathematics teaching, Stake and Easley concluded that "the source of knowledge authority was not so much the teacher—it was the textbook."[23] However, their reports do not contain sufficient information to sharpen our understanding of the match between textbook topics and instructional topics in other than a very global way. Several studies offer various kinds of evidence suggesting that textbooks play an important role in teacher planning and actual classroom instruction.[24] However, these studies do not explicitly describe the specific impact textbooks have on the topical content of instruction.

CONTENTS OF SECTIONS AND PAGES IN TEXTBOOKS

Another way to consider textbook use is to determine the sections or formats contained in them and then examine teachers' use of the various parts. Books differ in this aspect of textbook content as in others depending on the subject matter treated and the intended grade level of the pupils. For instance, basal readers consist primarily of reading passages which extend over a number of pages by the middle grades, comprehension questions to be answered after reading, and orienting questions at or near the beginning of the reading material. Some series also contain skill development exercises such as work on phonics or development of vocabulary, but others reserve such activities for workbooks that accompany the basal reader or suggest in the teacher's editions that teachers assign such activities.

The typical layout of a math book includes some pages of developmental material followed by problem sets or exercises. Challenge problems or brain teasers are also built into certain math textbooks, as are chapter reviews and "stay-up-to-date" sections which contain problems requiring the use of skills and concepts covered earlier in the book. End of chapter tests are also included in some series, and extra problem sets for students requiring additional practice are featured in some texts.

The most typical social studies textbooks consist of generously illustrated narrative text and sets of questions. In some books, questions are interspersed throughout the narrative material; there are also question sets at the end of each section and chapter. Some books contain certain skill development exercises, such as map and chart reading and vocabulary lists, and some contain a variety of suggested activities for students to pursue on the section topic. Chapter tests are also included in some social studies books.

Data that directly bear on the use of different portions of textbooks are scanty. The two subjects in which some empirical data speak to this issue are reading and math. In reading, the data suggest a rather close adherence to the book material in that the basal reading passages appear to be used in sequence and generally without omissions. The clearest evidence on this point is provided by Barr and Dreeben at the first-grade level.[25] Durkin's studies of first-, third-, and fifth-grade teachers also suggest that basal reading passages are used rather consistently, although she did not follow teachers over long instructional sequences.[26] Through her observations of individual lessons, Durkin provided evidence that the end-of-section comprehension questions and skill exercises are used regularly. Orienting questions and development of vocabulary, however, seem neglected in the classes she studied.

In math, it is commonly asserted that textbook sections (e.g., introduction, practice exercises, enrichment, review) are used differently. Data from two large national studies characterize math textbooks in use primarily as exercise books.[27] On questionnaires, students reported use of the problem sets in the books, but typically read only two out of every five pages in the textbooks. Students responding to national surveys claimed the developmental and introductory sections of math books were frequently skipped over during instruction.

In case studies of math teachers, Freeman and Porter gathered data regarding coverage of chapters, lessons, and parts of lessons.[28] On average, the four case study teachers used 58 percent of the chapters in their texts, with use defined as at least 25 percent of the lessons covered. On average, the teachers simply did not reach 29 percent of the chapters at the end of their texts. They skipped the remaining chapters deliberately.[29] It is not easy to compare the math and reading instructional data, but it seems that reading teachers cover chapters or pages of the basal readers in sequence. From Barr and Dreeben's work we can conclude that teachers do not consistently finish the text with every instructional group in reading.[30] In fact, one of the major correlates of ability grouping in reading is differential content coverage. Not enough data are available, however, to estimate the modal behavior of reading instructors with respect to chapters covered in basal readers.

In the Freeman and Porter study, the teachers' use of lessons and lesson sections was also investigated.[31] Consistent with the findings at the chapter level, the researchers found wide variation in lesson coverage across the four teachers. On average, about one-third of the lessons were used, at least in part, by the teachers. The range covered was 13.2 percent to 60.5 percent.

Freeman and Porter considered within-lesson use by examining five sections of the textbooks: student exercises, teacher-directed sections (e.g., introductory or developmental sections), enrichment, review, and additional practice. They found that when lessons were used the teachers utilized sections of the textbooks as follows: student exercises in 92.2 percent of those lessons; review sections in 86.3 percent; teacher-directed portions in 73.5 percent; enrichment in 56.4 percent; and additional practice in 23.6 percent. The researchers noted that the teachers displayed similar patterns in their use of student exercises, review activities, and practice problems at the end of the book, while they differed in their tendency to use enrichment and developmental (teacher-directed) sections.[32]

Except for our own case studies to be presented shortly, we are unaware of any systematic data on textbook use in social studies or science. Morrissett reviewed studies that show that textbooks are used during the majority of instructional class time and homework time by elementary school social studies pupils.[33] While systematic attention has been given to the content and composition of social studies textbooks, research targeted at documenting the specific ways they are used in classrooms is lacking.

SUGGESTIONS IN TEACHER'S EDITIONS

Some researchers have been interested in whether teachers follow suggestions in teacher's guides, not just if they use student textbook content. In reading instruction, the question is not whether basal content is read but whether the suggested instructional approach is followed. For example, Durkin investigated the use of basal reading series in first, third, and fifth grades.[34] She found that teachers did use the reading selections in the basals, but did not consistently follow the instructional practices suggested in the manuals. In particular, the teachers she studied did not use suggested prereading activities such as development of new vocabulary in context and guiding questions prior to student reading of basal selections. However, teachers did use comprehension assessment questions following reading and were rather consistent in their use of written exercises such as those dealing with phonics.

We have analyzed instructional suggestions in the teacher's guides of the most widely used math and social studies textbooks for fifth grade.[35] Most guides contain suggestions for activities that are considered essential (we termed these "core activities") and others that fall into an "optional" category. For example, the five most popular math series all expected student practice exercises to be a cornerstone of the instructional program. The use of calculators, manipulatives, contests and games generally was optional. In social studies, reading the text and answering questions were deemed core activities while group projects and field trips typically were optional. This general distinction may partially explain choices teachers make about which activities to include in their instructional program and which to eliminate, particularly when the teacher's own priorities are consonant with those of the text authors.

The influence of subject matter is apparent in reviewing the role and use of textbooks in classrooms. In the area of reading, the textbook selections are rather consistently used, although as Durkin demonstrated the readings are not always used in the ways suggested by teacher's manuals. Other investigators of reading instruction have also found that basal content per se is adhered to rather closely.[36] While it seems true that basal reading series are used in a regular and rather comprehensive way, reading may stand as the exception rather than the rule in the realm of textbook use. Variation in textbook use by subject matter deserves much more scrutiny than has heretofore been given to it.

Very little research has examined textbook use in other subject areas, although a study on writing instruction in elementary school by Bridge and Hiebert widens the scope of existing research.[37] The presence of textbooks in classrooms has been documented across most fields of study, even though the details of their use have not been adequately charted.[38] Since texts in different fields have distinctive features, research on their use needs to be tailored to the specific field of interest. Specific features also have to be considered in connection with individual curricula in a given school subject.

A Study of Textbook Use in Fifth-Grade
Math and Social Studies Classes

To explore further some of these issues and increase our empirical base, we examined textbook use in fifth-grade math and social studies classes through a reanalysis of observational materials collected for another purpose.[39] In all we looked at four math curricula and four social studies curricula in use by six math and six social studies teachers.[40] Teachers were in schools that served lower-class, working-class, middle-class, and upper-middle class pupils. The observed teachers were experienced; they had taught from six to thirty-six years. In two instances, we observed two teachers in the same school using the same curriculum (teachers A1 and A2 and B1 and B2 in math and teachers B1 and B2 and C1 and C2 in social studies), while the remaining curricula were each used by only one teacher in our sample. In three instances we analyzed both math and social studies instruction provided by the same teacher (B1, B2, and C1). In addition we analyzed the instruction of three other teachers in math (A1, A2, and D1) and social studies (C2, E1, F1). Thus, observations of nine teachers were analyzed for current purposes.

Written observations of the teachers were made during two consecutive weeks of instruction in midyear. The observation period was not selected on the basis of the content covered, nor was the original focus of the study textbook use. However, narrative records of the classroom activity structure were made during the observation period and can be used to add to our knowledge about how teachers use textbooks and curriculum packages.[41] However, due to the duration of the observations and some lack of relevant detail in the records, certain limitations must be acknowledged.

In examining instruction in the math and social studies classes we considered the ways in which the observed teachers used curricular materials from a number of points of view. Following our earlier analysis, we asked to what extent topics taught were from the book, what sections of the book or other materials were used, and if the suggestions in teacher's editions were followed. We also considered the specific nature of the materials available to the teacher in assessing the match between instruction and curricula.

SIX FIFTH-GRADE MATH CLASSES

Our six teachers exhibited a wide range of postures with respect to textbook use. We saw close adherence to the textbook, extreme autonomy from the adopted math textbook, and practices that fell between. For instance, both teachers (A1 and A2) who used the *Scott, Foresman Mathematics* text stayed close to the textbook topics, but one skipped over pages on problem solving with fractions and map reading. Neither of the two teachers (B1 and B2) who used *Exploring Elementary Mathematics* preserved the text topic sequence. Teacher B1 combined similar content from a number of chapters and skipped whole sections of chapters. Teacher B2 skipped a chapter on geometry that fell between two chapters on operations with fractions and combined material from the two fraction chapters. Teacher C1 who used *Discovery in Mathematics* focused most of her instruction on multiplication of fractional numbers and covered the topic in textbook order. In addition, she assigned students worksheets which contained basic computational operations such as three-column addition, presumably to maintain skills. Last, we observed teacher D1 whose classroom text was *Investigating School Mathematics*. We never saw him use the textbook during our two weeks of observation, although his instruction dealt with operations with fractions—topics covered in chapters 11 and 14 of the text.

At the very general level of topic, our math teachers behaved much as those studied by Freeman and by Freeman and Porter.[42] What was taught was almost always in their books, but most of them skipped topics and chapters and did not necessarily preserve text sequence. Of more interest is the extent to which the actual contents of the book were in evidence during instruction.

To examine this issue we looked at the various sections found in the student textbook lessons and determined how they were used by the teachers. Each of the four books contained introductory or developmental sections and exercise sections. Three of the books contained maintenance, review, and test sections, and two books had enrichment material. Table 1 displays each teacher's use of each section.

The pairs of teachers using the same books (the teachers across the hall) provide particularly interesting information. Teachers A1 and A2 both made use of the introductory sections in *Scott, Foresman Mathematics*. Teacher A1 did so explicitly with students actively using the text while teacher A2 used the same or similar material but did not regularly direct students' attention to the text section. Both teachers skipped word problems that were contained in the introductions and had students deal only with a numerical problem equivalent. For instance, teacher A2 omitted a story in the student text about children who lived different distances from school, a story intended to teach pupils how to compare the magnitudes of fractions. Instead, she went directly to the adjacent page on which such problems were presented in numerical form and solved them orally with the pupils. Teacher A2 also tended to ignore graphic and figural materials in the developmental portion, while teacher A1 used them occasionally.

Both these teachers regularly assigned student exercises from the text as homework or seatwork, but each also made up problems for students. Neither teacher used the enrichment sections of the textbook such as "side trips," laboratory exercises, calculator problems, and careers. One made use of a test and the other made use of a maintenance section. Both teachers stayed quite close to the text, particularly teacher A1 who tended to have pupils turn to every text page in order.

Teachers B1 and B2 used *Exploring Elementary Mathematics* in their classrooms. These teachers exhibited very different teaching styles and textbook use. Teacher B1, who was teaching equivalent fractions, used an actual textbook page on two days of observations. On those days she used a review section for a seatwork assignment and one introductory section of the text. She never used student exercises, maintenance, or test sections. Instead, she made extensive use of transparencies she prepared to introduce material, and worksheets of exercises and problems she created for student practice and recitations. When she used the introductory portion of the text she was selective and modified material. For example, she used the book's terminology of "parts" and "sets" but her own explanation for how to reduce fractions. Teacher B1 seemed aware of the explanations

TABLE 1
TEACHER USE OF SECTIONS OF MATHEMATICS TEXTBOOKS

SECTIONS OF TEXTS

TEACHER	INTRODUCTION (A.B.C.D.)*	EXERCISE (A.B.C.D.)	MAINTENANCE (A.B.D.)	REVIEW (B.C.D.)	TEST (A.B.C.)	ENRICHMENT (A.D.)
A1	Used (materials used; students directed to text)	Used	Not used		Used	Not used
A2	Used (materials used; text may not be open)	Used	Used		Not used	Not used
B1	Used (selectively used materials, modified the presentation; students may not be directed to text)	Not used (used teacher-made work sheets almost exclusively).	Not used (used teacher-made work sheets)	Used (as exercise)	Not used	
B2	Not used	Used	Not used (used teacher-made work sheets)	Not used	Not used	
C	Used (material used selectively; students may be directed to text)	Used	Not used (used teacher-made problems or con-tests)	Not used**	Not used** (used commercially prepared work sheets)	
D	Not used	Not used (used work book, work sheets, teacher-made problems, contests, and materials from other books)	Not used (used teacher-made problems or con-tests)	Not used		Not used

* Letters refer to texts used: A. Scott Foresman Mathematics; B. Exploring Elementary Mathematics; C. Discovery in Mathematics; D. Investigating School Mathematics.

** May be due to insufficient observation.

offered in the student text and the teacher's edition, but she used them selectively in conjunction with her own materials and instructional strategies. The students in her class spent over half their time in teacher-directed lessons.

Teacher B2 was also teaching operations with fractions. His use of the textbook, however, was very different from his in-school colleague. The only portion of the book used by teacher B2 was the student exercises which he assigned for both seatwork and homework and checked during classtime. He never directed students to any other portion of the book; students spent most of their time doing problem sets as seatwork. When seatwork exercises were not from the text, they were mostly commercially prepared worksheets that accompanied the textbook series. It is unclear if teacher B2 ever spent time on developmental activities during his classes; he did not do so in the two weeks we observed him.

Teacher C1, who used *Discovery in Mathematics*, rather consistently directed her students to the student textbook pages in their order of occurrence. With questions directed to the class she used a step-by-step approach in which she included some of the examples provided in the introductory and "oral" section of her textbook. However, she also ignored materials in those sections, particularly questions or diagrams, and primarily rehearsed necessary operations and rules with the class as emphasized in the book. Her seatwork and homework assignments were drawn from a variety of sources including exercises in the text, exercises in a workbook that accompanies the textbook series, another workbook she used regularly, and commercial dittoes that were frequently in game form from many other publishers. Her text did not contain many diagrams, pictures, and illustrations. It also lacked enrichment sections. Teacher C1's use of other commercial sources for student problems may have resulted in part from a need to supplement the book in these areas.

Investigating School Mathematics was the official text for teacher D1's class. However, during our observations he never used the textbook, although he briefly used an accompanying workbook page once for eight minutes during a lesson. Teacher D1 structured almost all his math periods as teacher-directed lessons during which he checked student homework, conducted recitations, and held many contests with students at the blackboard. When he used worksheets they were sometimes commercially prepared, but most of the time he selected problems from a wide variety of resource books or created his own. Teacher D1 expressed a strong conviction that students needed practice and mastery of basic arithmetic operations. Beyond the fact that he did not actually use the textbook adopted by his school, he also departed from its emphasis on discovery learning. His style and independent approach defined him as a teacher following his own beliefs about math teaching.

We have already seen that the teachers varied considerably in their use of the textbooks. We must also consider their use of the materials in the teacher's editions. Teacher A1, who adhered closely to student text material, incorporated a number of instructional suggestions in the teacher's edition—particularly explanations of concepts and skills and book terminology. Teacher A2, who was less consistent in her use of the student text than teacher A1, also modified and changed the purposes of introductory sections, was more selective in their use, and created her own explanations of material. Teacher A2 emphasized diagnosis and remediation and therefore spent considerable class time assisting individual pupils. The teacher's guide contained many enrichment and motivational techniques including using manipulatives, and recreational activities such as projects, experiments, games, contests, and the use of the calculator. Teachers A1 and A2 both ignored the enrichment and motivational material and suggestions.

Teachers B1 and B2 provided contrast in their use of the teacher's guide to *Exploring Elementary Mathematics* as they did in student textbook use. The teacher's guide itself describes the objectives of the text portion and offers procedures for explanation. Sometimes the guide also contains background explanations for the teacher. It does not contain suggestions for enrichment or additional activities for pupils. Teacher B1 basically handled the materials in her own way. She invented her own methods of explaining procedures and concepts, and used instructional strategies she thought effective such as having pupils take notes, recite definitions, and do mental arithmetic. These approaches were not suggested in the teacher's edition. She also defined terms in her own way. For instance, the teacher's edition states: "Reducing to simplest fractional numerals is having only 1 as a common factor of the numerator and denominator" (p. 225). Teacher B1 told her pupils, "Reducing to simplest fractional numerals is to find the *largest* number you can divide both numerator and denominator." As far as we could tell, teacher B2 completely ignored the suggestions in the teacher's guide. Since his textbook use was limited to student exercises with no use of introductory sections, we infer he was not influenced by the teacher's edition.

The teacher's guide provided with teacher C1's text contains very detailed suggestions on using textbook examples and explaining concepts, along with suggested classroom activities. Teacher C1 did not follow the suggestions in the teacher's guide; rather, she maintained her own recitation and seatwork style and produced her own explanations and rules for the operations under study. She emphasized student repetition of definitions and procedures—a practice consistent with the textbook orientation. However, this practice may have arisen from her own convictions rather than from adoption of the material and suggestions in the guide.

Since teacher D1 was completely independent of the textbook he did not use its accompanying teacher's edition.

Summary. The six teachers we observed varied considerably in their use of student and teacher's editions of their math textbooks. Overall, we observed the most agreement between textbook topics and instructional topics, although it did not usually extend to preserving topical sequence. The least agreement was in the use of the suggested activities in the teacher's editions and actual classroom practices. Most of the teachers departed significantly from the suggestions or did not even seem to have considered them in planning their instruction.

Certain parts of the textbooks and suggestions seemed dispensable to all of our teachers. In particular, manipulative activities and suggestions for enrichment did not find their way into practice during our period of observation. This result is consistent with prior research.[43] On the other hand, four of the six teachers did use student exercises for seatwork and homework assignments, although they were supplemented with problems and activities from other sources. The developmental or introductory sections were also used by four teachers; in one case, however, the use was very selective and the content was often modified. Interestingly, the most conformity and the more exclusive use of text content were exhibited by the pair of teachers in School A—an upper-middle class suburb with a strong math program directed by a math specialist. The adopted text was more varied in its content and instructional suggestions than some of the others we saw in use, although as we noted the teachers often omitted those distinctive activities. While school policy granted considerable autonomy to teachers in general, there was a commitment to keep to the same schedule of topics in all math classes. Consequently, teachers may have felt more constrained to stay with prescribed topics and materials than in other school settings.

Teacher D1 taught in a working-class suburban school, but exhibited complete autonomy from the prescribed text. His program was obviously acceptable in the school in which tight central control was present regarding grading, discipline, and educational objectives. In contrast, teachers B1 and B2 in another working-class school differed in teaching styles and textbook use. Teacher B1 created almost all her own materials and examples during instruction and spent considerable class time actively instructing her pupils. Teacher B2 used only student exercises and generally failed to sustain a developmentally oriented instructional program.

In sum, our cases suggest that teachers are very autonomous in their textbook use and that it is likely that only a minority of teachers really follow the text in the page-by-page manner suggested in the literature. Use is much more varied than usually suggested, particularly when one considers more than just the topics contained in the books. Even with regard to topics, we found, as Freeman and Porter did, that what teachers teach is in the books, but they do not teach everything that is in the books. Thus, math textbook content tends to place something like a cap on content coverage in classrooms, although putting something in a book does not guarantee instruction will be devoted to it.

Developers of teacher's editions might be sobered by our findings which suggest a weak link between their suggestions and actual classroom practices. However, it should be noted that we studied highly experienced teachers. It is perhaps true though that teacher's editions are not very effective influences on instructional practices, and this may be more true in certain areas of the curriculum. There is a rather convincing history of a disjunction between math educators' visions of math instruction and what classroom teachers do that suggests math is a domain in which the discrepancy may be particularly large. The omission of the more activity-based aspects of the curriculum by all our teachers is one symptom of this often noted disjunction.

Most of our students used more than just problem sets in their fifth-grade math books. At least occasionally some of our pupils were directed to the developmental portions of the book. In general, however, their experiences were restricted to written and oral activities that emphasized algorithmic mastery,[44] and did not involve materials other than paper, pencils, worksheets, textbooks, and the blackboard. When this routine was broken, it was to make room for a team contest or game focused on computation.

SIX FIFTH-GRADE SOCIAL STUDIES CLASSES

Using cases from the same database as the math classes, we examined teaching in six social studies classes in a similar manner. Teachers B1 and B2 were using *Inquiring about American History* (the Holt data bank system). Teachers C1 and C2 used the text *Man and Society*. Teacher E1 was using *Man: A Course of Study* (*MACOS*) and Teacher F1 had adopted a simulation curriculum, *Sailing to the New World*.

Our first analysis focused on the topics taught in the social studies classes and their match with the adopted text or curriculum package. In contrast to math texts, social studies texts do not seem to define the maximum range of topics covered during instruction. While text topics are taught, social studies teachers often conduct additional activities related and unrelated to the textbook or curriculum content.

In the case of teachers B1 and B2, we saw contrasting styles of curriculum use as we did in their math teaching. Teacher B1 made full use of the data bank system having students use the text and data sources in their study of the colonies and immigration. She also made a number of her own worksheets on aspects of government which were topically related to the study unit. Generally speaking, teacher B1 stayed close to the topics in the textbook and focused on the history of the colonial period.

Teacher B2 only used the textbook portion of the data bank system. On some observation days, the class was studying the Revolutionary period. Teacher B2 used topics in the student text but did not preserve the text sequence. On other days pupils were occupied with a map skills book from which they were to learn terminology such as "longitude" and "latitude," and how to copy maps. The work on maps did not seem connected to the history studied on adjacent days.

Teachers C1 and C2 both displayed topical coverage that extended beyond and could not be viewed as integrated with text topics. In fact, both teachers had a number of curricular streams going simultaneously. Thus, in a two-week period, teacher C1's students read about ancient and modern cities in their textbook, but also did a problem-solving exercise on immigration using another source, learned the abbreviations for the states, worked on graphing and table skills, worked on career project reports and posters, and reported on current events. Teacher C2's pupils engaged in almost as diverse a set of topics which included studying industrialism from the textbook, learning the names of the states, studying fine arts through worksheets on composers and dramatists, developing career project reports and posters, reading a news weekly about China and Taiwan (current events), and a "goods and services" problem-solving exercise. Both these teachers were equipped with a variety of resources for their social studies classes. As far as we could tell, topical integration of activities was not regularly sought and coverage went well beyond the primary adopted text.

Our other two teachers were using innovative curricula, both of which were structured for small work groups of students engaged in collaborative problem solving. Interestingly, it was teacher E1, using *MACOS*, and teacher F1, using *Sailing to the New World*, who were closest in topical coverage to their adopted curricula. In fact, although teacher E1 did not do all suggested activities in the *MACOS* unit on Eskimos, she did not devote any instruction to non-*MACOS* topics. Teacher F1 consistently and exclusively followed the simulation program dealing with preparation for colonization of the new world. In the presence of these curricular programs, the teachers did not devote instruction to other topics.

To summarize, three of the teachers (B1, E1, and F1) closely adhered to topics in their curriculum packages and materials, but sometimes teachers B1 and E1 were selective as both skipped some material. Both also occasionally created their own activities for students that were consistent with but not contained in their programs. The other three teachers, particularly C1 and C2, used their texts as only one component of their social studies instruction, and included various other unrelated topics on the days we observed. In the remaining case (teacher B2) two topical streams— Revolutionary history and map skills—were taught, each derived from a separate book.

We have already suggested that the teachers used the curricular materials in a variety of ways. In the Holt data bank system, a student textbook and data masters and data cards, which contain historical and tabular information, are provided. The data materials are meant to foster inquiry, concept attainment, and research skills. Teacher B1 told us that she liked the variety of materials and the concept approach and made full use of the system, assigning students data for individual and group research projects as well as using the text in connection with recitation and discussion. She also used some of the discussion topics suggested in the teacher's guide. However, she did not incorporate suggested enrichment activities and chose among the data materials provided. While staying within the spirit of the program, teacher B1 made some of her own worksheets and assignments and adapted the program to her own style and students.

Teacher B2 totally dropped the data materials and only used the textbook. In an interview, he stated the curriculum was too broad for his students and that they did not have the background for it. Most of his classes were devoted to lectures, recitations, or seatwork. He skipped around in the textbook and his lectures lacked close connection to the text topic. On one occasion he showed a film which was related to the study unit. His recitations tended to emphasize students' ability to define terms. For a number of days students worked individually on map skills from a workbook and were drilled orally on terminology. They also traced maps from the workbook. Teacher B2 did not use the suggestions in the teacher's guide that accompanied the data bank system. His instructional approach did not seem much affected by the particular materials adopted in his school.

Teachers C1 and C2 both used a wide variety of resources during instruction. Their text, *Man and Society*, was rather traditional in format with narrative material and some student questions and exercises. Both teachers used the textbook and its exercises for a portion of their instructional time, but it was one of a number of materials used in instruction. When in use, the textbook sequence was followed closely, although both teachers used a recitation format in which students took turns reading and then answered questions the teacher posed. Teacher C1 tended to ask more complex questions, while teacher C2 usually asked factual ones. This classroom procedure did not conform to the suggested activity in the teacher's guide and enrichment and extension activities were ignored. In both classes in school C the striking feature of social studies instruction was the diversity of sources used and topics covered. The text did not even appear to be an instructional anchor; it was simply one component of the social studies program.

We have already indicated that teachers E1 and F1—the users of nonconventional curricula—were more faithful to their adopted programs. Teacher E1 sometimes adapted activities in *MACOS*, but generally followed the suggested instructional procedures. We thus saw her pupils in small groups, watching films, putting on a play about Eskimo life, and generally engaged in the program as envisioned by its developers. Teacher F1, who was using *Sailing to the New World*, was unveering in her adherence to the suggested procedures for the program. Her students worked in small groups with the sheets and other materials supplied in an orderly simulation of preparing to colonize the new world.

Summary. The topics in social studies books, particularly traditional books meant to be the centerpiece of instruction, do not establish the set of topics to which social studies instruction is directed. In math, one can assume that almost everything taught is in the text although everything in the text is not taught. In social studies, the topics contained in the book are taught and usually taught in sequence; however, distinct and unrelated topical streams are covered simultaneously during instruction. Generally, more than topics in the textbook are the object of instruction in social studies.

From our limited number of cases, we suggest that more innovative curriculum packages may produce stricter adherence to content and procedure than standard textbooks in social studies. Innovative curricula also appear to provide a single and more exclusive focus for instruction and are not used in conjunction with other topics or content areas.

The use of multiple sources during instruction—including workbooks, other texts, newspapers, and films—is more common in social studies than in math. In the case of standard texts, other materials usually come from other publishers. Curriculum packages such as the Holt data bank system or *MACOS* provide a variety of types of materials for student use. Nevertheless, when textbooks are in use their narrative contents are used in order and completely. With one exception, our teachers did not skip around in the text or eliminate sections as we saw them do in math.

Teachers used more leeway in their teaching techniques and strategies when a standard textbook was adopted than when faced with an innovative program. As was true in math, enrichment suggestions in teacher's guides were ignored rather consistently as were most instructional suggestions. Our teachers used texts in the styles they felt most appropriate for themselves and their students, consistent with general school policies.

Conclusions

We have found little evidence in the literature or our case studies to support the idea that teachers teach strictly by the book. Instead, we have seen variation in practice that seems to result from teachers' own convictions and preferences, the nature of the materials they use, the school context in which they teach, the particular students in their class, and the subject matter and grade level they are teaching. Ball and

Feiman-Nemser have shown that student teachers receive conflicting advice about the use of textbooks.[45]

Our analysis of math and social studies teaching suggests that subject matter is a central determinant of the role of textbooks in instruction, along with the nature of the curriculum materials themselves. Our math teachers behaved very similarly to those studied by Porter and Freeman. But our social studies teachers behaved differently. From the literature we also infer that reading instructors make more comprehensive and ordered use of materials than we saw in either math or social studies.

With the innovative curricula in social studies as the only exception, we found a rather consistent disregard for many of the suggestions in teacher's guides—particularly those dealing with enrichment or motivational activities and specific questions and discussion topics. Teachers frequently made instruction more traditional (teacher-centered) by eliminating suggestions for group projects, for the use of manipulatives and exploratory activities, and for activities focused on higher mental processes. Our experienced teachers used their own styles of teaching and did not rely very much on the guides. As suggested by Graybeal, they tended to use core rather than optional suggestions from the teacher's guides.[46] Yet our strict adherents to the innovative curricula in social studies ran student-centered classrooms as dictated by their programs, reminding us that the nature of the program must be considered to judge fidelity.

A major difference between math and social studies is the extent to which the textbook content represents the *maximal* content coverage. In math this seems to be true; in social studies it is usually not true. Textbook content is supplemented and complemented routinely in social studies classes. Supplementation almost never occurs in math classes and probably not in reading classes either. On the other hand, when the text is in use, topical sequence is usually preserved in social studies. More skipping and departure from text sequence is found in math.

Our review and analysis suggests a real need for more study of textbook use, particularly in subjects other than the basic areas of reading and math. It also suggests that the common wisdom about textbooks pervading instructional decisions and actions must be tempered with more deliberate analysis of the specific ways in which such an assertion is valid and the conditions under which it is true. The popular vision of slavish adherence to texts does not seem supportable and may have arisen in part from overgeneralization of knowledge about primary reading instruction. The faulty assertions have also been bolstered by a lack of direct observation or other systematic data with which to verify or refute them.

NOTES

1. John I. Goodlad, *A Place Called School* (New York: McGraw Hill, 1984); P. Kenneth Komoski, "The Realities of Choosing and Using Instructional Materials," *Educational Leadership* 36 (October 1978): 46-50; Iris R. Weiss, *National Survey of Science, Mathematics, and Social Studies Education* (Washington, DC: National Science Foundation, 1978).

2. Donald J. Freeman, "Textbooks: Their Messages and Their Effects" (Unpublished manuscript, Michigan State University, 1986), p. 1.

3. Rebecca Barr and Robert Dreeben, *How Schools Work* (Chicago: University of Chicago Press, 1983).

4. Susan S. Stodolsky, *The Subject Matters: Classroom Activity in Math and Social Studies* (Chicago: University of Chicago Press, 1988).

5. Sheila S. Graybeal and Susan S. Stodolsky, "Instructional Practice in Fifth-grade Math and Social Studies: An Analysis of Teacher's Guides" (Paper presented at the Annual Meeting of the American Educational Research Association, San Francisco, 1986); idem, "Where's All the 'Good Stuff'? An Analysis of Fifth-grade Math and Social Studies Teacher's Guides" (Paper presented at the Annual Meeting of the American Educational Research Association, Washington, DC, 1987).

6. David L. Elliott, Kathleen C. Nagel, and Arthur Woodward, "Do Textbooks Belong in Elementary Social Studies?" *Educational Leadership* 42 (April 1985): 22-24.

7. Bruce DeSilva, "Schoolbooks: A Question of Quality," Special report, *Hartford Courant*, 15-18 June 1986.

8. Myra P. Sadker, David M. Sadker, and Tom Hicks, "The One-percent Solution? Sexism in Teacher Education Texts," *Phi Delta Kappan* 61 (April 1980): 550-53; Richard R. Powell and Jesus Garcia, "The Portrayal of Minorities and Women in Selected Elementary Science Series," *Journal of Research in Science Teaching* 22 (September 1985): 519-33.

9. Jean H. Osborn, Beau F. Jones, and Marcy Stein, "The Case for Improving Textbooks," *Educational Leadership* 42 (April 1985): 9-16; Bonnie Armbruster, "The Problem of the 'Inconsiderate Text'," in *Comprehension Instruction: Perspectives and Suggestions*, ed. Gerald G. Duffy, Laura R. Roehler, and Jana Mason (New York: Longman, 1984), pp. 202-17.

10. Jeanne S. Chall, "An Analysis of Textbooks in Relation to Declining SAT Scores" (Paper prepared for the Advisory Panel on the SAT Score Decline, jointly sponsored by the College Board and the Educational Testing Service. 1977).

11. Bonnie B. Armbruster and Thomas H. Anderson, "Structures of Explanations in History Textbooks, or So What if Governor Stanford Missed the Spike and Hit the Rail?" *Journal of Curriculum Studies* 16, no. 2 (1984): 181-94.

12. Bonnie B. Armbruster and Joyce Ostertag, "Questions in Elementary Science and Social Studies Textbooks" (Paper presented at the Annual Meeting of the American Educational Research Association, Washington, DC, 1987); Robert F. Nicely, Jr. "Higher-order Thinking Skills in Mathematics Textbooks," *Educational Leadership* 42 (April 1985): 26-30.

13. Barr and Dreeben, *How Schools Work*; Jana Mason, "A Schema-Theoretic View of the Reading Process as a Basis for Comprehension Instruction," in *Comprehension Instruction: Perspectives and Suggestions*, ed. Duffy, Roehler, and Mason (New York: Longman, 1984), pp. 26-38.

14. Barr and Dreeben, *How Schools Work.*

15. Andrew C. Porter, Robert E. Floden, Donald J. Freeman, William H. Schmidt, and John R. Schwille, *Content Determinants*, Research Series No. 179 (E. Lansing, MI: Institute for Research on Teaching, Michigan State University, 1986), unpaged abstract.

16. Donald J. Freeman, Therese M. Kuhs, Andrew Porter, Lucy B. Knappen, Robert E. Floden, William H. Schmidt, and John R. Schwille, *The Fourth-grade Mathematics Curriculum as Inferred from Textbooks and Tests*, Research Series No. 82 (E. Lansing, MI: Institute for Research on Teaching, Michigan State University, 1980), pp. 4-5.

17. Freeman, "Textbooks: Their Messages and Their Effects"; Donald J. Freeman and Andrew C. Porter, "Does the Content of Classroom Instruction Match the Content of Textbooks?" (Paper presented at the Annual Meeting of the American Educational Research Association, New Orleans, 1988).

18. Freeman, "Textbooks: Their Messages and Their Effects"; Freeman and Porter, "Does the Content of Classroom Instruction Match the Content of Textbooks?"

19. Freeman, "Textbooks: Their Messages and Their Effects."

20. Ibid.; Freeman and Porter, "Does the Content of Classroom Instruction Match the Content of Textbooks?"

21. Bonnie B. Armbruster, Robert J. Stevens, and Barak Rosenshine, *Analyzing Content Coverage and Emphasis: A Study of Three Curricula and Two Tests*, Technical Report No. 26 (Urbana, IL: Center for the Study of Reading, University of Illinois, 1977).

22. James R. Flanders, "How Much of the Content in Mathematics Textbooks Is New?" *Arithmetic Teacher* 35 (September 1987): 18-23.

23. Robert E. Stake and Jack A. Easley, *Case Studies in Science Education*, Vol. 2, *Design, Overview, and General Findings* (Washington, DC: U.S. Government Printing Office, 1978), ch. 13, p. 59.

24. EPIE (Educational Products Information Exchange) Institute, *Report on a National Study of the Nature and Quality of Instructional Materials Most Used by Teachers and Learners*, Report No. 76 (New York: EPIE, 1977); Goodlad, *A Place Called School*; Weiss, *National Survey of Science, Mathematics, and Social Studies Education*; Gail McCutcheon, "Elementary School Teachers' Planning for Social Studies and Other Subjects," *Theory and Research in Social Education* 9, no. 1 (1981): 45-66; Robert J. Yinger, "A Study of Teacher Planning," *Elementary School Journal* 80, no. 3 (1980): 107-27.

25. Barr and Dreeben, *How Schools Work.*

26. Dolores Durkin, "Is There a Match between What Elementary Teachers Do and What Basal Reader Manuals Recommend?" *Reading Teacher* 37 (April 1984): 734-44.

27. NACOME (National Advisory Committee on Mathematical Education), *Overview and Analysis of School Mathematics: K-12* (Washington, DC: Conference Board of the Mathematical Sciences, 1975); Thomas P. Carpenter, Mary K. Corbett, Henry S. Kepner, Mary M. Lindquist, and Robert E. Reys, *Results from the Second Mathematics Assessment of the National Assessment of Educational Progress* (Reston, Va: National Council of Teachers of Mathematics, 1981).

28. Freeman and Porter, "Does the Content of Classroom Instruction Match the Content of Textbooks?"

29. It is widely believed that math teachers do not reach a noticeable portion of chapters near the end of their books. Flanders analyzed new and old content in several

publishers' math series from grade one through algebra. He showed the first chapters in the series were consistently old material (that is, topics covered in the previous year or years) and, according to the authors, was there for review purposes. Flanders found that "on average the first half of a grade 1-8 book has 35 percent new conent, whereas the second half has 60 percent new content" (p. 22). Newer material was frequently not presented until the second third of the text and a number of new topics were never reached by teachers because they occurred in the end of the book as well. See Flanders, "How Much of the Content in Mathematics Textbooks Is New?"

30. Barr and Dreeben, *How Schools Work*.

31. Freeman and Porter, "Does the Content of Classroom Instruction Match the Content of Textbooks?"

32. Ibid.

33. Irving Morrissett, ed., *Social Studies in the 1980s: A Report of Project SPAN* (Alexandria, VA: Association for Supervision and Curriculum Development, 1982).

34. Durkin, "Is There a Match between What Elementary Teachers Do and What Basal Reader Manuals Recommend?"

35. Graybeal and Stodolsky, "Instructional Practice in Fifth-Grade Math and Social Studies"; idem, "Where's All the Good Stuff?"

36. Barr and Dreeben, *How Schools Work*; Mason, "A Schema-Theoretic View of the Reading Process as a Basis for Comprehension Instruction."

37. Connie A. Bridge and Elfrieda H. Hiebert, "A Comparison of Classroom Writing Practices, Teachers' Perceptions of Their Writing Instruction, and Textbook Recommendations on Writing Practices," *Elementary School Journal* 86, no. 2 (1985): 155-72.

38. Weiss, *National Survey of Science, Mathematics, and Social Studies Education*; Goodlad, *A Place Called School*; Stake and Easley, *Case Studies in Science Education*, Vol. 2, *Design, Overview, and General Findings*; Stodolsky, *The Subject Matters*.

39. Stodolsky, *The Subject Matters*.

40. The four math textbooks were: *Exploring Elementary Mathematics*, Holt, Rinehart and Winston, 1970; *Scott, Foresman Mathematics*, Scott, Foresman and Co., 1980; *Investigating School Mathematics*, Addison-Wesley, 1973; and *Discovery in Mathematics*, Laidlaw Brothers, 1972. The four social studies programs in use by observed teachers were: *Man and Society*, Silver Burdett, 1972; *Inquiring about American History*, Holt Data Bank System, Holt, Rinehart and Winston, 1976; *Man: A Course of Study (MACOS)*, Education Development Center, 1970; and *Sailing to the New World* (Discovery II), Interaction Publishers, 1976.

41. A full description of the observation procedures and the sample is available in Stodolsky, *The Subject Matters*.

42. See Freeman, "Textbooks: Their Messages and Their Effects" and Freeman and Porter, "Does the Content of Classroom Instruction Match the Content of Textbooks?"

43. Stake and Easley, *Case Studies in Science Education, Vol. 2, Design, Overview, and General Findings*.

44. Stodolsky, *The Subject Matters*.

45. Deborah L. Ball and Sharon Feiman-Nemser, "Using Textbooks and Teacher's Guides: A Dilemma for Beginning Teachers and Teacher Educators," *Curriculum Inquiry*, in press.

46. Sheila S. Graybeal, "A Study of Instructional Suggestions in Fifth-Grade Math and Social Studies Teacher's Guides and Textbooks" (Ph.D. diss., University of Chicago, 1988).

Introduction to Chapter VII

The planning of learning experiences is an integral part of the whole process of curriculum making. Developments in the field of computer technology have opened up a vast array of possibilities for learning activities that differ quite markedly from those that have dominated classroom practices in the past. As was the case when earlier technologies—film, radio, television—became available for classroom use, high expectations are now held for what computer technology can do to promote learning.

In the following chapter, Stephen Kerr reviews briefly how computer technology is typically used in schools, the effects of those uses on students' thinking, and how teachers learn to use this new technology. He shows how various applications of computer technology in education can be analyzed both in terms of what they make possible for teachers and students to do (i.e., affordances) and the sorts of activity that their use inhibits (i.e., constraints). He urges that similar analyses be undertaken with other potential applications.

Finally, Kerr outlines a vision for the introduction of technology in education that emphasizes education as a fundamentally human *activity rather than a technological or economic activity. He believes that how we think of technology in relation to education will determine whether or not "technology will have a more permanent place in education than it has found to date."*

Stephen T. Kerr is Professor of Education at the University of Washington. The chapter we reprint here originally appeared in the Society's 95th Yearbook, Part 2, Technology and the Future of Schooling, *edited by Stephen T. Kerr.*

CHAPTER VII

Visions of Sugarplums: The Future of Technology, Education, and the Schools

STEPHEN T. KERR

> The real problem is not whether machines think but whether men do.
>
> —B. F. Skinner (1969)

We are fascinated with technology. We expect it to make a difference in our lives, and particularly in education. We see its effects as beneficent. We look for it to change, and improve, what has come before. We await technological improvements in our lives, from better toaster ovens to improved (more effective, more efficient) schools and learning to rejuvenation of our bodies and protection from our enemies.

These images of what technology can do for us are peculiarly American, although not uniquely so. Americans, for a number of reasons, seem particularly susceptible to a set of related propositions: that technology is *good*, that it is *value-free*, that it *should* find application in *many* fields, disciplines, and aspects of our lives. Perhaps most troubling is the assumption that, if technology makes it possible to do something, then that thing *should* be done.

In our culture, the way in which technology is presented and framed in public forums mirrors these assumptions. The possibility of developing and using a "national information superhighway," of using "smart weapons" in the recent war in Iraq (and the probability of their increased use in the future), or of employing a variety of reproductive technologies to enable previously infertile couples to conceive children have been presented as basically value-free, scientifically neutral, and desirable options. The issues that are presented to us as problematic with regard to these changes (censorship and copyright questions

171

with regard to the information superhighway, concerns about commanders' possible desensitization in the case of smart weapons, worries over whether teenaged mothers can adequately care for their offspring) have typically come up for wider public discussion *after* the preliminary decision to deploy a particular technology had already been made.

So in education, the possibility (and desirability) of creating and using technologically based systems for teaching, learning, and provision of educational services are typically seen as basically transparent questions. Should we install large numbers of computers in the nation's classrooms? Should children use on those computers widely available commercial software packages (word processors, spreadsheets, databases, etc.)? Should we encourage the design, creation, and installation of a variety of new, multimedia instructional programs? Should we connect increasing numbers of schools, teachers, and students to the Internet? In almost every case, we answer "yes" before we can fully comprehend the costs or time involved, much less the more fundamental issues of learning, development, or social organization where the impact of these decisions may be felt.

A large part of the problem with technology in education seems to be our stance toward it, our impressions of what it is, what it is good for, and how we should think about it. Many of the failures of the past stem from this same problem: the films we expected to revolutionize teaching in the 1920s, the radio broadcasts that would bring the world into every school room in the 1930s, the "new media" of the 1950s and 1960s (television, Super-8 film loops, language laboratories), the passion for programmed instruction of the 1960s, the novelties of distance education and dial-access audio and video in the 1970s. In all these cases, we started with enormous expectations about what a particular set of technological devices, used in a particular way, might be able to accomplish. While there were a few successes (the overhead projector that rapidly spread into most of the classrooms in America, the somewhat slower but still wide-ranging dissemination of VCRs, the power of distance education and "open university" approaches to extend higher education to new audiences), there were certainly more problems and criticisms—the machines that were used once and consigned to the closet, the devices that teachers used once a year because they were too complex, the stigma that attached to teachers who used "too many films."

The problem of using new technologies was not made easier by the audio-visual (later instructional technology) establishment. After years of research studies that tried (and failed) to demonstrate an advantage for using one or another set of devices over "traditional instruction," practitioners were left with little guidance for selecting one approach over another. The field's response was to devise a new, overarching approach through systems theory, one that promised to focus attention not on devices but on design variables, development processes, and learning outcomes. While this new approach found many followers in business, military, and industrial training, it distanced technologists further from the public schools and from teachers, many of whom found the new "systems" emphasis confusing at best and threatening at worst.

The wave of interest in microcomputers and related devices that came in the early 1980s marked a shift away from the traditional concerns of technologists, and ushered in a period in which the interests of administrators, parents, community members, and teachers came to the fore. Whereas earlier technologies had either supported the educational status quo (films, television, overhead projectors) or challenged it in ways that were potentially too explosive for schools to handle (programmed instruction), computer technology seemed to be about more than simply teaching and learning. It was immediately associated with economics (employment prospects for graduates, based on the "skills needed for the information age"), with community pride ("Our school has six networked Mac labs!"), with concerns about gender, race, and class (Do minority students have as much access to software that encourages meaningful thought and action, as opposed to simply drill-and-practice, as their majority peers?), and with images of new kinds of classrooms and new types of schools (technology-in-the-service-of-reform, the movement to new kinds of student-teacher roles in classrooms organized in new ways). The small group of advocates for teaching about the computer as an object in itself (the teachers of programming and "computer studies") were quickly outnumbered by proponents of teaching programming for the sake of critical and logical thinking and problem solving, and an even larger number who saw the computer perhaps as a tool to improve performance in basic subjects, or perhaps merely as a slightly more worthy competitor to video games and Saturday morning cartoons. Among administrators and community members with an interest in education, the fascination with computers has often been expressed in terms of rationalization and improvements in efficiency: "If a computer can allow a secretary to type a letter 25 percent faster, it ought to allow a teacher to improve what happens in the classroom by the same margin."

In virtually all these cases, however, the discussion has gone forward without an examination of one central underlying assumption: that we *should* think of education, and schools, as sites for application of computers, software, networks, and associated technologies. Technology itself, rather than the particular goals and ends we wish to have students achieve by using it, often seems to have the priority. (I recall several years ago being asked to sit with a group of teachers from a local school who were interested, they said, in "doing some things with technology." At my first meeting with them, they showed me a document, several pages long, on which they had listed an impressive array of the latest computers, printers, modems, videodisc equipment, software, and so forth. There was no suggestion as to what these might be used for. When I asked about that, they replied, "We thought we'd figure that out later, once we actually get the computers.") We readily ask of technology "Can it do X?," but rarely seem to bring ourselves to ask "Do we really want it to do X? Why do we want it to do X?" The issues of what technology is "good for" are often either ignored or postponed until their consideration has become a moot point.

I want to suggest here that this approach to technology is fundamentally flawed, and that we ignore these concerns at our future peril. An approach to technology in education that puts hardware (or even software) in first place will ultimately lead to impoverished schools (in the moral, not the financial sense) where students learn things that are unimportant—but possible—to learn. Too, I want to suggest that wider use of computers (and associated new devices and technologies) in schools may have unanticipated results. This is because the ways in which we typically use them may define and limit, as well as extend, student (and teacher) perceptions. And I want to challenge the increasingly popular view that technology provides such power that we can use it to effectively eliminate schools altogether. This idea is so basically flawed, and so basically alien to our most central notions of what a good society is, how we should treat other persons in a democratic and civil society, and how we should educate citizens to live and work there, that we should do everything we can to defeat it.

Lest this prescription sound excessively Luddite, allow me to clarify several points. First, I am not against technology, I do not fear it, nor do I deny that we should introduce it into schools and use it there appropriately. Second, I see strong and important roles that technology can play; I view its effects as potentially significant and beneficial for individual teachers and students and for the education system more generally. Third, I maintain that the ways we think about technology—the attitudes we hold, the assumptions we make about what it is "good for"—are, in fact, as real and important as the CD-ROM drives and monitors of the computers themselves. Finally, I suggest that technology, as it grows and develops, will come to influence our lives in ways that we have great difficulty perceiving at the moment. This includes what happens in schools, among young people and adults, what emerges from those interactions, and how we value it.

Our History: Technology and Human Culture

The questions of what technology is "good for," and the place that it has in our consciousness as we think about our lives, have been addressed before, but perhaps not with quite the breadth or depth that we might expect. The scholars for whom these issues were central include Lewis Mumford, whose *Technics and Civilization* offered an analysis of the ways in which technology (at that time—the 1930s—primarily mechanical) had influenced human thought and action.[1] Mumford saw a pronounced effect from technology's focus on practicality, "matter-of-factness" as he put it, and consequent decline in "irrational and emotive" aspects of human behavior. His general attitude toward the increasing involvement of technology in human existence was sanguine. But Mumford also saw human existence as requiring something more than simply the coolly rational approach that technology encouraged; he saw technology's effects on human thought as offering a kind of basic minimum, a precondition for allowing humans to move on to more important, more "richly organic" human values.

Another perspective on technology is offered by the French sociologist and cultural historian Jacques Ellul.[2] Ellul saw technology somewhat less positively than Mumford, and was concerned by what he saw as the increased focus on efficiency as a goal in and of itself. For Ellul, the increasing reliance by society on engineers and "psychotechnicians," even in areas (such as education) formerly seen as the realm of other kinds of thought and sensibility, was problematic, an attempt to recapture through technology that which technology itself had taken away.

Specific aspects of technology's impact on society have intrigued some scholars. Of these, H. Marshall McLuhan may be best known to educators for his ideas about communication technology and its effects. McLuhan wrote in an aphoristic style that sometimes seemed deliberately designed to conceal rather than illuminate, and some of his ideas—"hot" and "cool" media, "the global village," "the medium is the message"—themselves became slogans. Arguments continue about the significance of McLuhan's work, but in one particular area, the impact of print technology on culture, his work was seminal for a series of other scholars.[3] Eisenstein examined the ways in which printing altered the relationships among the state, the individual, the church, and the academy in early modern Europe, and concluded that the spread of knowledge encouraged by printing radically democratized social life.[4] Luke considered the ways in which these factors affected the definition and construction of childhood.[5]

Others who have written on the technology-society question have considered how engineering and its products are perceived and used in society. Florman's analysis is basically exculpatory and suggests that critics often excoriate technology unfairly for exacerbating problems that are more properly described as social.[6] Winner, on the other hand, sees fundamental problems in the ways that technological artifacts are initially defined, especially in the typical lack of public participation in that process, which he sees as leading to fundamental problems after the technology is eventually deployed.[7] Petroski takes a somewhat different view, emphasizing the role of trial-and-error procedure and thus failure (sometimes admittedly catastrophic) in engineering design.[8]

Technology and Education

In the field of education, recent approaches to technology have stressed project descriptions, experimental evaluations of the success of a particular instructional product, or, more complexly, examinations of the ways in which technology can support cognition in various domains. Occasionally, there have been critics: Nunan, for example, saw instructional design as an attempt by educational technologists to preempt the teacher's role, a position echoed by Kerr.[9] A critique of the underlying assumptions present in notions of instructional design was provided by Streibel.[10] Richard Hooper, a former executive of the British Broadcasting Corporation, has written cogently about the problems educational technology has had in establishing itself as a field and the troubles it has had in defining which issues really warrant careful consideration.[11] Travers discussed the generally ineffectual approaches used by the field in coping with the changing political landscape in education.[12]

Some critics of the field have suggested that the problem of failed technological applications in education lies not with technologies or those who implement them, but rather with the entire system of schooling. Heinich criticized those working in educational technology for being too closely allied with the schools, and too little aware of the ways in which technology could be creatively applied in solving educational problems.[13] Perelman's arguments focus more on the ways in which current computer technology can do away radically with the need for schools as we have traditionally understood them, arguments that also undergirded the now uncertain attempts by financier and telecommunications entrepreneur Chris Whittle to create a new approach to schooling through the Edison Project.[14]

In almost all cases, the arguments for why we should want to introduce technology into the schools (or into education more generally, if the schools themselves are seen as irrelevant) are phrased in strictly utilitarian terms. We should "want to prepare workers for the competitive global economy" has been a popular formulation in recent years, although earlier it might have been "to prepare ourselves to fight the Cold War." Educational technology is almost universally discussed in terms of method, which is seen as having direct effects that are important to national purposes or the formation of citizens able to contribute in specified ways to the society and the economy.

The alternative would be to try to identify essential human concerns, make these the focus of the educational system, and make decisions within the framework of these concerns. In this kind of educational system, the primary focus of schools, and therefore of instruction, would be on human values, not economic utility. While some would fear that this sort of approach would too closely resemble the definition of a kind of "state morality" (or even worse, a "state religion"), in fact many school systems around the world operate with this sort of moral compass at the center of their image of the school. What kinds of concerns might qualify? I will suggest only four here, although there could easily be others: first, a focus on the acquisition of knowledge as a tool for self-discovery and liberation (rather than in the service of purposes defined by the state or other actors with an interest in the "products" of the schools); second, self-esteem and a feeling of self-worth; third, respect for others with differing values and characteristics; and fourth, what we might call a "democratic world view," a willingness to participate in the affairs of a democratic society.

While it has been rare for those concerned with the role of technology in our society to focus on such issues, some scholars have indeed seen them as important. The well-known theologian and philosopher, Martin Heidegger, for example, saw technology as a threat to fundamental human ways of relating to one another.[15] Neil Postman, a persistent critic of our society's unbridled fascination with technology, finds the subjugation of all social purposes and processes to technological determinism a sad and dangerous state.[16] Shoshana Zuboff explored the ways in which introduction of computer-based systems of management and control affected the careers of both professionals and blue-collar workers in various occupations. She found that the ways management typically used such systems led workers to feel that they were operating in a "panopticon of power," an environment in which all of their actions and decisions were much more open to scrutiny and analysis from outside than had ever been the case before.[17] But Ithiel de Sola Pool, a scholar who studied communication technology all his life, while critical, was also hopeful about technology's potential to effect social action beneficently.[18]

In the world of education and schools, relatively few have analyzed the ways in which the pervasive movement of computers into classrooms has been carried out. Noble examined the heritage of the educational technology community, especially its links with both the corporate and military sectors of American life. He found the connections omnipresent and saw them largely determining the nature of use of educational technology in the schools.[19] This view was reiterated, though in a nonjudgmental way, by *Power On!*, the U.S. government's own review of the effort to introduce computers into schools in the 1980s.[20] Sloan and Bowers offered generally critical assessments of the practices of computer-assisted instruction.[21] While there have occasionally been other discussions about the nature of the field and the ethical and moral quandaries inherent in applying technology in education, these have not had a central place in national discussions.[22]

To help advance discussion of these issues, it may be useful first to develop here a typology of the current situation—how technology is typically deployed for use in schools, by teachers, students, and administrators; how it is paid for, and, most important, what it is perceived by those involved to be "good for." We will therefore have to survey briefly:

- the ways in which technology is typically used in schools (e.g., types of software employed);
- the effects those uses have on students' thinking (e.g., effects on learning and belief);

- our teachers' ways of interacting with students and other teachers, the ways they have of learning about new practices (such as the use of technology), and their images of their professional work (what it means to be a teacher);

- the organization and structure of education (including how administrative and management decisions are made when technology is employed, technology as a vehicle for public engagement in education).

What Technology in Education Has Been Good For

Perhaps the primary thing we need to bear in mind about the interaction of technology and schooling is that the process has never resulted in the panacea that educators often hoped and assumed would follow. The reasons are varied, and some of them we touched on briefly above. A key determinant is the powerful set of social, political, and economic expectations borne by schools as a part (arguably the most important part) of the larger social institution we call education. As Cuban and Cohen have argued forcefully, technology does not succeed in classrooms the way we dream it might because of other expectations we have of schools. We have pervasive, powerful, and usually tacit images of how schools should work. We seem to think, for example, that having an adult teacher present to work with children is important, regardless of how sophisticated are the technological systems and devices we may create to circumvent this situation.[23] Such images are slow to change because they are powerful: they are widely circulated and broadly accepted in society. They are also shared by people from many different groups: educators, parents, politicians, business leaders, intellectuals. Because these images are so widely and deeply held, they are not easily changed, making it difficult to bring about change in schools.

A further aspect of the images we have of how a school ought to be organized is a strong component of control—a principal who is perceived to be "in charge" or an "instructional leader," a superintendent who is a "take command individual"—a feature that we are loath to give up, and may even want to strengthen (for example, through the current push toward greater teacher accountability, "high stakes" evaluation approaches, "outcome-based education," and state and national educational standards). These trends may conflict directly (though again, the conflicts are rarely discussed in the open) with technology as a mechanism for "flattening the pyramid," reducing the number of administrative layers in a school system, and generally fostering greater responsibility and "empowerment" for teachers at a local level.

These new expectations also make it difficult to pursue some of the things that technology might make available: greater individualization, more possibilities for students to explore their own agendas, teachers constructing new curricula that go outside the bounds of the usual.

Thus, schools as a part of the larger social institution of education have a kind of life of their own, an existence that we encourage and support through a myriad of public actions and private decisions even as we consider rather different images, based on technology, for what a school might be. It is important to keep this in mind as we examine both traditional images of how to use technology in schools, as well as some new images based on a rethinking of what technology in education might be "good for."

Technology as we know it. A number of surveys have defined typical uses for computer technology in schools. The machines were first organized in self-standing labs, but more recently have started to be dispersed to individual classrooms; various commercially available software application packages are used (word processors, spreadsheets, data bases, communications programs), as well as some purely instructional programs (science or social studies simulations, drill-and-practice exercises, and, occasionally, a few higher-powered interactive mathematics or science programs). Only in a small number of cases do students today learn about computers primarily in order to learn how to program them, an approach that originally seemed very promising to many in the field. And in even fewer cases do they work with instructional software that was created by their own teachers.

Technology other than computers is used in its own distinctive ways. Television, for example, has moved into virtually all the classrooms in the country, either through such programs as Whittle's "Channel One," or through the use of relatively inexpensive video cassette recorders. As was the case with other technological changes such as phonograph records and audio tapes, new technology made its way into classrooms most easily after it had first penetrated the home market and had thus become a part of most people's everyday existence. Surveys of video usage in the schools suggest that teachers typically use programming that is provided to their districts at no or reduced cost through local PBS stations; they use video programs freely and in relatively large numbers, but access to a wider variety of materials is neither easy nor terribly attractive for these teachers.

What is perhaps most significant about the ways technology has come to be used in schools is that it is almost universally thought of as an addition to or an extension of regular instruction rather than as a replacement for it. In spite of years of prediction that teachers, texts, schools would be put out of business by new technologies of teaching and learning, in fact schools as institutions seem to have grown ever more securely rooted over the years. Technology still plays a supplementary role in images carried around in the heads of most educators and most parents of how schooling ought to be organized.

Students and technology. Early arguments about the use of computers in education were framed, as had been virtually all preceding discussions about the use of educational technology, in terms of whether the new approach would "be better than 'traditional' instruction," or whether students would "learn different kinds of things." There were a good many very positive initial findings in the 1980s suggesting that using computers really did make a difference; students were found to improve test scores by large amounts (half a standard deviation or more) when they had the chance to work on a computer as opposed to listening to a traditional lecture. But later meta-analyses of these studies largely debunked the supposed advantage as an artifact of inappropriate assumptions and sloppy research; instead, the observed improvement was credited to the intense design work that underlies preparation of programs for computer-assisted instruction (CAI).

More recent studies of the effects of CAI on learning have shown that students can indeed benefit particularly from certain features of computer-based systems. These benefits come from the efficiency in presentation that comes from using a system that can rapidly and dynamically adapt to the specifics of a given user's pattern of responses, and that can present material that allows direct interaction and manipulation of a specific set of instructional variables. Software such as the "Geometric Supposer" in mathematics, a variety of similar software in the natural sciences, and powerful simulations in social studies can encourage students to think about problems in ways which, while they could likely be duplicated without a computer, would also be very difficult (time-consuming, expensive, dangerous) to arrange and present.

It has been more difficult to study the long-term effects of computer use on how students think, and on their deeper ways of perceiving the social and physical world. There were a number of early claims that using a computer regularly, especially for writing computer programs, would benefit students by improving logical thought or enhancing their abilities to solve problems. These have largely turned out to be unfounded.[24] The process of transfer from the very specific domain of programming to other arenas of problem solving turns out to be much more difficult than originally assumed. And there is even less information about the long-term impact of regular computer use on deeper images on oneself, one's interactions with others, one's purposes in life, the ways the world works.

There has been much enthusiasm about applying the Internet and other systems of digital telecommunication to the work of students and schools. Special attention has been given to possibilities for collaborative regional or international projects. Some of these have been quite successful, but overall results to date have been mixed. The principal problem seems to be how to decide upon particular, educationally relevant work to pursue, once the initial excitement of contact has worn off. Those projects that have defined such work (e.g., scientific analysis of air pollution data, comparative economic analysis of the cost of living) have generally been successful, while those that have not done so have often failed.[25] This is another area in which figuring out "what the technology is good for" is an important (if often untaken) step.

Teachers and technology. How teachers use technology (or don't) is a topic of enduring fascination to those who work within the field of educational technology. Until relatively recently, this issue was only peripherally interesting to other educators and administrators. Now, however, the resources committed to technology in the schools have increased exponentially, and so interest in how teachers perceive and use it has also increased.

Why people do or do not use certain practices in their work has been a concern to a broader community than just educators. Field extension agents and agricultural development workers in third world countries had a direct interest in encouraging those with whom they worked to adopt new practices. Another large literature on innovative practices and organizational change came from the business community. Many older models of educational change used these perspectives, and consequently suggested that individuals faced with a decision as to whether to change an established practice could basically be viewed as lying along a normal distribution, ranging from "early adapters," through the "majority" (early and late), down to "laggards" and "resisters."[26] The assumption here was that the decision to use a new practice is basically one-dimensional, and that knowledge about the benefits that would accrue from use would outweigh other barriers hindering adoption, propositions that came under critical analysis as the greater complexities of schools and teaching practices became evident.

More sophisticated treatments of the process of innovation appeared in the 1980s, at the same time that interest grew in looking at schools as "cultures" in and of themselves. Investigators who examined the uncertainties, problems, and fears of teachers vis à vis a particular change suggested using a "concerns-based adoption model" (CBAM), and urged that innovations be thought of not as a dichotomous choice for the potential user ("to adopt or not to adopt"), but rather as possibilities that would allow for a number of levels of use.[27]

Studies of teachers' interest in using computers quickly indicated why the earlier, simplistic models were insufficient. Whereas some earlier technological changes could be mastered by a teacher in a few hours (an overhead projector, for example, or even a 16 mm film projector) and their classroom implications relatively easily perceived and reconciled with existing practice, computers were something different. The complexity of the software involved, its "invisibility" to the naked eye, the variety of different approaches one could take when using the hardware, and the potential implications for organization of classroom practice—all these were both complex and troubling for many teachers. Faced with textual and multimedia materials that might include the equivalent of several encyclopedias in a single package, many teachers were concerned about merely identifying what was there, let alone having students master the content in the ways that they might use in working with a traditional text.

Confronting a machine that some suggested could radically restructure classroom organization was also a challenge for many teachers. If one was in fact to move from working as a direct instructor to being more of a mentor and guide, then how was one to learn how to do that, and how was one to assure that one's students were in fact progressing as they should and not using their own (often superior) ability with technology to create merely a Potemkin village of progress?

The difficulties inherent in starting to use computers in classrooms were assuredly real, and teachers found few easy ways to cope. The in-service training opportunities that districts offered were in many cases inadequate, with brief workshops and one-day seminars providing only scant information on topics that many teachers found puzzling and complex. Several studies of how teachers worked in these new environments suggested that rather than thinking in terms of hours or even weeks of teacher in-service preparation for using new technologies appropriately, the time scale ought better be thought of in terms of years.[28]

A major issue in teachers' coming to use technology in their work has had to do with how that work is defined both by teachers themselves and by those who influence their work (professors in colleges of education, local and state educational administrators, union officials, and other influential teachers from the same or neighboring districts). The problem of how to prepare teachers is thrown into especially sharp focus here, since colleges of education generally have not themselves rushed to embrace new technology. The few programs that have been carried out around the nation to enhance teacher education with technology have not revealed any special secrets in this regard.

Ultimately, the principal issue in working with teachers must be how they themselves define their work. That image may be slowly changing under the impact of technology, but it responds to other influences as well, and it is too early to tell what ultimately might result. Perhaps the central problem here is not so much in technology as it is in the social form of the school—whether the school will continue to be an empire of solo practitioners, with teachers who retreat to largely isolated and self-contained classrooms to "do their own thing," with students who are relatively passive, sit in rows, and listen to the teacher talk, and with bureaucratically oriented principals and superintendents, or whether collaborative practice among teachers, more flexible patterns of school organization, and students able to work with each other and independently of the teacher will come to be more the norm. If such changes as these are to come about, there will need to be more support (and enthusiasm) for them from all sides than has been the case to date.

Technology and the management of schools as organizations. Technology in its current form may have an impact not only on teaching practice but also on the administration and organization of schools as workplaces. Some of these changes affect the ways teachers might work with their colleagues, as mentioned above. But some will lie in more traditionally administrative realms—how to manage schools and districts, how to plan school finance, and how to kindle and track public involvement in making decisions about new programs, new buildings, new purposes in education.

While many districts have rushed to install computer systems for collecting and processing information about students, teachers, and finances, relatively few studies exist of the ways in which these new systems have affected the organizational structure of districts. Perhaps the advent of electronic mail and the changes in communication patterns that accompany it, for example, will eventually have more impact than the computers themselves, though this is not clear from current experience. Where people—teachers, for example—historically have had no involvement in making decisions about the school budget, simple access to an e-mail system and the opportunity to comment on a draft plan for expenditures will not automatically transform them into experienced budget analysts.[29] If technology is to "flatten the pyramid" of hierarchical bureaucracy found in most school districts, there must be intentional efforts to bring that about. These might include new patterns of information flow, new ways in which information is used within the organization, and training for educators in how to create, analyze, and use that information in making collaborative decisions. Similarly, the opportunity for teachers to work together in technology-intensive classrooms will probably not automatically result in radically new patterns of instruction unless specific guidance is provided on how to accomplish those changes.

The involvement of the public in decisions regarding education is another area in which technology holds much as-yet-unrealized promise. It would seem that the possibility of circulating large amounts of information rapidly to a circle of interested parties would be a useful way to gather reactions to proposed policy initiatives, or to collect public opinions about controversial curricular or program matters. Virtually no research has been done on these issues, perhaps because there are still very few public school districts with the needed wherewithal to mount such an initiative, and perhaps also because the issue of selective access is still problematic. For example, could a district claim that it had reasonably "sampled public opinion" if it restricted that process to electronic means of dissemination and collection, and thus perhaps excluded segments of the population that did not have access?

Too, the issue of "electronic referenda," while superficially attractive, also raises some cautionary flags. Should "hot" public issues (e.g., adoption of a sex-education curriculum, a proposed teacher pay increase, or funding for a new building) be settled via a quick public vote? Is there something in the way of deliberation that might be lost in such a process? (These same issues were raised a few years ago during the 1992 presidential campaign by independent candidate Ross Perot, who proposed "electronic plebiscites" on important public questions.) Many who have explored the significance of our current procedures for making public decisions emphasize that representative democracy was intended to provide a cushion against the demands of particular groups for swift action to resolve what are perceived as the pressing problems of the moment.

Ultimately, though, there is some evidence that technology's most pronounced effects on education may be on organizational structures. There is widespread public sentiment that the present pattern of hierarchical bureaucracy that characterizes education in many Western countries is counterproductive and outmoded. For technology to break those patterns, support will be needed not only from educators but also from the public, legislative bodies, and the business community.[30]

Constraints on What Technology in Education Might Be Good For

If we want to describe a more fully human vision for what technology might contribute to education, we need to consider not only what has been done to date, but also what the constraints are—what technology, by its very form and function, encourages us to do, and what by those same features it keeps us from doing.[31] This is an interesting and complex issue, and a complete examination would require more space than we have here. A suggestion of how this kind of analysis might be managed is provided here through a look at the typical range of application-oriented computer software commonly used in schools and the sorts of activity their structure encourages (affordances) and inhibits (constraints).

Spreadsheets. Using spreadsheets (or their derivatives, "gradebook" programs) to calculate the grades students are to receive in a course was an early success in the campaign to have teachers use computers in classrooms. This has been especially so for those teachers who think of the process of determining grades in ways that would be approved by authors of textbooks on measurement and evaluation: gather a number of component elements, weight each one appropriately, and combine them to yield a final grade. To calculate grades in this way by hand or calculator is a process that is both time-consuming and error-prone; with a spreadsheet, the task is quick and relatively effortless, once an initial template has been designed.

The problem, if there is one, lies in the assumptions that underlie this way of thinking about grades. Are students' activities in fact so easily decomposed into a set of subparts? More important, *should* we think of them in this way? Might it be the case that human thought and action are better thought of as wholes, not so easily broken into pieces, and requiring a different kind of analysis, a different method of evaluation, than the spreadsheet model supposes?

The debate is less an empirical one than philosophical, for our purposes in evaluating students are linked intimately with our sense of what schools are for, what purposes evaluation serves in the wider social context, and how we want students themselves to think about the work that they have done in school once they leave. The debate is especially intense at the moment, when some scholars writing on evaluation suggest that the existing (spreadsheet) model is really a holdover from an earlier approach to schooling that itself presupposed a kind of Taylorist, early-twentieth century image of the school as factory, and teachers as producers of knowledge in the same sense that a factory worker might produce railway cars or motors. If one rivet or connecting rod was incorrectly placed, that should be determined, and should affect the evaluation of the overall quality of the finished product. But models of schooling that presuppose a different kind of endproduct—an educated person, rather than a cog in a machine—may require different forms of evaluation, and our current spreadsheet models are not easily matched to such an image.

Word processors and desk-top publishing. The introduction of wordprocessing software and desk-top publishing packages into classrooms has been hailed by teachers of writing and language arts as a great boon. By allowing children to revise their work easily, the claim goes, computers have enabled students to move beyond the agonizing process of hand-written or typed rewrites of a composition and focus on the substance of what they want to say. In cases where the software used is sophisticated, it may allow the student not only to manipulate the text itself, but may also provide the student with hints, guidance, and gentle correction of spelling, grammar, and syntax. The addition of desk-top publishing capabilities—embedded pictures, graphs, varied type faces and sizes, borders and columns—allows the student to produce a document that may rival what a full-fledged print shop could have done twenty years ago.

The problem here may lie in the support that such environments provide for focusing on the details of a composition, whether having to do with grammar or lay-out, rather than the substance of the thoughts expressed. As the Canadian writer Stephen Leacock once said when asked by a young correspondent how he could become as famous a writer as Leacock, "Don't try to *write*: try to *think*: then when you really have something to say and want to say it very much, say it. That process is called *writing*."[32] This sort of deep reflection is not made impossible by word-processing software, but neither is it encouraged.

Desk-top publishing programs lead to a similar kind of fascination with form over function. As a number of observers have noted, the initial use of such software tools in organizations led to the appearance of a plethora of ugly, unreadable newsletters and memos as authors and public-relations specialists immediately experimented with the full range of fonts, dingbats, graphic images, and page layout designs available, often combining numerous different forms in one document.[33]

The point is not to deny the possibility that many teachers and students will be able to use these new tools to create instructional products characterized by elegant composition and attractive layout. Rather, it is to suggest that such software carries within it both affordances (the possibility of checking spelling, of moving text around, etc.) as well as constraints (the lack of any way of checking the quality of arguments made, the organization of the discussion; the focus on variety of presentation mode rather than on clarity). The affordances are what we typically attend to, and they are also what the advertisements for such products often feature; the constraints are not only invisible, but their existence, which an earlier generation would have taken for granted and compensated for in other ways, is now increasingly ignored. It is as if we have somehow collectively decided that the form and presentation shall be given not just equal, but superior, weight as compared to the quality of thought, the force of argument, the elegance and simplicity of presentation.

Databases and hypermedia. Using a database to store, organize, and retrieve information seems a natural addition to the teacher's armamentarium. Teachers concerned to help their charges master these skills have often built such activities into their classroom practice, either through use of materials that require students to think about gaining access to and using the information, or simply by taking the students to the school library and having them learn the necessary skills. Databases facilitate this process by allowing students themselves to define the structure of the information, identify what is to be recorded, and then work with the resulting set of information in various ways. Already existing databases (electronic card catalogues and other kinds of data on CD-ROM increasingly found in school libraries) offer students similar experiences but without the initial step of defining the content.

While none of these approaches is bad, they do impose certain kinds of constraints that are not usually noted by proponents of their use. If students themselves construct databases, for example, they are limited to the particular specifications of given database software for the kinds and formats of information that can be entered (e.g., the length of a field, alphabetic vs. numeric information). Too, the ways in which information can be organized and retrieved must conform to what the system makes possible. The spread of ready-made macros, bundled together with commercial software, exacerbates this problem, making it ever easier for the user to accept someone else's predesigned "solution." Likewise, in library systems and CD-ROMs, the way the material is structured largely determines what work can be done with it and what can be extracted. Hypermedia (combinations of video, text, graphics, music, and animation) allow the user to follow varied, nonlinear links among chunks of information, but the set of possible links is often itself prespecified by the designer of the materials. These constraints may not be problems at all, but they may emerge as issues if the material is not naturally presented in the ways the student wishes to work with it.

The affordances of databases also need special attention. As with the possibility of placing form over function in work with word processors, the ability instantly to retrieve large amounts of information about a topic becomes something of an end in itself. Quantity is confused with quality, and the more subtle clues that formerly allowed (and encouraged) students to make judgments about the real value of a book or other information (a known and trustworthy source, the strength and completeness of the supporting evidence, the reasonableness of conclusions drawn, the quality of organization, the rhetorical strength of argument) often wash out in electronic form.

The issue, as in the case of spreadsheets, is whether we wish to encourage students to think of information as an ultimately fungible, reducible commodity, one which, to be useful, needs constantly to be recast in different ways (abbreviated, cross-referenced into predefined categories) so as to make it manipulable, accessible. The separate issue of confusing quantity for quality is similar to that for desk-top publishing, where we are encouraged to mistake variety and flash for substance. These hurdles are not insurmountable, but they require teachers to provide guidance and to fill in cues about the quality of information that may have been removed when it is made available electronically.

Communication and connectivity. As more and more students are able to connect through their school computers with networks, either locally (throughout the school or the district) or on a broader scale (around the nation or the world), new issues surface as regards the value and purpose of such links. As noted above, many interesting things can happen if the connections are carefully thought through in advance. But there is also a risk here, that the fact of connection will be seen in and of itself as a good thing. As Richard Hooper notes, a kind of fetish of interactive communication has emerged, making the link itself the ultimate purpose.[34]

The constraints here are obvious; one can only link electronically with someone who has similar capacities. Likewise, if one party has access to that part of the World-Wide Web (part of the Internet) using an audiographical "browser" interface such as Mosaic or Netscape, and the other party is using a text-only interface, one may be able to create and send materials to which one's partner will remain blind.

The affordances also need careful thought. Several studies of how people react to each other when working in an e-mail environment suggest that what happens there is a new kind of communication, especially in comparison to earlier written forms—less carefully structured, more informal, more intense, less bound by typical social conventions as to what is permissible and what is not, more open to "flaming" (*ad hominem* attacks on individuals for the content of their messages).[35] Some maintain that the resulting "communication culture" is more similar to what existed in predominantly oral cultures before the advent of written communication and record keeping. Walter Ong, for example, notes that discourse in preliterate cultures was often characterized by an "agonistic" tone, repetitious content, features that also characterize communication in contemporary electronic culture.[36]

Issues of copyright and intellectual property constitute a further set of affordances and constraints of electronic interchange of information. The possibility here is one of rapidly copying and disseminating materials thousands of times at the push of a few keys, and also includes editing or altering original content before passing material along. When we consider the question of copyright in such environments, the rules and ethical principles which ought to apply are not yet settled. When one is working with children and young people, the situation suggests special caution in making sure that there is an understanding that with the freedom to "publish" and exchange electronically comes a corresponding responsibility to those whose materials are circulated. Issues of access and censorship also come strongly to the fore when making electronic materials available on-line to children. Internet databases were not designed, for the most part, with a K-12 audience in mind, and giving young people access to a resource, parts of which may well offend community standards, is sure to be a contentious issue for parents, educators, and school boards.

Instructional programs and CAI. Early instructional software often consisted of "electronic workbooks," materials that had been originally prepared for print dissemination and which were simply transferred, often without careful reworking, to the screen. While current CAI (computer-assisted instruction) relies less heavily on such programs (save, perhaps, in so-called Integrated Learning Systems, where the curriculum often still relies on them), the image that they provide for how to organize and present instructional materials to students is still powerful. Indeed, that image itself, and the form of much CAI software, recalls in a more automated environment the form that was typical of materials for programmed instruction in the 1960s.

The constraints of the traditional CAI approach are easy to identify: they usually limit student responses to a few predefined categories; action is restricted to selection from a small number of alternatives, by pushing the appropriate letter or number on a keyboard; the world is presented in a way that suggests it has been thoroughly organized, predigested, reduced to just those elements that are the concern of the invisible, distant instructor. The material itself indicates to the student that the world is ultimately reducible to a set of elements like those contained in the program. Knowledge is presented as a plastic, fungible commodity, dispensed and categorized so that the same number of problems always appears in part I as in part II of the lesson.

The affordances of typical CAI are potentially positive, yet also carry their own distinctive message. The student works in an environment that is immediately defined and controlled by a machine, rather than by another human being. This, for many children, may be a great advantage, for the nonjudgmental and patient tutelage of the computer frees them from the social stigma of being critiqued by a human teacher. Yet the interaction runs the risk of becoming sterile, essentially inhuman. The artist George Tooker provides immediate, powerful images of a world of isolates, people who are shorn of their humanity through lack of humane interaction with their fellows. It is this quality that the radical enthusiasts for more extensive use of technologically based instruction seem not to see.

Simulations. The variety of simulations has increased dramatically in the past few years, and includes programs that allow their users to seem to be "inside" real historical events (e.g., MECC's "Oregon Trail"), chemical processes (much software from TERC—the Technology

Education Resource Center), mathematical equations (the "Geometric Supposer"), and so on. Creating simulated worlds is a major focus for developers working with virtual reality—computer-based systems with which one interacts using specially fitted goggles that display a seemingly three-dimensional reality in front of one's eyes, and a glove or other device that allows one to maneuver in cyberspace, grasp objects and manipulate them, etc.

The affordances here are significant. Events that take place on planes too small, too dangerous, too distant in time or space, too fast or too slow to be ordinarily perceptible can, through the use of simulations, be made real. The graphic demonstration of particular ways of representing the world can provide important models of cognitive processes for those unable to generate such models for themselves. Too, simulations can provide opportunities for children to work collaboratively on projects and to think jointly about solution strategies.

The constraints likely to be encountered in working with simulations are subtle, but real nonetheless. They can probably be overcome with some attention and care on the part of a teacher. First and foremost is the need to realize that this is not reality, that the world of the simulation may not in fact reflect the way the real world works. Particularly in historical reenactments but also in some biological environments, the variables that are given great weight by the designer of a simulation may not in fact be those that link with key differences in reality. The ways in which variables interact may also be artificially limited by the computer-based environment. A further property of simulations is that there is usually a defined conclusion of some sort, that is, a finish to the game or process. One knows if one has succeeded, and in many cases just *how* successful one has been (via some system of keeping score). Reality is not necessarily so neat.

Multimedia and graphics. Multimedia and graphics are not so much variants on instructional approaches as they are production variables—elements that a designer may or may not include in any of the other types of programs discussed above. Nonetheless, they have particular attractiveness, and also particular problems, in computer-based environments, and so it is worth our while to treat them separately here.

The affordances of these features are that they can promote interest, as well as provide for unusual ways of representing information, particularly in demonstrating dynamic states whose essence is not well captured in static displays. They capture the user's attention, and (especially in the case of multimedia) they provide for a more complete kind of experience than can be obtained through text, audio, or video alone.

The problems of these approaches are mostly in the kind of habituation they provide to young people, the sense they convey that this is how the world should be presented, as an entertaining, exciting package, with graphics, sound, and other elements routinely vying for attention, whether they add to the learning value of the content being presented or not. Such possibly gratuitous use of graphics, media, and glitz for the sake of entertainment has worried a number of researchers in the field.[37] Additionally, in many programs (CD-ROM encyclopedias seem to be especially susceptible to this problem), the space taken up by the multimedia components (particularly video) is often a significant portion of all the space available on the disk, thus limiting the amount of other information which the user can access.

Summary: Constraints and affordances in educational technology. The values and limitations discussed above give us a somewhat different picture of educational technology than that found in many popular treatments (and a surprising number of scholarly ones) of what technology in education may be "good for." While there are certainly things that technology in classrooms can accomplish, there are also several cautions that need to be addressed. Many of these have to do with the contrast between, on the one hand, the alluring aspects of technology as toy and as environment, an attractive world in which all variables seem controllable, all errors retractable, and the world generally a sure and knowable place and, on the other, the messy, unpredictable, eclectic, serendipitous, heavily context-dependent nature of the real world. These qualities are not negative in and of themselves, but they need to be recognized consciously and handled by a sensitive teacher if technology in education is to develop a more human face. What such a vision might actually look like in practice is sketched out briefly below.

Toward a Person-Centered Vision for Technology in Education

The above analysis of constraints and affordances suggests that we have problems not so much in thinking up intriguing uses for technology in education as in reminding ourselves that education is fundamentally a human, not a technical or economic, activity. It is, or should be in a free and democratic society, concerned radically with the nurturance of human beings who will, because of the ways in which they have been encouraged to develop within the educational system, willingly choose an appropriate life for themselves that will enhance both their own well-being and the economic and social well-being of others.

To make of education primarily an economic activity, the generation of "well-trained, competitive workers for the global economy," is to put the cart before the horse. This state of affairs, while arguably important, should be a sought-for consequence of our having done reasonably well at educating human beings, not the primary goal in and of itself.

Nor should we allow ourselves to slip into the hacker's dream world where the program and its effects on individual consciousness become ends in themselves. While generation of particular cognitive effects is clearly a desirable goal, there are many cases in which the learning promoted by such programs appears to have been seen by the program's designer in ways that are decontextualized, separated from social intents and consequences, unconnected with life.

To introduce and use technology for educational ends, I would argue that the system we should want has roughly these qualities:

1. It places human values and educational purposes over and above economic or other socially expedient ends for education, as well as over and above a fascination with technology as an end unto itself;

2. It makes educational ends the criteria for selecting and using software (and hardware), and for encouraging certain experiences that software may support. It also focuses on how these kinds of applications support the fundamental development of those who use them (students and teachers), rather than taking their use in business settings as a sufficient reason to introduce them into classrooms;

3. It recognizes that, for teachers and others who work with children, the process of coming to grips with technology in their work is not one of merely adding a "quick fix" to their classroom repertoires. Such approaches have a long history, particularly in American education, and teachers have become used to thinking that this is how professional self-development should proceed. But our experience to date suggests that technology is qualitatively and quantitatively different from other kinds of classroom innovations, that it requires a radical shift in both teaching style and the teacher's vision of what classroom life is all about. The time required to assimilate these new images, particularly for older teachers, will be significant—on the order of years rather than hours or days. Too, this new vision is one that changes the teacher's role in basic ways, reducing the importance of "chalk and talk," increasing the need for sensitivity to individual students' problems and achievements, shifting how classrooms are laid out, how evaluation is conducted, how teachers relate to their colleagues, and a hundred other particulars of daily life in schools.

4. Administratively, the advent of technology raises the question of how information about the school ought to be collected and shared within the organization. Creating processes that feature open collection and sharing of information, and even more so new ways of acting and relating to one another as professionals engaged in a common enterprise, will require extraordinary support and sensitivity. The challenge for administrators, many of whom have spent all their lives in systems that are thoroughly bureaucratic, is no less than that for teachers; the problematic features of bureaucratic systems are less amenable to individual solution (as are many of teachers' practices) and more often codified in various sorts of district regulation, administrative code, and state law.

Addressing this complex of issues will not be easy. Education is characterized today by countervailing forces. Some interpret technology as merely a tool for improving the ways we do things now, a set of devices and procedures that allow us to extend the efficiency and the effectiveness of schooling without altering underlying assumptions about the roles and relationships of the students, teachers, parents, and administrators involved. The possibility of seeing technology as a very different kind of tool—one oriented toward the development of individual capacities in a social context and toward restructuring the work of schools—is more rarely suggested. Yet it is this set of properties of technology that may ultimately win it a more permanent place in education than it has found to date. The task of reconceiving how we think about technology is not a small one, but it is one we need to confront.

NOTES

1. Lewis Mumford, *Technics and Civilization* (New York: Harcourt Brace, 1963).

2. Jacques Ellul, *The Technological Society* (New York: Knopf, 1964).

3. H. Marshall McLuhan, *The Gutenberg Galaxy* (Toronto: University of Toronto Press, 1962).

4. Elizabeth Eisenstein, *The Printing Press as an Agent of Change*, 2 vols. (New York: Cambridge, 1979).

5. Carmen Luke, *Pedagogy, Printing, and Protestantism: The Discourse on Childhood* (Albany, N.Y.: SUNY Press, 1989).

6. Samuel C. Florman, *Blaming Technology: The Irrational Search for Scapegoats* (New York: St. Martin's, 1981).

7. Langdon Winner, *Autonomous Technology* (Cambridge: MIT Press, 1977); see also, idem, "Do Artifacts Have Politics?" *Daedalus* 109, no. 1 (1980): 121-136.

8. Henry Petroski, *To Engineer Is Human: The Role of Failure in Successful Design* (New York: St. Martin's, 1985).

9. Ted Nunan, *Countering Educational Design* (New York: Nichols, 1983); Stephen T. Kerr, "Technology, Teachers, and the Search for School Reform," *Educational Technology: Research and Development* 37, no. 4 (1989): 5-17.

10. Michael Streibel, "A Critical Analysis of the Use of Computers in Education," *Educational Communication and Technology Journal* 34, no. 3 (1986): 137-161.

11. Richard Hooper, "A Diagnosis of Failure," *AV Communication Review* 17, no. 3 (1969): 245-264; idem, "Computers and Sacred Cows," *Journal of Computer Assisted Learning* 6, no. 1 (1990): 2-13.

12. Robert M. W. Travers, "Educational Technology and Related Research Viewed as a Political Force," in *Second Handbook of Research on Teaching*, ed. Robert M. W. Travers (Chicago: Rand McNally, 1973), pp. 979-996.

13. Robert Heinich, "The Proper Study of Instructional Technology," *Educational Communication and Technology Journal* 32, no. 2 (1984): 67-87; idem, "Instructional Technology and the Structure of Education," *Educational Communication and Technology Journal* 33, no. 1 (1985): 9-15.

14. Lewis Perelman, *School's Out: Hyperlearning, The New Technology and the End of Education* (New York: Morrow, 1992).

15. Martin Heidegger, *The Question Concerning Technology, and Other Essays* (New York: Garland, 1977).

16. Neil Postman, *Technopoly: The Surrender of Culture to Technology* (New York: Knopf, 1992).

17. Shoshanna Zuboff, *In the Age of the Smart Machine: The Future of Work and Power* (New York: Basic, 1988).

18. Ithiel de Sola Pool, *Technologies of Freedom* (Cambridge, Mass.: Belknap Press, 1983).

19. Douglas Noble, *The Classroom Arsenal: Military Research, Information Technology, and Public Education* (New York: Falmer, 1991).

20. Office of Technology Assessment, U.S. Congress, *Power On!* (Washington, D.C.: Office of Technology Assessment, 1988).

21. Douglas Sloan, *The Computer in Education: A Critical Perspective* (New York: Teachers College Press, 1985); C. A. Bowers, *The Cultural Dimensions of Educational Computing: Understanding the Nonneutrality of Technology* (New York: Teachers College Press, 1988).

22. For a collection of articles evaluating Whittle's Channel One project from a variety of disciplinary and ideological perspectives, see Ann DeVaney, ed., *Watching Channel One: The Convergence of Students, Technology, and Private Business* (Albany, N.Y.: SUNY Press, 1994). For a collection of papers that raise a number of similar issues, see Robert Muffoletto and Nancy Knupfer, eds., *Computers in Education: Social, Political, and Historical Perspectives* (Cresskill, N.J.: Hampton Press, 1993. For a set of papers that consider the field of educational technology through a variety of unusual conceptual lenses, see Denis Hlynka and John Belland, eds., *Paradigms Regained: The Uses of Illuminative, Semiotic, and Postmodern Criticism as Modes of Inquiry in Educational Technology* (Englewood Cliffs, N.J.: Educational Technology Publications, 1991).

23. See Larry Cuban, *Teachers and Machines: The Classroom Use of Technology Since 1920* (New York: Teachers College Press, 1986); idem, "Computers Meet Classroom: Classroom Wins," *Teachers College Record* 95, no. 2 (1993): 185-210; David K. Cohen, "Educational Technology, Policy, and Practice," *Educational Evaluation and Policy Analysis* 9, no. 2 (1987): 153-170.

24. Papert's basic ideas were set forth in Seymour Papert, *Mindstorms: Children, Computers, and Powerful Ideas* (New York: Basic, 1980).

25. For a treatment of this issue that shows how such projects can both succeed and fail, see Alexander Uvarov and A. A. Prussakova, "The International Telecommunication Project in the Schools of Moscow (Russia) and New York State (USA)," *Educational Technology: Research and Development* 40, no. 4 (1992): 111-118.

26. The classical treatment of innovation viewed as dissemination of practice over a normal distribution is Everett Rogers, *Diffusion of Innovations* (New York: Free Press, 1963; 3rd ed., 1983).

27. The teacher-concerns and levels-of-use typologies are in Gene Hall and Shirley Hord, "Analyzing What Change Facilitators Do: The Intervention Taxonomy," *Knowledge* 5, no. 3 (1984): 275-307, and in Gene Hall and Susan Loucks, "Teacher Concerns as a Basis for Facilitating and Personalizing Staff Development," *Teachers College Record* 80, no. 1 (1978): 36-53.

28. For two studies that characterize the emerging patterns of teachers' use of technology based on observation of real classrooms, see Karen Sheingold and Martha Hadley, *Accomplished Teachers: Integrating Computers into Classroom Practice* (New York: Bank Street College of Education, Center for Technology in Education, 1990), and Stephen T. Kerr, "Lever and Fulcrum: Educational Technology in Teachers' Thinking," *Teachers College Record* 93, no. 1 (1991): 114-136.

29. J. A. Brown, "Implications of Technology for the Enhancement of Decisions in School-based Management Schools," *International Journal of Educational Media* 21, no. 2 (1994): 87-95.

30. Stephen T. Kerr, "Toward a Sociology of Educational Technology," in David Jonassen, ed., *Handbook of Educational Technology Research* (New York: Macmillan, in press).

31. The notion of constraints inherent in a technology is strongly portrayed in the works of both Langdon Winner, *Autonomous Technology* and Donald Norman, *The Psychology of Everyday Things* (New York: Basic, 1988); idem, *Turn Signals are the Facial Expressions of Automobiles* (Reading, Mass.: Addison-Wesley, 1992); idem, *Things That Make Us Smart: Defending Human Attributes in the Age of the Machine* (Reading, Mass.: Addison-Wesley, 1993).

32. Stephen Leacock, letter to W. Leslie Barnette, September 8, 1927.

33. This issue has become a *bête noire* of graphic designer and theorist Edward Tufte. See Edward Tufte, *The Visual Display of Quantitative Information* (Cheshire, Conn.: Graphic Press, 1984).

34. Hooper, "Computers and Sacred Cows."

35. Sarah Kiesler, Jane Siegel, and Timothy W. McGuire, "Social Psychological Impacts of Computer-mediated Communication," *American Psychologist* 39, no. 10 (1984): 1123-1134.

36. Walter Ong, *Orality and Literacy: The Technologizing of the Word* (New York: Methuen, 1982).

37. Gavriel Salomon, "TV is 'Easy' and Print is 'Tough'": The Differential Investment of Mental Effort in Learning as a Function of Perceptions and Attributions," *Journal of Educational Psychology* 76 (1984): 647-658.

Introduction to Chapter VIII

In the following chapter, Professors Thomas Romberg and Gary Price examine problems involved in bringing about planned change in the curriculum. While the successful implementation of a curricular innovation is dependent upon many factors, the authors concentrate on how change in the curriculum affects, and is affected by, the culture of the school. They argue that major changes in the curriculum are challenges to the cultural traditions of schools, including the way in which the curriculum is to be viewed. These traditions and the importance attached to them are not easily altered.

Yet in many cases, well-established and traditional views of the curriculum need to be reconsidered in responding to a significant innovation. If that innovation is to have a lasting effect it may be that a commitment must be made to ideas contrary to traditional notions. Romberg and Price cite examples of changes that failed to have a longtime impact because cultural traditions of the schools had not been taken into account.

Their own experience and their review of well-known efforts to effect curriculum change lead the authors to offer three general recommendations for dealing with problems encountered when implementing innovations. These recommendations deserve the attention of teachers, curriculum developers, and administrators who are interested in bringing about major curricular change.

Thomas Romberg and Gary Price are both Professors of Education at the University of Wisconsin at Madison. The chapter we reprint here is from the Society's 82nd Yearbook, Part 2, Staff Development, *which was edited by Gary Griffin.*

CHAPTER VIII

Curriculum Implementation and Staff Development as Cultural Change

THOMAS A. ROMBERG AND GARY G. PRICE

There has been a long history in the United States of moral imperatives for schools to change their practices. The reasons for those imperatives have varied, but the ongoing obligation to change has not.[1] Under this constant pressure to change, it has become a tradition in education to make change by adopting or developing a new curriculum. Implicit in that tradition is an assumption that the adoption or development of a new curriculum is the easiest or best way to change school practices.

Although the adoption of new curriculum materials may involve only minimal changes in school practices, it is nevertheless a form of change that is visible to parents and other groups pressing for change. Many teachers view the pressures for change as illegitimate. As unwilling partners to much change, teachers are sometimes attracted to changes of window dressing (for example, purchasing a revised text series adorned with new, four-color pictures). Such prophylactic changes help to fend off those seemingly illegitimate pressures to change.

Thus, teachers are often cast as defenders of curricular traditions. That role is not all bad, because curricular traditions are important. In the first place, curricular traditions are inevitable facts of life in schools. Furthermore, they do have the virtue of bringing rational order

The material in this chapter is based upon work supported by the National Institute of Education under Grant No. NIE-G-81-0009 to the Wisconsin Center for Education Research. Any opinions, findings, and conclusions or recommendations expressed are those of the authors and do not necessarily reflect the views of the Institute or the Department of Education.

and predictability to schools (for example, teaching a year of geometry to fifteen-year-old students).

However, legitimate changes are made difficult to implement because they challenge curricular traditions that have outlived their usefulness. As satirically narrated by J. Abner Peddiwell in his classic, *The Saber-Tooth Curriculum*,[2] traditions such as a course on "saber-tooth-tiger-scaring-with-fire" sometimes outlive their usefulness (that is, "scaring-with-fire" continues to be taught even after saber-tooth tigers have become extinct). Today, interpolation of logarithms is still being taught, even though calculators and computers have replaced its use in all aspects of engineering. And elementary statistics is often taught using obsolete (precomputer) paper-and-pencil computational shortcuts that interfere with statistical insight. Demands for new educational programs that challenge the curricula of schools must be examined and, if valid, must be met. For example, the demands of scientists and mathematicians to have school programs that reflected their disciplines were authentic in 1957. Funding of the "modern" science and mathematics programs by the federal government led to the curriculum reform movement of the 1960s.

In similar manner today, the microprocessor "chip" and the blossoming worldwide technological revolution in computing is now demanding the attention of schools and is generating an everbroadening need for both computer literacy and mathematical literacy. These needs create pressure for innovation in schools. Also, advances in computing are making possible instructional innovations such as rapid tailoring of drills,[3] complex diagnostic procedures,[4] and two-dimensional simulations.[5] Instructional technologies like these provide another type of pressure for innovation in schools. Again, both new curricula and new instructional procedures need to be—and will be—developed and implemented.

In summary, efforts to change curricula in schools must be viewed as natural phenomena the impetus for which comes from personal, professional, community, and other social sources. Curricula that respond to legitimate pressures need to be developed and implemented. However, the successful implementation of such programs will not just happen. Our purpose in this chapter is to examine the problems involved in planned curricular change with particular reference to staff development in schools.

To that end, we first attempt to shed light on the differing perspectives about a curriculum. Second, we will characterize curriculum innovation in terms of its effect on school life. In particular, we want to draw attention to the need to consider the culture of schools. Third, we will discuss sources of information on the diffusion of innovations, and present various theoretical models of the change process. From that discussion, we will identify some of the problems of implementing change, including those factors that make educational innovation so difficult. Fourth, based on this knowledge of planned educational change, we will offer a set of recommendations concerning the staff development needs for curriculum implementation. Finally, we will present an example from a school district that has developed a curriculum monitoring procedure that meets our recommendations.

Curriculum

The notion basic to this section is that a curriculum is an operational plan detailing what content is to be taught to students and how the students are to acquire and use that content. One's perspective of curriculum is due in part to one's distance from the act of learning. As Goodlad pointed out, a curriculum can

be viewed from many different vantage points and at several levels of generality or specificity. For a student, the curriculum is what he perceives to be intended for him in his courses and classes, including assigned readings, homework exercises, field trips, and so on. For the teacher, it is what he intends for the students; at one level of insight, a perceived means for changing student behavior. For teachers (and administrators) in concert, the curriculum is the whole body of courses offered by the institution or all planned activities including besides courses of study, organized play, athletics, dramatics, clubs, and other programs. For citizens and policymakers, the curriculum is the body of educational offerings available to whatever groups of students or kinds of educational institutions concern them. For a philosopher, theologian, or educational reformer, the curriculum might be in the learnings to which groups of students, in his judgment, should be exposed. All of these perspectives concern themselves with end products in the form of intended learnings.[6]

This is somewhat analogous to industrial planning. Corporate operational plans are viewed quite differently by assembly-line workers and members of the board of directors. Although production operations are carried out only at the assembly-line level, planning takes place at several levels. As distance from actual operation increases, plans are less specific and show a greater emphasis on general structure and relationships. Similarly, planning in schools takes place at several levels. For clarification, four levels of curriculum planning are identified in Figure 1—design, blueprint, concrete interpretation, and utilization.

LEVEL	EDUCATIONAL PLANNERS (AND ANALOGUES IN INDUSTRY)	NATURE OF PLANS
Design	National Committees (Board of Directors)	General Specification of Needs and Priorities
Blueprint	Publishers and Curriculum Groups (Vice President)	Package of Curriculum Materials—texts, materials, software
Concrete interpretation	Local Curriculum Committees (Shop Foreman)	Guidelines to Teacher for Sequencing Topics and Grouping Children
Utilization	Teacher or Instructional Team (Worker)	Lesson Plans

Fig. 1. Levels of curriculum planning

The design level is analogous to that of a board of directors in corporate planning. From the perspective of this level, curriculum is considered the general course of study—an outline of the content to be covered, specifying the needs and priorities to be served. The main topics to be covered are mentioned, but little is said about instruction. In education, planning at this level is usually done by national committees.

The next level of planning, the blueprint or vice-presidential level, goes beyond the bare outline of content to a carefully detailed listing of what is to be covered, what order is to be followed, and what resources can be used to achieve the intended learnings. The curriculum becomes a detailed set of specifications. The expected interactions are central to the planning; however, the way the interactions are to take place is not spelled out. Most texts can be considered operational definitions of a curriculum at this level.

The third level of curriculum planning, the concrete interpretation or shop-foreman level, goes beyond specification of materials and resources to specification of how humans should use and interact with those materials and resources. Here a curriculum becomes "the organization and sequence of a subject matter in which statements about the subject, methods of teaching, and the activities of the learners are intricately interrelated to form a single entity."[7] Both what is to be done and the way it is to be done are spelled out. The key to this conceptualization of the curriculum is the elements other than content and objectives that are included in the detailed planning.

The last level of curriculum planning, the utilization level, involves those interactions each child actually takes part in. The curriculum here is an individual set of lesson plans that must be developed in terms of the specific instructional setting. The focus is now not on what or how but on whom.

Thus, since the intended learnings remain fixed, a single curriculum can be viewed as a different set of operational plans at each of these levels. The thing that varies over the levels is the specificity of the plans.

This matter of the perspective one takes in relation to a curriculum has been raised for two reasons. First, it illustrates the variety of views on the subject. Second, it underscores the fact that, while different persons have different curricular perspectives, it is the teacher who has the final say about what is actually taught. That fact makes teachers' perceptions of a new curriculum critical to the determination of whether and how it is implemented.

Culture and Change

Our purpose in this section is to examine the problems involved in planned curriculum change. We begin by examining curriculum change in terms of its effect on the lives of persons in schools. We argue that schools have a culture of their own that affects and is affected by efforts at curriculum development. In our experience, to adopt a curriculum change is not necessarily to use it. Moreover, if a curricular innovation *is* used by an adopting school, it is rarely assimilated into the school in the manner intended by the developer. We recommend that curriculum development be considered, in general, as an effort to change the culture of a school, and, in particular, as an effort to change the belief structures and work habits of the school staff.

CURRICULUM CHANGE AS CULTURAL CHANGE

The difficulty of implementing a particular innovation depends on many factors, ranging from the characteristics of the innovation itself to the structure of the culture affected by the change. McClelland discussed how the effective implementation of an innovation may involve different levels of cultural restructuring.[8] The simplest level of restructuring is the substitution of one isolated component of a system for another, such as a change in textbook. If this simplest of changes causes further systemic alterations, such as the purchase of manipulative materials for the classroom, that is a higher level of change. The most complex of all changes deals with values, such as asking teachers to value an active classroom over a quiet one.

This way of characterizing curriculum changes focuses on the degree of restructuring they involve. Arranging curriculum changes on a continuum from least to most restructuring, we have labeled the poles of this continuum *ameliorative innovation* and *radical innovation*. *Ameliorative innovations* are designed (or are perceived as designed) to make some ongoing practice better or more efficient, but do not challenge the values and traditions associated with the school culture. For example, the nonprogrammable calculator as a replacement for the slide rule in engineering classes does not challenge how knowledge of engineering is defined in that culture, or how teachers are to work. Thus, it is an ameliorative innovation.

At the other extreme, *radical innovations* are designed to challenge the cultural traditions of schools, and are perceived as doing that. For instance, "modern mathematics" texts asked schools to define the proper content of school mathematics differently. In another instance, "team teaching" asked schools to develop new staff relationships. The infusion of computers into classrooms, though often marked by ameliorative innovations like computer-mediated drill, will also invite radical innovations like the decoupling of penmanship from composition, wholesale individualization of certain curriculum strands, and the use of dynamic simulations to convey complex concepts. The technologically inexorable infusion of computers will create an especially visible context for the introduction of both amelioratively innovative and radically innovative curriculum change.

CULTURE IN SCHOOLS

Our basic premise is that curriculum development should be planned with the culture of the school deliberately in mind. The need for systematic procedures for disseminating innovations into the culture of schools is evident in the growing literature on school stability. Education in the United States has been remarkably refractory, despite massive efforts sponsored by foundations and the federal government to engineer and implement changes such as team teaching, programmed learning, individualized curriculum programs, modern mathematics, modern science, and open multigraded schools.

In reviewing major educational reform efforts, Goodlad maintains that the work of teachers and students has hardly changed since the turn of the century.[9] Bellack argues convincingly that the most interesting phenomenon of reform is the schools' remarkable resistance to change.[10] Stability, not change, seems to be the dominant characteristic. From an analysis of one reform effort, Romberg states that most change, however well intended, ends up being nominal (with changes in labels, but not practices).[11] From a case study, Gross demonstrated how enthusiasm and dedication are eroded in a very short time, after which practitioners revert to old habits.[12] In a review of the modern mathematics movement, the Conference Board of Mathematical Sciences was forced to conclude that modern mathematics was not a major component of contemporary education in the United States, and that there was no evidence it had even been given a fair trial.[13]

To discuss the culture of schools, we will follow the sociological notions used by Popkewitz, Tabachnick, and Wehlage in their examination of exemplary Individually Guided Education (IGE) schools—a part of the IGE Evaluation Project.[14] "First, school is a place of work where students and teachers act to alter and improve their world, produce social relations, and realize human purposes. Second, schools are places where conceptions of knowledge are distributed and maintained. . . . Third, schools contain an occupational group whose conduct gives legitimacy to the forms of work and knowledge that enter into schooling. Often that group uses the slogan 'professional' to establish its status, privileges, and control."[15]

These three institutional dimensions—work, knowledge, and professionalism—were used because they direct attention to the social assumptions and values that underlie school practices and constrain the implementation of innovations. By our definition, *radical innovations* challenge basic assumptions about work, knowledge, and professionalism.

Work. First, school should be seen as a place of work. Children in schools are doing work when they do assignments, manipulate objects such as microscopes, build things in an industrial arts class, and answer questions on a test. Teachers in schools are doing work when they take attendance, plan lessons, lead discussions, read stories, and evaluate children's performance.

The nature of school work becomes apparent when we look at the initial school experiences of children. Apple and King showed that kindergarten children are taught particular distinctions between work and play.[16] Work was what the teacher gave directions for children to do. Accordingly, children perceived work as coloring, drawing, waiting in line, cleaning up, and singing. The definition of work did not concern specific accomplishments but instead concerned the motivation of the activity. Play activities were those permitted only if time allowed, only after children had finished assigned work. Classroom work was related to certain classroom social relations. All work activities were compulsory, done simultaneously by children, and directed toward identical products. The purpose of classroom work was always defined by the teachers. Diligence, perseverance, participation, and obedience were paramount as evaluative criteria.

In a similar vein, Jackson characterized the teacher as one whose work involves being a supply sergeant, a dispenser of special privileges, an official timekeeper, and a traffic manager.[17] The need to control great numbers of individuals in schools produces a form of spectatorship in which students spend much of their time waiting for the teacher's directions. Although these aspects of schooling may not be viewed fondly by teachers, they are nonetheless embedded in teacher training, school architecture, and definitions of professional competence.

Some computer-based innovations challenge traditional conceptions of school work. Altered conceptions of students' work are involved when students turn their attention to a computer display, whether they do so as consumers of a program or as programmers. The work of teachers is also changed to include diverse new responsibilities like scheduling computer use, interpreting computer output, learning certain uses of a computer and its peripherals, helping students to use computers, and tolerating the absorption many students exhibit when interacting with a computer.

An innovation can sustain, modify, or otherwise interact with conventional patterns of work. Consequently, we must consider the relationships between curriculum change and elements of institutional work in order to make apparent the significance of intervention.

Knowledge. The second institutional dimension of school culture concerns the conception of knowledge. Young and others pursuing the sociology of knowledge have characterized schools as institutions that distribute and maintain certain types of knowledge.[18] Young argues that the relationship between teachers and students is essentially a reality-sharing, world-view-building enterprise. As teachers and students interact, they develop a shared vocabulary and shared ways of reasoning which give sense to one another's actions and provide a framework applicable to future experiences. This shared understanding is based upon an implicit value structure that defines "being educated."

Curriculum changes are radical to the extent that they change the knowledge distributed by schools or the way in which that knowledge is distributed. Curriculum changes (if radical) may change the way teachers allocate their efforts (that is, the way teachers work) and they may also undermine conventional notions of what it means to be educated.

Professionalism. The professional position of teachers is our third dimension of school culture. Professional educators are vested with the authority and power to define pedagogical practice. The label "professional" is used by occupational groups to express the belief that they are highly trained, competent, specialized, dedicated, and effectively serve the public trust. But the label is more than a declaration of public trust. It is also a social category that implies status and privilege. The label "professional teacher" signifies not only technical knowledge and service, but also the power of teachers to bestow a social identity upon their clients (students), a social identity that can affect students' subsequent status as adults.

Like other professional groups, teachers use their power to preserve and expand control, and to resist disadvantageous changes in power relationships. For example, in Becker's study of parent involvement in Chicago schools, teachers reacted to parent involvement in ways that preserved their own control and status in the institution.[19]

Much of the bureaucratization of schooling in recent years has been to the benefit of teacher professionalism at the expense of lay involvement. Technical language, increased specialization, and greater hierarchical differentiation of school personnel make the work of teaching seem esoteric and immune to outside influence. For example, in a study of a Teacher Corps project, technical jargon set apart the initiated (teachers, university professors, school administrators) from the outsiders (lay members of a Native American community).[20] Shibboleths like "competencies," "modules," "cycles," and "learning styles" forced the Indians to look to experts for interpretations of school experiences. The technical language introduced a perception of efficiency and prevented critical scrutiny of educators' priorities and beliefs.

In summary, our argument is that schools are complex social institutions which are not easily altered. The faltering implementation of an innovation into school culture can be examined in terms of its effects on the work of teachers and children, the knowledge dispensed, and the professional position of teachers.

PERSONS IN SCHOOLS

As explained earlier, teachers' perceptions of a new curriculum are critically important. Institutional resistance to innovation can be understood by considering the perspectives held by the persons involved. Their perspectives are important because they govern the way innovations are ultimately used. Innovations are introduced into social situations in which people have beliefs, hopes, desires, and interests, and into institutional contexts that structure actions. The net effect of an innovation can easily be a surface change congenial to existing values and assumptions. Innovations tend to be assimilated into existing patterns of behavior and belief, frequently coming to function as little more than slogan systems that legitimize the values and assumptions underlying the status quo.

If curriculum developers want the essence of their innovation to be implemented, they must assure that its effects on the work of teachers and children, on the nature of knowledge dispensed, and on the professional position of teachers are understood by all persons involved. Innovations not understood in this way have generally failed to endure in a form that would please developers. At best, they have been assimilated into the existing school culture without affecting that culture. If administrators, teachers, the immediate community of the school, or the general public misconstrue the innovation, it likely will be implemented in a distorted form, if at all. This was the fate of many reform programs of the past twenty years.

Our colleagues in the IGE Evaluation Project have documented in rich detail how this fate befell IGE, even in some schools that were reputed exemplars of IGE.[21] One of us was made sadder but wiser to see a similar fate befall *Developing Mathematical Processes*.[22] Other examples abound. The matrix algebra materials of the School Mathematics Study Group[23] and *The Man Made World*[24] are other examples of well-conceived, federally funded projects that were never widely implemented. Despite their virtues, these curriculum changes contradicted certain aspects of conventional school culture. The beliefs of high school mathematics teachers concerning which parts of high school mathematics are indispensable left no room for the intrusion of matrix algebra, a content previously not taught in high school. *The Man Made World*, an excellent introduction to engineering for high school students, was seldom used, largely because no high school teachers regarded themselves as teachers of engineering.

The rejection of *Man: A Course of Study (MACOS)*[25] by religious groups in local communities is an instance where persons other than professional educators have helped make the culture of schools refractory to change. Innovations can even run afoul because they contradict children's beliefs about the nature of work or teacher-child relations. The Au and Jordan study of culture-bound participation structures is a case in point.[26] Questioning strategies used successfully by teachers with white, middle-class children failed with children of Hawaiian background, reportedly because the children attach different meaning to adults' behavior and expect something different of them. Heath's study of a black community in the piedmont Carolinas similarly illustrates how children assimilate school events to the culture of their community.[27]

School administrators', teachers', parents', community groups', and even children's understanding of an innovation and its challenges to the existing culture of schools must be considered when developing and implementing curriculum change.

PLANNED CHANGE

Curriculum development is a form of planned change. The extensive research literature on planned change includes many classic references.[28] In that literature are many attempts to develop guidelines for planning educational change.[29] As noted by Havelock in his review, such models of planned change can be grouped into three main classes: the *research-development-diffusion perspective*, the *social interaction perspective*, and the *user-as-problem-solver perspective*.[30]

The research-development-diffusion perspective, which is associated particularly with Guba,[31] is characterized by a sequence of planned, coordinated activities, a division of labor, and a rather passive target population. This model is often criticized for giving little heed to users' own perceptions of their needs. Also, it fails to recognize the importance of schools in generating worthwhile problems for research and development, as has been noted elsewhere.[32]

During the past decade, many innovations based upon this model were advertised and adopted, then dismissed by teachers as badly matched to the student population of their school system. Hamilton has argued that lack of significant curriculum change is in part due to the inadequacies of this "center → out" development-implementation process. New programs are developed by a few central individuals, who prepare implementation procedures.[33] School staffs, unaware of the problems, assumptions, and alternatives considered in development gradually modify the new program back to fit old habits. In an example offered by Romberg, primary school staffs assigned to new open-plan schools inevitably introduced partitions and other permanent fixtures so that, within a couple of years, the schools operated as if walls were there.[34]

The social interaction perspective is basically sociological in nature, and considers the path taken by a preidentified innovation as it moves through a social system. This model has guided a great deal of empirical research in agriculture,[35] education,[36] and medicine,[37] and emphasizes characteristics of innovators[38] and theories of rejection[39] as well as adoption. Also stressed are important aspects of the social structure, such as group membership and opinion leadership.

The weaknesses of this model include lack of concern with how the innovation is developed and with the adaptations the user may make. While education is a social enterprise, there has been a failure by many to consider the organizational structure of the school.[40] Different curricula make different assumptions about learners, about the system of delivering knowledge to students, and about the technology of the instructional system. Failure to appreciate these assumptions may make adaptation of the new program very difficult.

The *user-as-a-problem-solver perspective* stresses (a) starting with the user's need and its diagnosis, (b) providing nondirective help from outside, and (c) encouraging the user to develop his or her own internal resources and capacity for change. The main drawbacks of this perspective, according to Havelock, are that it puts great strain on the user, it minimizes the importance of outside resources, and it is not suited for large-scale implementation.[41] The possibility of generally applicable guidelines for planned change has been called into question by Broudy, Cronbach, Phillips, and others.[42] In essence, the point is that the social sciences at best produce short-lived generalizations, and at worst, can never generalize beyond the situation studied.

While none of these three perspectives is perfect, each identifies factors that should be considered when planning educational change.

THE OCCURRENCE OF RADICAL CHANGE IN SCHOOLS: STAFF DEVELOPMENT

Ameliorative innovations are commonplace and are readily implemented, so their implementation is seldom a concern of curriculum developers. Radical curriculum development is concerned with a change in the culture of the school. But the crux of the matter is that the developer's view of a radical innovation is ultimately not what matters. Ultimately what matters is the mix of actual responses in a school to the innovation.

From our shared experience in the evaluation of Individually

Guided Education (IGE) and from Romberg's experiences in the evaluations of the School Mathematics Study Group and *Developing Mathematical Processes*, we find it useful to consider the different sorts of school responses to radical innovation that get viewed and labeled as "change."[43] Responses to radical innovations can be loosely divided into nominal change and actual change.

Nominal change. Nominal change is the most prevalent type of response to innovations. It involves adopting nothing but labels. Educators are good at this. If team teaching is in fashion this year, we label groups of teachers as "Team Red," "Team Blue," and so on. Next year, when individualization is in vogue, the new term gets prominence in the school reports. But the routines are not changed. We do not fault school staffs for this strategy. As institutions, schools are under considerable political and social pressure to do things they were never designed to do; nor do they have personnel trained to do them. To maintain political viability or to keep pressure groups at bay, nominal change is often reasonable.

Nominal change is recognized and admitted by practitioners. For example, many principals of IGE schools admitted that they really did not have regular Unit meetings, did not have an operative Instructional Improvement Committee, and did not group and regroup students on a regular basis. All of these features were central to orthodox operation of IGE schools. Reasons or excuses why such practices were not operative were freely offered. Such statements were usually accompanied by a promise or a wish that in the future things would be changed.

Actual change. Actual change occurs where the school staff understand that a radical innovation is expected and attempt to implement it as such. But even when the staff perceive themselves as having actually changed, we must distinguish between different kinds of actual change. We present here a three-part taxonomy that emerged in the IGE Evaluation as a useful way to describe different kinds of IGE implementation.[44] The kinds of actual change are labeled technical change, constructive change, and illusory change.

Technical change describes a situation in which practitioners have adopted not just the labels but also the rituals and routines of a new program. However, this implementation is done without fully grasping or taking to heart the values and principles that guided the development of the program. Technical change is analogous to following the letter of a law, but not understanding its intent.

Technical change is unquestionably actual change at the procedural level, and procedural change is not inconsequential. Most educational programs specify procedures to be followed. For example, in most modern mathematics texts a chapter on sets was added, and often one on other number bases, and so forth. Technical adopters dutifully cover those chapters. However, their coverage is mechanical, done without understanding the purpose of the chapter. Drilling on "base 7" addition facts is not what the authors had in mind. Likewise, in the IGE program, we found schools in which the staff dutifully specified instructional objectives, grouped students according to need, assessed progress, kept records, and so forth. What was missing was reflection, common sense, and an understanding of the purposes of the routines.

Given what Hamilton has characterized as a "center → out" approach to planned change, this shallow form of implementation is understandable.[45] In a center's efforts to convince practitioners to adopt a new program, the "how" of implementation is usually emphasized. The assumptions, practical compromises, and inevitable arguments that were involved in developing the program are not mentioned. Hence, the staff of an adopting school has little sense of the reason for change.

In schools exhibiting technical change, there is a strong sense of efficacy. That is, teachers are convinced that children are benefitting from the innovation in demonstrable ways. Their defense of the program may not cite the developer's broader educational purposes, but will make reference to outcomes other than the teachers' own successful acquisition of vocabulary, rituals, and routines.

Constructive change refers to those instances that most please a curriculum developer. The staff of a school adopting the innovation understands its underlying values and principles, and appreciates its larger educational purpose. The language, rituals, and procedures of the innovation are used in light of that purpose. The staff's grasp of the purpose of the innovation enables schools like this to rise beyond orthodoxy and to construct local adjustments for the purpose of better serving the ends of the program. In schools that have responded to a radical innovation with constructive change, deviations from the letter of the law are sometimes made for the purpose of better serving the intent of law. It is this kind of change that Goodlad and others are seeking.[46] In the IGE evaluation, a few instances of constructive change were found.[47]

In *illusory change* the trappings of a radical innovation, its language and rituals, are adopted, but teachers show no conviction that the effects of the innovation will be demonstrable in their own right. In other words, only ipso facto justifications are given for the innovative program. In such a context, doing a good job becomes equated with trying hard and with employing state-of-the-art techniques, regardless of the net effect on children. Teachers find solace as participants in the innovation. If children are not shown to benefit, then their failure to respond is rationalized as inevitable. In this regard, the developer and the school staff may have discrepant beliefs about the capabilities of children and the kind of knowledge the school should offer them. The developer's innovation gets assimilated into the teacher's world view.

This situation invites slippage of procedures, despite staff sincerity about implementing the innovation. The surface trappings can lead a casual observer to believe that the innovation has been fully implemented, which makes this type of change insidious. Careful and repeated observation in the IGE evaluation revealed that some reputed exemplars of IGE fit this description.[48] As prescribed by IGE rituals, teams of teachers were formed, a team leader was chosen, and team meetings were held at scheduled times. Unfortunately, the team meetings were not devoted to the kinds of activities recommended in IGE procedural guidelines—activities like sharing ideas about instruction and making decisions about how to group and regroup children. The casual observer is not the only one affected by the illusion. Surprisingly, the teachers themselves in these schools believed that bona fide implementation of IGE had occurred.

Distorted conceptions of education can arise in illusory change. Some teachers in the IGE evaluation equated the learning of rituals with being educated (for example, how well children read was not important, so long as they acted like children who could read). Similarly, many educators in the past considered that they were teaching a "modern mathematics" course by adding a chapter on sets. We are particularly afraid that in many schools, *computer literacy* will be approached as nothing more than an additional topic in some mathematics class. Unless computer technology permeates school culture beyond that level, the schools will be deluding themselves about fostering computer literacy. Frankly, we are haunted by the unfortunate prospect of computer equipment being wheeled into a classroom with the announcement, "It's your week to cover computers."

Recommendations

Based on our experience and upon this review, we make three general recommendations. The recommendations are meant to address problems that are commonly, perhaps inevitably, involved in planned curriculum change. The recommendations are couched in the language of a "center → out" orientation with respect to the generation and dissemination of innovations, but they are not limited to that orientation. The problems of planned change and general recommendations for dealing with those problems would be applicable to any strategy for implementing change.

1. IDENTIFY TRADITIONS THAT ARE BEING CHALLENGED

Our first recommendation is that innovators identify cultural traditions that will be challenged by an innovation. This may or may not spark conflict. Perfectly reasonable innovations can be subverted by unexamined cultural traditions that, if they were examined, could be changed. As Popper argued, criticism of a cultural tradition can lead to change, but criticism presupposes that the tradition has been identified and brought to consciousness.[49] Whereas some cultural traditions may be found on examination to have low priority in everyone's eyes, some traditions can be challenged successfully only by explicating and arguing about the trade-offs that they involve with other traditions.

Essentially, this is a recommendation that innovators anticipate the various ways in which a planned change will affect the lives of persons in schools, and give a forthright description of those anticipated effects. Innovators who neglect to do this, we would argue, fail to appreciate the inertia of curriculum traditions in schools and the role of persons in schools (particularly teachers) as defenders of curriculum traditions. Even though a curriculum change may have been developed with its effects on children as the paramount concern, its successful implementation must involve changes in the belief structures and work habits of school staff. It is our experience that belief structures and work habits do not change easily, especially when left unexamined and unchallenged.

For innovators to anticipate the effects of an innovation on the lives of persons in schools, they must be well acquainted with the belief structures and work habits of persons in schools. More generally, they must give ample attention to the culture of schools.

2. DEVELOP A DISSEMINATION PLAN AND MATERIALS TO SUPPORT DISSEMINATION

Our second recommendation is not to abandon proven practices in staff development. There are proven ways of recruiting schools and introducing them to a curriculum change. Among those proven ways are a dissemination plan and materials developed to support dissemination.

Dissemination plan. A dissemination plan divides the process of disseminating an innovation into a sequence of stages, and it provides for the unique requirements of each stage. A simple distinction can be made between an initial *awareness stage* and a subsequent *installation stage.* The awareness stage of a dissemination plan introduces the new program and provides school staff with the information they need to decide whether to adopt or reject the program. Teachers and school leaders will certainly be included in plans to generate awareness of a program. Less obvious but equally important targets are the clients of schools—children, parents, and community groups. Indeed, staff are inadequately informed of the ramifications of a program if they are unacquainted with the prospective reactions of school clients to the changes it will bring.

Providing for the requirements of the awareness stage is a challenging task that few curriculum developers have done well. One problem is the "pollyannaism" of the initiated. Persons who are immersed in a new development and are knowledgeable about it tend to be overly forgiving in their appraisal of it. Besides that lack of objectivity, they also tend to see the virtues of the development as self-evident, and consequently they have a hard time communicating with persons who lack their enthusiasm for the new development.

The new program is initially put into practice during the installation stage. Staff development techniques applicable to the installation stage include in-service training, group discussions, and workshops for teachers on materials development. Group discussions appear to be valuable in helping participants to identify the particular changes that they hope to achieve through the new program.[50] Inasmuch as few innovations survive without the ongoing support of the school principal,[51] it is also important to provide for the needs of administrators, particularly principals.

Staff development techniques should do more than acquaint staff with the program and persuade them to try it. Enthusiasm for a new program is not enough. There must also be training—most typically, in-service training of existing staff. Belief structures and work habits do not change easily or quickly; to change them, a well-designed and unhurriedly executed training program is a virtual necessity. We will not elaborate on features that distinguish effective training programs, but we do want to underscore the importance of staff training as an often neglected ingredient of curriculum change.

Materials to support dissemination. One proven practice in staff development is the provision of materials that support the training of staff to use an innovation. Such materials are typically coupled with a description of how, on a procedural level, the new program is distinct from others that may have preceded it. As described in our earlier discussion, surface procedural differences can easily become the focus of persons who encounter and use the materials. For constructive change to occur, it is necessary for the staff to grasp the purpose of the innovation.

Obviously, then, dissemination materials must go beyond descriptions of procedures and provide a statement of purpose. The dissemination materials of IGE did provide a positive statement of the purposes that motivated that innovation. That "positive sell" approach to recruitment and motivation is evidently successful at initiating a change. However, it often fails to identify how certain aspects of the innovation are intended to remedy what curriculum developers saw as deficiencies of existing practices. If criticism of existing practices (that is, "negative sell") is omitted, radical innovations will soon be deflected and modified to include some features that curriculum developers hoped to supplant.

We recommend that dissemination materials include the "negative sell," in combination, of course, with a "positive sell." Dissemination materials must tell persons what *not* to do (and why), in addition to telling them what they *should* do (and why).

Dissemination materials often overlook the idea that, to make change, something must be given up. We recommend that dissemination materials be explicit about traditions with which the innovation is incompatible. Traditions that the innovation is meant to supplant are obviously in this category. Incompatibilities of that kind are *deliberate incompatibilities*. There can be other traditions that must also be changed if the innovation is implemented, even though the innovation was not specifically designed to supplant them. These easily overlooked *tangential incompatibilities* between an innovation and traditions can disrupt the implementation of the innovation if they are not dealt with explicitly as a part of staff development. To summarize this point, the "hit list" of things that must be given up will include both deliberately incompatible traditions and tangentially incompatible traditions.

3. USE A SYSTEMATIC MONITORING PLAN

Our third recommendation is that a systematic monitoring procedure be planned and implemented for any innovation. To monitor something means to gather information about it at several times. The procedure would monitor the expected effects of the innovation. The term "expected effects" is not limited to student outcomes, which are conventionally monitored. It can certainly include student outcomes, but it should also include other expected effects on the lives of persons in schools. Moreover, it should include the monitoring of anticipated problems.

There is an a priori tone to this recommendation that is deliberate. There is prior specification of what is to be monitored. Things specified to be monitored are the expected effects, and not the unexpected effects. It is difficult to monitor systematically things that are unexpected, so the benefits of systematic monitoring stem mainly from knowledge about prespecified, expected effects. Developments that occur unexpectedly during the implementation of a new program certainly should not be ignored. Our point is simply that awareness of a development is a precondition to focused, systematic tracking of it.

Monitoring and the tracking that it permits of selected aspects of life in schools involves a different conceptual framework (and more data) than conventional pretest-posttest approaches. Campbell and Stanley made a strong case for an interrupted time-series design to study the effects of planned change on single populations.[52] Two measures (pretest and posttest) on a single population simply do not give enough information to demonstrate effects due to implementation. At least four observations (two before implementation and two after) are necessary to distinguish between change due to implementation and change due to natural growth. At least six are needed to discern drift, decay, cycles, and so forth. Obviously, the larger the number of observations, the more we can detect.

As a part of such a plan, we suggest causal modeling to specify the variables to be observed, to identify expected relationships, and to assist in communicating the expected changes. This approach can be used to study the ongoing nature of schooling events, and it permits us to focus on the effects of a change on various characteristics.

If key elements are identified from a causal model, a reasonable monitoring scheme following an interrupted time-series framework can be developed. Our motive is not to advocate statistical esoterica. The kernel of our recommendation is the suggestion that developers attempt to be explicit about the chain of events they would expect to occur, pursuant to implementation of their innovation. Through doing that, they will acquire a better grasp of what phenomena to monitor.

Furthermore, communication with potential users of the innovation may be improved. If a developer provides explicit speculation about diverse effects of an innovation, schools adopting it will be better informed and more likely to show constructive change.

Systematic Monitoring of Planned School Changes: An Example

To demonstrate that our recommendations are plausible, we have chosen to conclude this chapter by examining the efforts of one school district to produce planned curricular change. The Berea (Ohio) City School District serves a working- and middle-class suburban community bordering on Cleveland. It is typical of many districts in that it has experienced a decline in enrollment, a gradual change in population due to outmigration from a troubled major city, and an aging staff with little opportunity for administrative advancement. Yet, its staff is committed to a quality instructional program. In 1975, the district's Board of Education and its superintendent made a commitment to a project called "Curriculum Review."

CURRICULUM REVIEW

The purpose of the Curriculum Review project was to develop a comprehensive scope and sequence of skills and content for kindergarten through grade twelve for all subject areas and to have those curriculum programs understood and implemented by all teachers.

Conventionally separated subject areas (for example, Language Arts, Mathematics, Home Economics) were placed into a five-year cyclical schedule. In each year of the schedule, approximately one-fifth of the subject areas were singled out for intensive review, with each subject area reviewed by an area-specific review team composed of teachers on leave and administrators. The review team for each subject area was responsible for identifying a manageable set of high priority objectives for which teachers in *all* subject areas would be responsible.

The process in each subject area involved formation of the review team, attendance of team members at workshops and seminars, review of current practice, review of pertinent research, selection of top priority objectives, preparation of a program guide for meeting those objectives, reaction to drafts of the program guide by teachers in the school district, reactions of nationally recruited consultants, and formal adoption of the program guides by the Board of Education. It was clearly understood that, once a program guide was adopted, all teachers in all subject areas were to use it as a basis for their classroom planning and instruction. During the year following formal adoption of a program guide (year two), it was expected that all teachers would be helped to understand the program guide. It was also expected that all teachers would incorporate suggestions of the guide into their lesson plans. In the year after that (year three), changes in classroom practice (observable by a supervisor) were expected. Only in the fourth and fifth years of the cycle were the curricular changes expected to manifest themselves in students' behavior (construed broadly to include such things as recreational reading as well as test performance).

At this level of description, the Curriculum Review project sounds typical of many programs developed in other school systems. However, the approach taken to the project was unique in that they attempted to deal with the three recommendations we proposed in the last section.

First, they knew they were challenging many traditions surrounding the professional specialization and autonomy of teachers. Indeed, they were expecting *radical change* on the part of teachers. Although changes in student outcomes were the ultimate goal, they were consciously expecting teachers to change their work habits (and, in turn, the students' work habits). For example, *all* teachers were expected to implement the writing program. This meant that teachers of science, mathematics, shop, homemaking, and so forth were to know the program and its objectives and to implement it by correcting spelling, grammar, and organization of paragraphs in their courses. Similarly, social studies and science teachers (not just mathematics teachers) were responsible for teaching students to interpret data from tables. Thus, although the program developers did not systematically attempt to identify traditions that were being challenged (as we recommend), they were aware that some common habits of teachers would need to be changed. In particular, *all* teachers were responsible for all curricular changes.

Second, they were concerned with dissemination and implementation. In fact, a long-term commitment to the Curriculum Review process was expressed. For each curriculum program, a five-year commitment to implementation was made by all administrators. For each new program, the expected changes in staff planning and teacher behavior were specified, carefully considered, then formally adopted. These expectations became part of staff evaluation. The curricular changes were not viewed as fads. Thus, an implementation plan and materials were made, and staff in-service training was carried out. The school board did not assume that teachers would automatically use Curriculum Review materials. Nor did they assume that improvement in student learning would be a pro forma occurrence. Student changes were expected to occur only with changes in teachers and their teaching. The school board recognized that in the past curricular changes often ended with adoption, publication, and distribution of a guide or manual. Once classroom doors had been closed, the innovation had remained on a bookshelf. The activities of teaching had continued unchanged. Thus, staff development was seen as essential.

Third, systematic monitoring was seen as part of the Curriculum Review process. In each succeeding year after the adoption of a curriculum guide, more information was monitored. This expansion from lesson plans to teachers' behavior to students' behavior reflects a realistic, unhurried commitment to change. The intent was to document actual, gradual change. Evaluation was not a summative judgment external to the implementation, but an integral part of and stimulus for curriculum change.

THE SYSTEMATIC MONITORING PROCESS FOR LEARNING (SMPL) STRATEGY

In 1978, as Curriculum Review programs were being completed, the Curriculum Review staff of the district realized that they must develop and put into practice a self-monitoring scheme. What evolved was a strategy for monitoring and evaluation, which they called the "Systematic Monitoring Process for Learning" (the SMPL strategy).

Traditionally, to evaluate the introduction of a new curriculum or program, schools have relied primarily on assessments of pupil performance. In SMPL, that is still done. However, SMPL also monitors, documents, and assesses changes in teacher and student activities that occur *between* the introduction of a new program and the evaluation of student achievement in a content area. The ongoing process of monitoring maintained an incentive for staff to internalize the changes into their daily routines. District administrators also hoped that the monitoring would provide documentation of any real change that did occur, and that it would help to restore community faith in the ability of public schools to chart, adjust, and reach their goals. The district administrators were confident that the SMPL strategy would demonstrate that each new curriculum program was actually implemented and that the money, time, and effort were indeed worthwhile.

The actual use of the SMPL strategy by administrators and staff involved gathering, summarizing, and analyzing information concerning four basic questions: (a) What related background information is available? (b) How are the new curriculum programs being used? (c) What data describe the processes of student learning in classrooms? (d) Have students reached desired outcomes? Information concerning each of those questions is described below.

Background. The first question addressed by SMPL deals with background information about students, staff, and the community. As a first step, that information needed to be gathered and studied. The context of the new program or curriculum change was examined to identify factors that were believed either to facilitate or restrain implementation. For this question, the staff of each school wrote descriptive summaries of the school's students, staff, and social environment. The staff then decided upon goals for the school and upon means that might be used to reach those goals. The exercise provoked self-analysis, identification of priorities, and reflection on environmental factors that might affect innovation.

Program use. District administrators were determined not to overlook the second question—how programs were being used—because they believed bona fide implementation of new curriculum programs was necessary to improve student outcomes. The administration assumed that student achievement (in particular) would not improve unless three conditions were met.

The first condition is that teachers understand the rationale and philosophy of each new Curriculum Change program. This includes not only a grasp of its content, but also a grasp of its underlying philosophy, its techniques and strategies, and the changes it involves.

The second contention is that targeted aspects of the new program be reflected in teachers' lesson plans and classroom activities. Teachers tend to achieve what they plan; therefore, daily and long-range planning were seen as critical. Lesson plans must include the new content or skills, the new priorities, appropriate materials and strategies, and means of assessing the student growth expected in the new program. In addition, teachers were to work collaboratively to make their daily plans consonant with long-range goals.

The third condition is that teacher-student interactions and student-student interactions should follow certain principles suggested by instructional research. According to the first principle, *structuring*, the teacher should explain in advance the purposes of a lesson and the connection of activities to the purposes. According to the second principle, *feedback*, the teacher should inform students of their successes, strengths, and needs. According to the third principle, *motivation*, the teacher should create a learning environment that is interesting and supportive and one in which mutual respect is practiced by the teacher and students. According to the fourth principle, *individualiza-*

tion, the teacher should assess the needs and interests of individual students, then match students with appropriate activities and resources during instruction. According to the fifth principle, *peer relations*, cooperative peer relations conducive to learning are recognized and fostered by the teacher.

Classroom learning. The third question in the SMPL strategy— gathering data to describe classroom learning—provides monitoring of the actual interaction of the new program with students. The data collected included: (a) *Allocated Time*: How much time is allocated for teaching a new Curriculum Review program? (b) *Engaged Time*: How much student time is actually engaged with a particular skill, concept, or content area? (c) *Quality and the Appropriateness of Teaching Activities*: What activities are basic to the new program? Which activities best develop a skill or teach a concept? Which activities do not work? Which activities involve factors of effective classrooms identified from research?

The collection of such data involved a myriad of monitoring procedures and data sources: classroom observations, work samples, lesson plans, teacher logs or diaries, faculty discussions, grade level and department sharing sessions, regular status report forms, and individual teacher-principal conferences.

Student outcomes. The fourth question—how well students reached desired outcomes—was to be answered unhurriedly. Student outcomes were to be examined only after the district administration had determined that a new Curriculum Review program was implemented as planned. Berea decided that at least three years were needed for this process of implementation. A premature leap to demonstrating student achievement without first documenting significant changes in instruction would presumably have produced little evidence of improvement.

Also, school administrators were well aware that their program goals would not be reflected in standardized achievement tests alone. One goal, for example, was to increase the time children spend reading "classroom libraries." Time spent in free reading was seen as a valuable outcome, regardless of its relationship with performance on standardized reading tests.

Summary. The SMPL strategy begun in 1979 by the Berea Schools is a longitudinal, systematic change model. The monitoring activity is thoroughly integrated with the implementation of newly refined curriculum programs. While initially concerned with changes made by teachers, its eventual concern is with students. Based on the Berea experience, as reported by Langer and Romberg,[53] SMPL has helped improve the educational process in at least six major areas.

1. SMPL has caused principals, staff, and program supervisors to study their implementation plans, procedures, goals, and actions continuously.

2. A detailed examination of planning has resulted in a totally new assessment of teachers' lesson plans. Each school has examined the role of planning. The school system has stressed the need to have new programs reflected in all planning—particularly long-range planning. The quality of lesson plans has improved.

3. Time is now more carefully considered and used. Not only has allocated time been documented, but teachers and principals are more aware of engaged time. In effect, the use of time is now viewed more critically as a key element in learning.

4. SMPL has changed staff documentation of the implementation of Curriculum Review. Every teacher, kindergarten through grade twelve, has set goals in reading, mathematics, written communication, and social studies and provided a status summary of these goals.

5. The relationship of principal to teacher and of principal to staff to program has changed. The use of SMPL has returned to the principal a critical role, that of instructional leader and evaluator. Monitoring the new Curriculum Review program has become a high priority job for the school leadership. As a result, classroom observations have increased, and the staff and principal regularly discuss curriculum and school goals.

6. SMPL has placed curriculum and instruction in the spotlight. It has assured that Curriculum Review programs enter into teachers' thinking and planning. Preliminary data indicate that the new programs are indeed being used and are indeed the basis for teacher planning. Principal, staff, and new programs have merged cooperatively to assure that students are taught according to the priorities of Curriculum Review.

Curriculum implementation and evaluation in Berea has been more than talk, more than promises, and more than educational jargon. It has involved the hard work of perseverance, of setting priorities, of assuring and assessing educational change for the improvement of learning. The community has observed a school system committed to long-range planning, staff development, and systematic improvement through professional monitoring.

Concluding Comment

There is no question that schools are and will continue to be under considerable pressure to change their practices. In particular, changes made by adopting or developing a new curriculum will occur, but the success of their implementation will not just happen. The obstacles that school staffs face in order to make a curriculum change a success are many. To facilitate planned curriculum change, we have made three recommendations based on our analysis and experience:

1. Identify traditions that are being challenged.

2. Develop a dissemination plan and materials to support dissemination.

3. Use a systematic monitoring plan.

Furthermore, to demonstrate that such recommendations are feasible, we have examined curriculum review and monitoring procedures developed in one school district. The culture of a school is more likely to change if our recommendations are followed.

NOTES

1. Lawrence A. Cremin, *The Transformation of the School: Progressivism in American Education, 1876-1957* (New York: Alfred A. Knopf, 1961); Herbert M. Kliebard, "Education at the Turn of the Century: A Crucible for Curriculum Change," *Educational Researcher* 11 (January 1982): 16-24.

2. J. Abner Peddiwell [pseud.], *The Saber-Tooth Curriculum* (New York: McGraw-Hill, 1939).

3. Richard C. Atkinson, "Ingredient for a Theory of Instruction," *American Psychologist* 27 (October 1972): 921-31.

4. John S. Brown and Curt VanLehn, "Towards a Generative Theory of 'Bugs'," in *Addition and Subtraction: A Developmental Perspective*, ed. Thomas C. Carpenter, James M. Moser, and Thomas A. Romberg (Hillsdale, N.J.: Lawrence Erlbaum Associates, 1982).

5. J. Olin Campbell, "2d Simulation: Educational Breakthrough," *Interface Age* 5 (1980): 86-90.

6. John I. Goodlad, *The Development of a Conceptual System for Dealing with Problems of Curriculum and Instruction* (Washington, D.C.: Office of Education, U.S. Department of Health, Education, and Welfare, June 1966), pp. 2-3.

7. Evan R. Keislar and Lee S. Shulman, "The Problem of Discovery: Conference in Retrospect," in *Learning by Discovery*, ed. Evan R. Keislar and Lee S. Shulman (Chicago: Rand McNally and Co., 1966), p. 190.

8. William A. McClelland, *The Process of Effecting Change*, Professional Paper 32-68 (Alexandria, Va.: Human Resources Research Office, 1968).

9. John I. Goodlad, "Schooling and Education," in *The Great Ideas Today*, ed. Robert M. Hutchins (New York: Encyclopedia Britannica, 1976).

10. Arno Bellack, *Competing Ideologies in Research on Teaching*, University Reports on Education 1 (Uppsala, Sweden: Department of Education, University of Uppsala, September 1978).

11. Thomas A. Romberg, "Systematic Monitoring of Planned School Change" (Invited address at the University of Tasmania, October 1979).

12. Neal Gross, "The Fate of a Major Educational Innovation" (Paper read at the Conference on Improvement of Schools through Educational Innovation sponsored by the Wisconsin Research and Development Center for Individualized Schooling, University of Wisconsin, Madison, October 1969).

13. Conference Board of Mathematical Sciences, *Overview and Analysis of School Mathematics, Grades K-12* (Washington, D.C.: Conference Board of Mathematical Sciences, 1975).

14. Thomas S. Popkewitz, B. Robert Tabachnick, and Gary G. Wehlage, *The Myth of Educational Reform: School Responses to Planned Educational Change* (Madison: University of Wisconsin Press, 1982); Thomas A. Romberg, "IGE Evaluation: Perspectives and a Plan," Working paper no. 183 (Madison: Wisconsin Research and Development Center for Individualized Schooling, 1976).

15. Popkewitz, Tabachnick, and Wehlage, *The Myth of Educational Reform*, p. 11.

16. Michael W. Apple and Nancy King, "What Do Schools Teach?" in *Qualitative Evaluation: Concepts and Cases in Curriculum Criticism*, ed. George Willis (Berkeley, Calif.: McCutchan Publishing Corp., 1978).

17. Philip H. Jackson, *Life in Classrooms* (New York: Holt, Rinehart and Winston, 1968).

18. Michael Young, ed., *Knowledge and Control: New Directions for the Sociology of Education* (London, England: Collier-MacMillan, 1971).

19. Howard S. Becker, "The Career of the Chicago Public School Teacher," *American Journal of Sociology* 57 (March 1952): 470-77.

20. Thomas S. Popkewitz, "Reform as Political Discourse: A Case Study," *School Review* 84 (November 1975): 43-69.

21. Popkewitz, Tabachnick, and Wehlage, *The Myth of Educational Reform*.

22. Thomas A. Romberg, "Developing Mathematical Processes: The Elementary Mathematics Program for Individually Guided Education," in *Individually Guided Education*, ed. Richard Rossmiller, Herbert Klausmeier, and Mary Saily (New York: Academic Press, 1977).

23. School Mathematics Study Group, *Introduction to Matrix Algebra* (Stanford, Calif.: School Mathematics Study Group, 1965).

24. Engineering Concepts Curriculum Project, *The Man Made World* (New York: McGraw-Hill, 1968).

25. Jerome S. Bruner, "Man: A Course of Study," in Jerome S. Bruner, *Toward a Theory of Instruction* (New York: W. W. Norton and Co., 1968).

26. Kathryn H. Au and Catherine Jordan, "Teaching Reading to Hawaiian Children: Finding a Culturally Appropriate Solution," in *Culture in the Bilingual Classroom*, ed. H. Treuba, G. P. Guthrie, and Kathryn H. Au (Rowley, Mass.: Newbury House, 1981).

230 CURRICULUM CHANGE AS CULTURAL CHANGE

27. Shirley Brice Heath, "Questioning at Home and at School: A Comparative Study," in *Doing the Ethnography of Schooling,* ed. G. D. Spindler (New York: Holt, Rinehart and Winston, 1982).

28. See, for example, Warren G. Bennis, Kenneth D. Benne, and Robert Chin, eds., *The Planning of Change,* 2d ed. (New York: Holt, Rinehart and Winston, 1961); Ronald G. Havelock, *A Guide to Innovation in Education* (Ann Arbor, Mich.: Institute for Social Research, 1970); Ronald R. Lippitt, Jeanne Watson, and Bruce Westley, *The Dynamics of Planned Change* (New York: Harcourt, Brace and World, 1958); Eleanor E. Maccoby, Theodore M. Newcomb, and Eugene L. Hartley, eds., *Readings in Social Psychology* (New York: Holt, Rinehart and Winston, 1958); Matthew B. Miles, ed., *Innovation in Education* (New York: Bureau of Publications, Teachers College, Columbia University, 1964); Everett M. Rogers, *Diffusion of Innovations* (New York: Free Press of Glencoe, 1962).

29. See, for example, J. Victor Baldridge, *Organizational Change Processes: A Bibliography with Commentary,* Research and Development Memo no. 57 (Stanford, Calif.: Stanford Center for Research and Development in Teaching, 1970); Ronald G. Havelock, James C. Hueber, and Steven Zimmermann, *Major Works on Change in Education: An Annotated Bibliography with Author and Subject Indexes* (Ann Arbor, Mich.: Institute for Social Research, 1969); McClelland, *The Process of Effecting Change.*

30. Havelock, *A Guide to Innovation in Education.*

31. Egon F. Guba, "Development Diffusion and Evaluation," in *Knowledge Production and Utilization in Educational Administration,* ed. T. L. Eidell and J. M. Kitchel (Eugene, Oreg.: University of Oregon Press, 1968).

32. See especially, Herbert J. Klausmeier, "Research and Development Strategies in Education," in *Research and Development Strategies in Theory Refinement and Educational Improvement,* Theoretical Paper no. 15, ed. Herbert J. Klausmeier, J. L. Wardrop, Mary R. Quilling, Thomas A. Romberg, and R. E. Schutz (Madison: Wisconsin Research and Development Center for Individualized Schooling, 1968); Dennis C. Phillips, "What Do the Researcher and the Practitioner Have to Offer Each Other?" *Educational Researcher* 11 (December 1980): 17-20, 24; Thomas A. Romberg, *Examples of the Use of Various Strategies for Relating Research and Development to Educational Improvement Through Individually Guided Education* (Madison: Wisconsin Research and Development Center for Individualized Schooling, 1970).

33. David Hamilton, "Making Sense of Curriculum Evaluation: Continuities and Discontinuities in an Educational Idea," in *Review of Research in Education,* ed. Lee Shulman (Itasca, Ill.: F. W. Peacock Publishers, 1978).

34. Romberg, *Examples of the Use of Various Strategies for Relating Research and Development to Educational Improvement.*

35. Rogers, *Diffusion of Innovations.*

36. Richard O. Carlson, *Adoption of Educational Innovations* (Eugene, Oreg.: University of Oregon Press, 1965).

37. Herbert Menzel and Elihu Katz, "Social Relations and Innovations in the Medical Profession: The Epidemiology of a New Drug," in *Readings in Social Psychology,* ed. Maccoby, Newcomb, and Hartley.

38. Rogers, *Diffusion of Innovation.*

39. Gerhard C. Eichholz, "Why Do Teachers Reject Change?" *Theory Into Practice* 2 (December 1963): 264-68.

40. Charles Perrow, "A Framework for the Comparative Analysis of Organization," *American Sociological Review* 32 (April 1967): 194-208.

41. Havelock, *A Guide to Innovation in Education.*

42. Harry S. Broudy, "Criteria for the Theoretical Adequacy for the Conceptual

Framework of Planned Educational Change" (Paper prepared for the Conference on Strategies for Educational Change, Washington, D.C., November 1965); Lee J. Cronbach, "Beyond the Two Disciplines of Scientific Psychology," *American Psychologist* 30 (February 1975): 116-27; Phillips, "What Do the Researcher and the Practitioner Have to Offer Each Other?"

43. Romberg, "Developing Mathematical Processes."

44. Popkewitz, Tabachnick, and Wehlage, *The Myth of Educational Reform.*

45. Hamilton, "Making Sense of Curriculum Evaluation."

46. Goodlad, *The Development of a Conceptual System.*

47. Popkewitz, Tabachnick, and Wehlage, *The Myth of Educational Reform.*

48. Ibid.

49. Karl Popper, *Conjectures and Refutations: The Growth of Scientific Knowledge* (New York: Harper and Row, 1963).

50. Havelock, *A Guide to Innovation in Education.*

51. Mark A. Chesler, Richard Schmuck, and Ronald Lippitt, "The Principal's Role in Facilitating Innovation," *Theory Into Practice* 2 (December 1963): 269-77.

52. Donald T. Campbell and Julian C. Stanley, "Experimental and Quasi-experimental Designs for Research on Teaching," in *Handbook of Research on Teaching*, ed. N. L. Gage (Chicago: Rand McNally, 1963).

53. James W. Langer and Thomas A. Romberg, "The Systematic Monitoring Process for Learning," *Educational Leadership* 39 (November 1981): 140-42.

Introduction to Chapter IX

An example of how the implementation of a curricular innovation involves changing the culture of the school is provided in the following account of an effort to redefine vocational education at the Rindge School of Technical Arts in Cambridge, Massachusetts.

Adria Steinberg and Larry Rosenstock, both of whom were associated with that school when this chapter was written, describe the challenge presented by a veteran vocational education faculty that had to be helped "to move outside the century-old paradigm of training workers for industrialization and to embrace new curricular priorities and instructional policies and practices."

Motivated by a desire to enhance the low status then accorded to students and teachers in vocational education and encouraged by federal policies (through the Perkins Vocational and Applied Technology Education Act of 1990) to promote the integration of vocational and academic education, the staff at the Rindge School of Technical Arts undertook a complete redesign of its vocational program. The new program required a professional culture quite different from that which prevailed in the well-established traditional vocational program in the school. Steinberg and Rosenstock describe strategies employed to create this new professional culture.

Adria Steinberg is now Program Director for Jobs for the Future in Boston, Massachusetts. Her forthcoming book with David Stephen provides a full description of the CityWorks program. Larry Rosenstock is now President of Price Charities in San Diego, California. Their chapter originally appeared in the Society's 94th Yearbook, Part 1, Creating New Educational Communities, *edited by* Jeannie Oakes and Karen Hunter Quartz.

CHAPTER IX

CityWorks: Redefining Vocational Education

ADRIA STEINBERG AND LARRY ROSENSTOCK

Some people seem to have a problem with the Rindge School of Technical Arts. They are always putting RSTA down and stereotyping us. . . . the students in RSTA are dumb; they will not go to college; they are going to drop out. Well, I will not take this any more. . . . Being a freshman in RSTA, I am positive that I will go to college, and a lot of my confidence has come from my teachers. RSTA students have worked hard, demonstrated enthusiasm and displayed some great exhibits. We are smart, not only in mind, but also with our hands. We have, or will have shortly, an advanced technological mind as well as an academic mind. . . . We give respect, so we expect respect. Success demands it!

In March, 1993, Paulina Mauras published this statement in the newspaper of the Cambridge Rindge and Latin High School. Her anger is not surprising. Why would anyone want to be labeled "non-college-bound"—especially in Cambridge, Massachusetts, the premier college town in the United States? As a ninth grader in the Rindge School of Technical Arts, the vocational wing of Cambridge's comprehensive high school, Paulina suffers from the low status accorded to vocational education and all who enter it.

What is worth noting is that this fourteen-year-old is ready to do something about it. She knows she is smart; she feels ready to tackle anything or anybody at the high school; and she believes that she has the right to voice her thoughts and feelings in a public forum. Perhaps most striking, Paulina has become an articulate spokesperson for a new definition of vocational education—one that is not based on a prediction about a child's future (for example, non-college-bound) but rather on challenging the conventional conceptions of ability.

Not surprisingly, this reconceptualization is difficult to achieve in daily practice. Paulina puts particular blame on the "put downs" of those outside her school program. Certainly she is right that old stereotypes must be attacked. But in this chapter we focus on another more subtle and difficult challenge: how to help a veteran vocational faculty to move outside the century-old paradigm of training workers for industrialization and to embrace new curricular priorities and instructional policies and practices.

Like Paulina, the authors of this chapter are writing "from the inside." In 1990, Larry Rosenstock became the executive director of the Rindge School of Technical Arts (RSTA), where he had previously worked for eight years as a carpentry teacher. He entered this new role with the explicit goal of tearing down the walls between academic and vocational education—a goal he had just spent two years helping to embed in federal law as a staff attorney for the Center for Law and Education. Adria Steinberg, then editor of the *Harvard Education Letter*, entered first as a consultant to the process and then stayed on as the full-time academic coordinator. Combining an intimate knowledge of "business as usual" with a strong vision of a very different kind of vocational education, the authors have worked with a veteran faculty to put the rhetoric of academic and vocational integration into daily practice.

We decided to begin with the ninth grade program, the entry point for students into our vocational school. In the spring of 1991, a small design team of faculty created the framework for a new program called "CityWorks." The idea was to replace the traditional ninth grade exploration of different shops and trades offered at the school with an exploration of local community needs and resources. Although we began without a blueprint of what we hoped to accomplish, we were guided by a key assumption about school change: if we wanted a school where all students could be smart, we would have to restructure it in ways that would call upon all teachers to be smart. While this statement seems almost a truism, teachers have a very hard time believing that anyone really wants them to think or will listen to their ideas.

Acutely aware of their low status within the comprehensive high school, Rindge teachers were especially cynical. They had seen reforms and reformers come and go. What they had never experienced was a change effort in which they would be encouraged to use everything they knew and understood, not just about students, learning, and schools, but about the world outside of school, where they had developed considerable expertise as parents, community members, and, in many cases, as entrepreneurs and independent contractors.

The pages that follow provide an account of what happened when teachers at Rindge became engaged in redesigning the ninth grade program. In the first section we focus on the technical aspects of this innovation, the curricular projects, activities, and content that give CityWorks its definition and that differentiate it from the model of vocational training it replaced. The second section provides a sketch of how political and economic events have shaped vocational education, and how recent changes at the federal level are helping to create fertile ground for "growing" this local innovation. In the remainder of the chapter we focus on the process of change, outlining both the strategies we used to try to create a professional culture within a vocational school and the lessons we learned about the dynamics of political and normative change.

Beyond Shop Class: Reinventing Curriculum

THE CITY IS THE TEXT

Paulina's notion of combining hands and minds comes directly from her experiences in CityWorks, the centerpiece of the ninth grade program at the Rindge School of Technical Arts (Rindge). Cambridge is the "text" as students investigate the neighborhoods, the systems, the people, and the needs that comprise an urban community. Students work on individual and group projects, bringing aspects of their community into the classroom by creating numerous "artifacts" of Cambridge—maps, photographs, tapes, oral histories, and three-dimensional models.

Several features make this program unusual. First, CityWorks combines key characteristics of vocational programs—a project approach, apprentice-master relationships, and real clients—with the broader content and essential skills of academic education. Projects involve "hands on" work, like making a wall-sized map of the city and wiring it to light up selected landmarks. At the same time, students engage in problem solving, like deciding where on the map to locate a new teen center that would attract youth from all ethnic and racial communities of the city.

Second, CityWorks is taught in a space designed for collaborative learning projects. Looking for an alternative to both shops and classrooms, we borrowed the notion of "studios" from design schools. An open area at one end of the room is used for large-group activities such as demonstrations and exhibitions, but most of the room is subdivided into studios where teachers work on projects with small groups of students. This arrangement gives participants the flexibility to regroup, team up, or borrow tools and materials as the project necessitates.

Third, community representatives are invited to help create a context for students' efforts. Staff members from city agencies and programs identify unmet community needs that students could address and also serve as an authentic audience for students' finished products and presentations. For example, at a recent exhibition of students' work, several teams of students displayed drawings and scale models of a heritage museum they had designed for Cambridge. Each group had a different conception of where the museum might be located and how it should be designed. The museum builders sat with their models to explain their ideas as audiences of parents, city officials, and local businesspeople wandered through the exhibit.

In making the models, the museum builders were responding to a request from the city's tourist agency that is actually in the process of raising funds for a museum. Six weeks before the exhibit, the agency director had come to speak to CityWorks students and ask for their help in this effort. With thousands of people visiting the city each year, it was important for students to understand the tourism industry and to help plan its development in a way that would take the needs of residents into account.

In addition to the museum builders, several other groups of students involved themselves in the question of what visitors to the city should see and do. Rejecting existing brochures featuring "Old Cambridge" and Harvard University, one group designed a tour featuring places of interest to visiting teens, while another created a "Sweet Tour" for visitors seeking the best desserts in town.

A third group of students liked the idea of highlighting the efforts of a "local hero." They videotaped an interview with John E. Gittens, a founder of the Cambridge National Association for the Advancement of Colored People, and learned that he had led a neighborhood organizing effort to get the city to open a new playground named after a child who was struck by a car because he was playing in the street. Their brochure featured a map locating the playground as well as the story of its creation. All three brochures, along with a T-shirt that another group of CityWorks students designed, have since been adopted by the board of the tourist agency as products they will distribute and market.

The goal of CityWorks projects is to help students understand their community and its needs, and ultimately to see themselves as people who can affect that community and create new opportunities for themselves and others who live or work there. Through the lens of community development, students arrive at a very different and more positive vision of what it means to be a vocational student. The point is not just to make things, learn some skills and get a job, but rather to become thinkers and solvers of problems, who work well together in teams and communicate well with various audiences.

WRITE IT DOWN; WRITE IT UP

The work that Paulina and her classmates do in CityWorks is complemented and reinforced by two other multidisciplinary courses: CityLife (humanities) and CitySystems (integrated mathematics and science). This means that freshmen at RSTA spend five of their seven periods each day in integrated study.

In CityWorks, students explore the dynamics that affect them and their community. In CityLife, a double-period humanities course, they read texts describing how young people in other times and places have thought about and fashioned their lives and futures—from Benjamin Franklin's "Advice to a Young Tradesman" to Jay MacLeod's ethnographic portrayal of the "Hallway Hangers" in a housing project in Cambridge.[1] The model building and other hands-on skills emphasized in CityWorks are reinforced in CityLife through group projects in which students are required to combine library research, construction, and public presentation. For example, in one project students investigate cities in other countries and time periods, building models to illustrate what they have learned. These, too, become part of the CityWorks exhibitions.

Because many students entering Rindge are reluctant writers, emphasis is also placed on giving them a new way to think about what is involved in putting pencil to paper. The approach is two-pronged: "Write it down" and "Write it up."[2] Students learn the habit and value of reflection and thinking on paper through keeping journals and work logs (write it down) and they also learn what is involved in preparing their writings for public presentation (write it up). The work logs students keep in CityWorks can also be brought to the humanities class if they want to "write up" any of the entries in more finished form for either an exhibition or inclusion in a final portfolio.

CitySystems is ambitious not only in its integration of academic with vocational education, but also as the only course in the high school to attempt a full integration of mathematics and science. Studying many of the same concepts covered in the schoolwide freshman course, Scientific Principles, students learn to use mathematical reasoning, patterns, and equations as a quantitatively accurate "language" for describing these principles. Whenever possible, the vocational shops are used as the laboratories for this learning.

For example, the voltage meter in the electrical shop becomes a tool for teaching positive and negative numbers. Visits to this shop also feed into a study of mechanics: students build small electric motors, using only wire, batteries, cups, rubber bands, and copper wire. The autobody shop is a place to begin the study of the principles of force. Students puzzle over why it is easier to break the window of a car than the fender. ("We took a beat-up car and started hitting it with a sledge hammer to see how force works," explains one delighted student in his photo essay of this trip). Visits to the autobody shop also afford an opportunity to compare the structure (skeleton) and organic systems of a human body to the frame and systems of a car.

Such visits are intended to serve a dual purpose. By exposing students to "real world" applications, lessons taught in the shops help them to understand scientific theories and concepts as well as the importance of quantitative accuracy. At the same time, investigations in the shops help students to see the high level of academic skills required in technical work.

The Dual System: Changing the Rules

THE OLD RINDGE

If Paulina had entered Rindge several years ago, her experience would have been almost totally different. She and her classmates would have been placed in an "exploratory," spending two periods per day, for two to three weeks at a time, rotating through each of the shops offered in the school. The rest of the day would have been spent in the typical fragmented, academic schedule of a high school freshman. At the end of the year Paulina would have chosen a "major"—the shop in which she would spend half of her school time for the next three years in narrow skill training for a specific occupation.

There was virtually no integration of the exploratory with academic subjects. In fact, Rindge students "went out" to the other parts of the high school for academics. Although this was supposed to eliminate social isolation and bring vocational students into contact with a wide range of peers, the reality was that they were mixed primarily with other low-income students in low-level academic classes. Rindge students faced all the problems associated with the bottom track in high school: watered-down curriculum with minimal academic content, teachers who would rather be working with a more motivated set of students, and negative labeling (such as Paulina describes) by other students and teachers.

The traditional Rindge program was justified in terms of appropriateness for its clientele. Since they were considered non-college-bound, Rindge students had to choose—at age fifteen—what they were "going to be" for the rest of their lives so that they could work on the skills necessary to their chosen occupation. The justification harked back to 1888 when Frederick Rindge bequeathed money and land to the city with the stipulation that it be used for a manual training school for boys. The sons of the city's merchants, businessmen, and professors already had their school (Cambridge High and Latin). The philanthropist Rindge wanted to ensure that a broader base of young men would be prepared to work in the rapidly growing manufacturing industries of New England. The now merged comprehensive high school (Cambridge Rindge and Latin) still displays his sentiments, carved in granite over the front door: "Work is one of our greatest blessings. Everyone should have an honest occupation."

ORIGINS OF THE DUAL SYSTEM

Massachusetts was one of the first states to institutionalize two separate curricula: one to educate middle and upper level managers for the new industrial firms, the other to train laborers and clerical workers. But the early history of vocational education also contained a more democratic impulse. Seeking to realize Horace Mann's vision of a common school system that included children from all backgrounds, local school boards found that they could attract Irish immigrant and rural families by introducing vocational programs focusing on agriculture and mechanical trades.

By the late nineteenth century the fundamental contradiction of vocational education was evident. On the one hand, it was and remains a means of providing an education to students who would not otherwise attend school. The Massachusetts Commission on Industrial and Technical Education reported that high school enrollment in Massachusetts rose from 6.7 percent of those fourteen to seventeen years old in 1888 to 32.3 percent of that population by 1906.[3] On the other hand, it created a dual system in which lower-income students were tracked into vocational classes and away from the academic courses which prepared others for future education and higher income, white-collar jobs.

A 1906 report by the Massachusetts Commission on Industrial and Technical Education triggered a debate between John Dewey and David Snedden, the Commissioner of Education in Massachusetts. Believing that vocational education could "do more to make public education truly democratic than any other agency now under consideration," Dewey argued vehemently against Snedden's defense of the efficiency of a dual system.[4] As Dewey noted: "Nothing in the history of education is more touching than to hear some successful leaders denounce as undemocratic the attempt to give all the children at public expense the fuller education which their own children enjoy as a matter of course."[5]

Despite such deep disagreement about the direction of vocational education, it garnered wide support. A powerful lobbying organization, the National Society for the Promotion of Industrial Education, was supported by a broad range of groups, including educators, the Chamber of Commerce, the National Association of Manufacturers, major farm organizations, and settlement workers. After initial suspicions about vocational education, even organized labor jumped on the bandwagon. Sensing the inevitability of vocational education, the American Federation of Labor wanted a voice in redirecting its antiunion bias.

The campaign culminated in the passage of the Smith-Hughes Act in 1917. For the first time, federal money was available for high schools to use in preparing students for employment in the major occupations of an emerging industrial society. In addition to the availability of federal money, two other factors assured the growth of vocational education. First, the compulsory education laws of 1923 captured into vocational programs many students who were now required to go to school. Second, intelligence tests such as the Stanford-Binet were developed and used to justify relegating some students to "work with their hands," separated from those who would presumably benefit from academic pursuits.

THE PERKINS ACT OF 1990

The Carl D. Perkins Vocational and Applied Technology Education Act of 1990 created a federal legislative mandate to reopen the conversation about the purposes and content of vocational education.

As recently as the previous reauthorization hearings in 1984, it was practically blasphemous to suggest that schools integrate vocational and academic education. But by 1990 some disturbing facts had begun to emerge. The job entrance rates and wage rates of vocational school graduates were only marginally better than those of students graduating from the high school's general track; only 27 percent of all secondary students in the United States who were majoring in a technical area ever worked in a related field. Widespread dissatisfaction with the outcomes of vocational education, combined with strong pressure from a coalition of national advocacy groups led by the Center for Law and Education, galvanized support for change.[6]

In its final form the Perkins Act requires that vocational and academic education be broadly integrated and that vocational programs move from occupationally specific, narrow, skill-based training to offer instruction in "all aspects of an industry." Through its participatory planning mechanisms the Act also increases the opportunity for vocational education to forge links with community economic development efforts.

In theory, the Perkins Act makes available federal money that could potentially affect the direction of schooling for 4.3 million vocational students. CityWorks is one of the first efforts to work out the ideas embodied in the Perkins Act in a real school setting. As the mandates of the Perkins Act trickle down to the local level, educators call and write, asking us to please "send CityWorks." Although we oblige such requests by mailing out curriculum packets, we suspect that these materials by themselves will do little to help our colleagues.

What is important about CityWorks is not the lesson plans or the specific projects that each group of teachers and students does. At best, these represent a way to bring technical improvements to a school. The process of detracking, staff development, and restructuring that CityWorks exemplifies and necessitates is much more at the heart of what it means to put the Perkins Act into practice. Vocational programs supposedly exist for the benefit of those who wish to enter the skilled labor market. But in too many cases, such programs have become dumping grounds, barely distinguishable from the "general track." The Perkins Act could be a powerful tool, not just for improving vocational education, but for challenging the social class biases and assumptions about intelligence that lie behind the sorting itself.

Changing the Norms

VOCATIONAL EDUCATION FOR EVERYONE

In Cambridge Rindge and Latin High School, as in most urban comprehensive high schools, the measure of quality is in the percentage of students going on to higher education. The Cambridge Public Schools pride themselves on having eliminated the general track and having achieved a 75 to 80 percent college-going rate. Basically, it is assumed that the non-college-bound go into the vocational track, and everyone else is preparing for college.

But these statistics are deceiving. What happens to the students who are supposedly college bound? How many leave high school really prepared to succeed in college and how many ever attain a degree? Although not collected on a local level, the national data tell a depressing story. Of those entering two-year colleges, the majority leave within the first six months. Only about half of those entering a four-year college or university graduate within a six-year period.

As we thought about who would benefit from a redefinition of vocational education, we looked not just at the students coming into our program but at the much larger group of young people who could benefit from broadly integrated academic and vocational education, from the creation of new career pathways and apprenticeships, from opportunities to contribute to the revitalization of their own depressed communities. In a very real sense, we saw our potential clientele as encompassing the whole student body, rather than the 15 to 20 percent willing to identify themselves with a program for the "non-college-bound."

We began with the ninth grade, not simply because it is the entry point for students into the social sorting mechanism of the high school, but also because changes in the ninth grade program would, of necessity, involve most of the vocational teachers. Although they taught the "exploratory" course in the autonomous isolation of their own shops, these teachers each had a strong interest in getting to know all of the freshmen. The exploratory course had long been the recruiting ground for future shop "majors."

The system functioned rather like a series of blind dates: students went from shop to shop trying to decide with which teacher (and technical area) they would enter into a relationship. Not surprisingly, this bred competition among the areas. Teachers in each area suspected the other areas of "courting" students too vigorously and of making unrealistic promises. Although teachers did not propose a change, there was a recognition that a competitive norm was not particularly healthy. There was also a growing feeling of futility and desperation as the total enrollment continued to drop, and students who entered seemed less and less interested in vocational pursuits.

SETTING GROUND RULES

In January, 1991, we took our first step: informing the staff about key provisions of the Perkins Act and explaining a proposed strategy for addressing these at Rindge. We would begin by undertaking a complete overhaul of the ninth grade program, and then, as the first group of freshmen proceeded through the school, revamp the program offerings in each successive grade level. It was, we hoped, a suitably ambitious, but not totally overwhelming way to proceed. The superintendent supported us by publicly declaring her desire for Rindge to be "turned on its head."

According to our timetable, the staff had the spring and summer of 1991 to design a new ninth grade program for the fall of 1991. For the plan to succeed, the new ninth grade program not only had to work for students but also had to function as effective staff development for teachers. A curriculum had to be designed that would introduce the whole staff to what we envisioned as the core idea of a revamped four-year program: academic-vocational integration within a community development framework. As soon as possible, staff needed not just to talk about but to *experience* what it was like to work together across trades and to combine methods that they used regularly in their shop with content that was less familiar.

In embarking on program redesign, we set ourselves three ground rules. The first was to keep everyone in the department informed of all that we were doing. The second was that no one would have to participate who did not want to. And the third was that those who did not want to participate would not be allowed to interfere with the efforts of those who did. When the first call went out for teachers to join a design team, six volunteered.

By the fall of 1991, the team had come up with an overall conceptual framework for CityWorks, had fiddled with the schedule to create unprecedented daily meeting time for teachers, and had begun the construction of a space that would house the new program. Although our goal had been to establish a full academic program, in the first year students continued to go to the main campus for most of their academic subjects. It took us until the fall of 1992 to find a way to fund and schedule the CityLife and CitySystems components.

RELYING ON TEACHERS

In all, we began the school year in 1992 with enough classroom activities to last only about one month. The rest would have to come from the CityTeam meetings in which everyone teaching the course would participate. Although it was a bit terrifying not to have all of CityWorks plotted out, we also knew it would be a mistake to hand teachers a finished curriculum. Teachers, like students, are not empty vessels into which the current wisdom can be poured.

For years vocational teachers at Rindge had spent virtually all of their time at school teaching narrow technical skills that were occupationally specific. Most believed that this is what it meant to be a vocational teacher. State mandated curricula reinforced this notion. Vocational teachers received manuals for their shop areas listing duties and tasks that students in that area were expected to undertake. If we wanted our school to be a place where all students could be smart, we would have to structure a program where all teachers could be smart. This meant encouraging teachers to unearth the reasons behind their current practice, and to reconsider that practice in the light of changing economic and social realities. In other words, it was important to respect and make room for them as thinkers as well as doers.

We suspected that Rindge teachers were experiencing a kind of cognitive dissonance. Certainly the curriculum they were teaching at school left out much of what they knew to be important in their own work and lives outside of school. This was brought home to us early on in our reform efforts in a conversation with a teacher who had taught carpentry at Rindge for many years. Like many vocational teachers, he was an independent contractor outside of school. He explained that he would very much like to turn his business over to his sons, both of whom were skilled carpenters. The problem was that neither seemed to be good at most of the other tasks associated with running a successful contracting business, for example, making good estimates, writing contracts, dealing with clients and subcontractors, and getting variances from the local zoning board.

This teacher held within his own experiences the seeds of a new approach to practice. The challenge for us has been to create a professional culture which encourages teachers to share their experiences and reflect on their practice. Three strategies have been particularly critical to that effort. These are described below, with further discussion of the political and normative dimensions of such strategies in the sections that follow.

1. *Carving out time and space for teachers to meet.* The most basic thing that we have done is to give teachers both informal and formal opportunities to work together. Their close physical proximity in the CityWorks room opens up the possibility of joint projects. Required daily CityTeam meetings ensure that such possibilities will be discussed.

To create a meeting time in the daily schedule necessitated closing the shops for a period, not a popular move either with our own teachers or counselors who signed students up for shops as personal-interest electives. But it is critical to what we are trying to accomplish. The meetings are a time to reflect on what is happening in CityWorks, to review, revise, and propose curriculum activities, and more generally, to get to know one another and explore the possibilities for collaboration. As the facilitators of the daily meetings, the authors have played a key role in steering the meetings away from gripe sessions and a focus on logistical concerns to a broader conversation about teaching and learning.

2. *Including people from outside the department and the school.* From the beginning, the vocational teachers who staffed CityWorks have been joined by a variety of people from very different backgrounds who bring other perspectives and experiences to the task. The "others" have included several academic teachers, a loaned employee from the Polaroid Corporation, bilingual technical assistants, and, as needed, consultants to assist staff, first in their work on curriculum, later on group dynamics and issues of organizational development.

This mixture creates a forum for reexamining assumptions and for moving beyond the specific skills involved in particular trades or subjects to what it is important for all students to know and be able to do by the time they leave the program. At one critical juncture, for example, when vocational teachers were resisting collaborative projects in the name of craft specialization, the Polaroid employee talked about the multicraft perspective at his company and at other high-performance workplaces.

3. *Creating a situation of genuine interdependence.* The meetings are productive because they have to be. Everyone knows that they are about to go in and teach CityWorks the next day (or the next hour). In a very real sense, they sink or swim together. If the program works, it will eventually increase enrollments and attract a broader clientele of students. If it does not, Rindge will suffer the kinds of staff cutbacks of other vocational programs. As of this writing, the program *has*

worked. Freshman enrollments at Rindge for 1994-1995 have doubled. The competitive ethic of the old exploratory does not die easily, but it really is counterproductive in the new structure. It makes much more sense to collaborate, to nurture and support new ideas, and to look to one another for project ideas and strategies.

Learning the Politics of Change

NOT A SECRET

There is a tendency in school reform efforts to build a protective wall around what you are doing. If you do not, you might get accused by parents, or worse, by school board members of "experimenting with our children." Although it is possible to hide for a while, in the long run the only real protection is in convincing key stakeholders of the value and perhaps the inevitability of what you are doing.

CityWorks has never been a secret. Staff members and students have made presentations at parents' nights, spoken at each of the junior high schools, and hosted hundreds of people at the exhibitions of student work. The interest in CityWorks expressed by the larger community has given an added impetus to the staff both to make the new program work well and to be able to describe it well to others.

The "publicness" of what we are doing has caused political problems locally. Speaking for a small but vocal constituency of parents, one school board member accused Rindge of misdirecting working-class students by offering them liberal arts rather than the manual training that they need. One critic noted that Rindge is preparing "Renaissance people, not plumbers." There has also been an attempt to get the state to decertify our program.

Thus far, such attacks have tied up time and energy, but they have also solidified the staff, students, and parents behind the new program. Fortunately, we also receive very positive feedback about what we are doing, both from within the district and around the country. As awareness of the Perkins Act has grown, so have requests to visit our program or to send our teachers out as workshop leaders and presenters. In fact, the requests became so great that we set up our own formal mechanism for handling them: the Hands and Minds Collaborative[7]— a joint effort of Rindge and the Center for Law and Education.

YARDSTICK FOR MEASURING CHANGE

Contact with "outsiders" has brought major benefits to our staff. The attitudes, questions, and comments of teachers from other districts have become yardsticks against which Rindge teachers can measure the distance they have come. In June of 1993, a dozen Rindge teachers served as workshop leaders at a national conference cosponsored by the Center for Law and Education, the Massachusetts Institute of Technology, and the Hands and Minds Collaborative. It was the job of the workshop leaders to assist the nearly two hundred participants in developing projects that would help them implement the Perkins Act in their own schools.

At the last session, after listening to a number of teachers express concerns about the loss of time for trade-specific training, Tom Lividoti, the electrical teacher at Rindge, spoke up: "I used to sound just like that. I was the loudest one complaining about fewer hours in the electrical shop. But what we're doing now brings out creative juices I didn't know kids had; I see developments on the academic end that I never dreamed were possible. I may not be able to turn out second-year apprentice electricians, but I know we are turning out better all-round students."

Academic teachers working with the CityWorks program have also found that they have important messages to share with their colleagues. Alif Muhammad, the CitySystems teacher, convened a workshop series for Cambridge teachers called: "Put the action back into math and science." In these sessions mathematics and science teachers learned to use new tabletop physics equipment being constructed by students in the woodshop. Rob Riordan, a member of the Rindge humanities team, echoed Dewey last year when he addressed teachers and scholars at a national meeting sponsored by the American Council of Learned Societies: "I started the year thinking it was my mission to bring humanities into vocational education. Now I believe we must bring vocational methodologies into the humanities."

TOWARD INTERDEPENDENCE

During the first few months of CityWorks team meetings, teachers would almost never comment on a teaching or learning issue without prefacing it with a disclaimer: "I would never say what's right for anyone else" or "This is just the way I do things" or "I know that everyone has his or her own way of doing things and that's fine." The frequency of such statements provided clues to an underlying group norm that can best be characterized as "noninterference" (that is, I won't look too closely at what you're up to or tell you what to do; and you won't scrutinize me).[8] The conditions of teaching make teachers view their work with the sometimes fierce independence of artisans.[9] For vocational teachers, this perspective is reinforced by their highly specialized work within the school (and outside) as trade artisans.

In the past, Rindge teachers defended the separateness of their shops in terms of the differences among their trades, each with its own specific skill requirements. Shop autonomy seemed a natural and even necessary condition of vocational education. The most obvious negative side effect was the competition for students noted earlier. But perhaps an even more serious problem was that teachers had no reason to identify the broader educational needs of their students, nor any real way to address those needs. They focused on finding ways to interest students in a specific technical area, but did not feel responsible for ensuring that all students become better problem solvers or communicators, or gain a good solid basis of reading, writing, and quantitative and scientific reasoning skills.

It is impossible to pinpoint a moment when the focus changed, but after two years of team meetings a sense of broader responsibility is now evident within the group. It can be seen in an increased sharing of information and in a willingness to identify competencies that students need regardless of their schooling or career choices. Staff members are more likely to team up for multicraft projects, and, sometimes even design classroom projects that do not involve their trade specialty at all.

In early planning stages for CityWorks there was a tendency to swing from cynical skepticism ("This will never work") to unrealistic enthusiasm ("We're almost done"). Now teachers approach the task of restructuring with a kind of rolling up of the collective sleeve. There is a noticeably greater tolerance for ambiguity. People are more willing to bring issues to the team for group problem solving and have found ways to deal constructively with disagreements. Teachers are evolving a shared language for talking about how they work together and for getting through the inevitable crises. Perhaps more important, we now have a picture of what we could and should become: a high performance workplace where staff members are highly interdependent yet each is an active participant, focusing energy on the tasks at hand.

WHEN TEACHERS CARE

The amount of time devoted to meetings and the intensity of the staff work have, at times, created a worry that we might become too adult-focused. Fortunately, this is not what students seem to feel. When freshmen are asked what is most noticeable or important to them about Rindge, most students begin with the simple statement: "The teachers here really care about you."

Of course, the teachers cared about students before too, but the scope of what they care about has broadened considerably and hence is more evident to the students. In the old way of doing business, teachers had little patience with students who were not ready to make a choice about what they wanted to be and were not motivated to learn all of the skills of that particular trade. They felt their identities as skilled craftspeople slipping away, to be replaced by a much less desirable identity as "caretakers of marginal students."[10]

CityWorks gives teachers a new identity. Even if students do not express interest in particular trades, teachers no longer feel like mere caretakers. They know that they can help students develop competencies, interests, and attitudes that will serve them well in future schooling or work. This feeling of self-efficacy on the part of their teachers is evident to students. Several freshmen recently surprised a visiting reporter by telling her that what makes CityWorks teachers different is that they *like* what they are doing.

Not surprisingly, students respond by becoming more engaged with school; their "creative juices" get going and teachers see them at their best. The caring and mutual respect go beyond the classroom walls. For example, during the summer a group of students who had just completed their CityWorks year responded to the invitation from one of their teachers to come up with ways to smooth the entry of incoming freshmen. Using the acronym R.S.T.A. (the abbreviation for the Rindge School of Technical Arts), they named themselves "Responsible Students Take Action."

When Paulina and her cohort entered Rindge, they received a new student handbook, covering all of the things the older students wished someone had told them, and they found immediate support in the form of R.S.T.A. student mentors who had set up a table in the hall to help freshmen with everything from coping with sticky locks on lockers to dealing with hazing.

Impressed by such efforts, staff members have become willing to carve out even more unusual forums for student participation and input. Rindge is probably the only vocational school in the United States to have its own Innovations Board, with equal membership (and votes) of students and staff. The Board was created in late 1991, soon after CityWorks received an Innovations Award from the Ford Foundation. One of ten innovations in state and local government selected nationally from over 1,700 applicants, CityWorks was given $100,000 to "broaden and deepen" the work.

The staff agreed to set aside one third of this award to be given out over three years in small grants to other innovations in the Cambridge Schools that would further the CityWorks mission. The process would be overseen by a board with equal representation of students and staff, and several slots reserved for community representatives. At its first few meetings, the board hammered out a mission statement and a set of priorities. Student members were outspoken in these discussions, insisting, for example, that all proposals be submitted by at least one teacher and one student, and that proposals specify the ways in which students would be involved in carrying out the program.

By the spring, board members were reading and evaluating nearly two dozen proposals from all over the school district. After selecting and interviewing the finalists, the board selected nine winners, with proposals ranging from a new student-run radio program to a special summer school for bilingual students. Questioned by teachers and classmates as to why they did not use more of the money internally for Rindge projects and programs, several students spoke passionately of the need to end the isolation of the vocational program. They want the Innovations fund to encourage teachers and students throughout the school district to try new ways to join hands and minds. Their hope echoes the note sounded by Paulina at the end of her statement to the school: "We give respect, so we expect respect. Success demands it!"

NOTES

1. Jay MacLeod, *Ain't No Making It* (Boulder, Colorado: Westview Press, 1987).

2. Rob Riordan, English Department Coordinator of the Cambridge public schools, coined this phrase.

3. Edward Krug, *The Shaping of the American High School, 1880-1920* (Madison: University of Wisconsin Press, 1969), p. 220.

4. John Dewey, "Some Dangers in the Present Movement for Industrial Education," *Middle Works* 7 (1913): 99, 102.

5. Robert Westbrook, *John Dewey and American Democracy* (Ithaca: Cornell University Press, 1991), p. 178.

6. The Center for Law and Education, based in Cambridge, Massachusetts and Washington, D.C., provides support services on education issues to advocates working on behalf of low-income students and parents. Paul Weckstein of the Center played a lead role in advocating academic and vocational integration in the 1990 reauthorization of the Perkins Act.

7. The Hands and Minds Collaborative is open to educators and community partners interested in redefining vocational education. It is based at the Rindge School of Technical Arts, and is funded by the Dewitt Wallace-Readers Digest Fund and the Stewart Mott Foundation.

8. Judith Warren Little, "The Persistence of Privacy: Autonomy and Initiative in Teachers' Professional Relations," *Teachers College Record* 91, no. 4 (Summer 1990): 509-535.

9. Michael Huberman, "The Social Construct of Instruction in Schools," *Teachers College Record* 91, no. 1 (Fall 1989): 32-58.

10. Judith Warren Little, "Two Worlds: Vocational and Academic Teachers in Comprehensive High Schools," National Center for Research on Vocational Education, University of California at Berkeley, June 1992.

Introduction to Chapter X

Curriculum developers and teachers are often under pressure to include subjects, innovations, or features in the curriculum that are perceived by some as controversial. Controversies may arise because of different views as to the purpose of the innovation, the nature of the innovation itself, or the instructional materials to be used. As Christine Sleeter points out in the following chapter, multicultural education can be seen as controversial for these as well as other reasons. If the potential for controversy is not acknowledged at the outset, there is the possibility of curricular decisions that are uninformed and perhaps unwise.

One way of handling such matters is to undertake a systematic inquiry that will identify aspects of the proposed innovation that could result in controversy and to identify as precisely as possible where difficulties may arise. Professor Sleeter's article is such an inquiry. She asks what multicultural education is and where it came from. She describes various approaches to instruction in this area and various instructional materials designed for use in that instruction. She summarizes major criticisms of multicultural education and responds to those criticisms. Finally, she draws implications for educators from her analysis.

Professor Sleeter's essay provides an example of how any controversial issue pertaining to a proposed innovation could be examined prior to a decision to make it a part of the curriculum. The reader can obtain a broad view of issues involved even though the author's own position on multicultural education, as she defines it, is never in doubt.

Christine Sleeter is Professor in the Center for Collaborative and Professional Studies at California State University Monterey Bay. Her chapter is reprinted from the Society's 94th Yearbook, Part 2, Changing Populations/Changing Schools, *edited by Erwin Flaxman and A. Harry Passow.*

CHAPTER X

Curriculum Controversies in Multicultural Education

CHRISTINE E. SLEETER

The community in which I live is wrestling currently with multicultural education in a manner similar to that of many communities today. Most of the schools are predominantly white, although populations of color are growing rapidly and student bodies in many schools are becoming diverse. The community itself has historically been a volatile "melting pot" for European ethnic groups, and most residents use the template of the European ethnic immigrant experience to attempt to understand non-European groups, in the process denying alternative perspectives about race relations put forth by people of color. When called upon to provide information about multicultural education I encounter questions such as these: "Is it a new program?" "Does it work?" "Could you suggest some good international speakers or performers for a school's 'cultural' week?" "Isn't multicultural education unfair by asking teachers to bend over backward for 'those' children?" "Doesn't it retard rather than help the assimilation process?" "Isn't it just another form of 'political correctness'?"

In this chapter I briefly situate multicultural education in its historical context, and in the process I attempt to provide a broad conceptualization of what multicultural education means. I review criticisms of multicultural education that have permeated the media during the late 1980s and early 1990s, focusing on debates about curriculum, since these criticisms inform many educators' understanding of multicultural education. I then counter the criticisms with the research and theory undergirding multicultural education. I will argue (1) that multicultural education represents a challenge to historic forms of racial oppression in the United States more than a response to recent demographic

257

changes; (2) that it attempts to shift power in educational decision making toward groups of color rather than being merely a program that one can "adopt"; and (3) that practices recommended by theorists of multicultural education rest on a growing base of research and theory.

What is Multicultural Education?
Where Did It Come From?

Multicultural education emerged seriously in the context of the Civil Rights movement of the 1960s. As African Americans, joined by other oppressed racial groups, demanded access to various institutions from which whites had historically excluded them, they formulated agendas for changing those institutions to support inclusiveness. In higher education, students demanded courses in ethnic studies as well as other programs and policies in support of diverse cultures. At the K-12 level, as schools began to experience desegregation, parents and educators criticized (1) the exclusion of people of color from curricula and from decision-making roles and (2) the low academic expectations white educators had for children of color, expectations which were buttressed by assumptions about cultural deprivation.[1]

As educators and community activists of color articulated their concerns about schooling, "multicultural education" became a term designating recommended changes. The prefix "multi" was adopted as an umbrella to include diverse groups of color. The term "multiethnic education" linked common concerns of diverse racial and ethnic minority groups; "multicultural education" expanded the umbrella to include gender, disability, and other forms of diversity.[2]

An Intergroup Education movement, which had been active during the 1940s and 1950s, is regarded by some educators as a precursor to multicultural education. Banks, however, locates the roots of multicultural education in the Civil Rights movement and the development of Black Studies, distinguishing these from Intergroup Education in this way:

Intergroup educators, most of whom are liberal white academics who worked in mainstream American institutions, placed more emphasis on a shared American identity than did black scholars, who were more concerned about creating accurate images of African Americans, empowering African Americans, and building African-American institutions.[3]

Multicultural education at its inception attempted mainly to synthesize the work of African-American, Latino, Native American, and Asian-American scholars and activists.

Since the early 1970s, a great deal of material has been produced that articulates and develops changes that should be made in schools to support the strengths and aspirations of diverse groups. For example, in the ERIC listings of journal publications between January 1982 and June 1992, the descriptor "multicultural education" retrieves 911 entries; this does not include books, nor all resources catalogued under related descriptors such as "bilingual education" or "Asian Americans and education."

Clearly, the field of multicultural education is not new. Educators new to the field often derive their understanding of the term "multicultural education" from their notions about the term "culture" with the prefix "multi." They too often disregard (or assume a lack of) scholarship that has been developed in the field over the past twenty-five years. Many white educators also assume that multicultural education is related mainly to new immigrants, and they dissociate it from a critique of historical patterns of racism in schooling and society. For example, white teachers sometimes tell me that they already know "all about" African Americans and Hispanics, resent a stress on "them," and want some information about Hindu or Japanese culture. Part of the problem is that most teachers lack substantive knowledge of a nonwhite American group. In the absence of such knowledge, most teachers greatly underestimate what there is to know. In addition, any individual who has not lived in a racial minority community (as is the case with most whites and some educators of color) is less likely to view such communities in terms of strengths and resources than are the community members themselves.

So what is multicultural education? It is a process of school reform that is based on reciprocal dialog among diverse sociocultural groups and on genuine power sharing among groups. Historically, school structures, processes, and research have been framed largely by white middle- to upper-class educators and policymakers. The literature in multicultural education, although contributed to by a wide variety of people, has mainly represented attempts by educators of color to articulate the kinds of changes schools should make to reverse oppression based on race, language, ethnicity, and gender. Banks argues that multicultural education should entail a process of school reform that requires transformation of the school as a whole: "[To] transform the school to bring about educational equality, all the major components of the school must be substantially changed. A focus on any one variable in the school, such as the formalized curriculum, will not implement multicultural education."[4] Major components include relations with the community, teaching and learning styles, assessment programs, instructional materials, school policies, and the school staff. Grant terms this reform an "education that is multicultural" rather than multicultural education, since what is required is not the addition of a program, but the transformation of an institution.[5]

Institutional reforms discussed in the literature on multicultural education are supported by ethnographic research that documents various forms of inequality in schooling. Whether or not schools contribute to the reproduction of unequal relationships is an issue educators debate; multicultural education as a field takes the position that in many ways most schools do reproduce inequality, but could operate differently. Oakes's research, for example, critiques tracking, including its institutionalization of racial and social class disparities in access to education.[6] Rist documents processes by which African-American children were rendered "invisible" in a white desegregated school.[7] Grant and Sleeter portray various forms of racial, social class, and gender inequality found in many facets of a junior high school.[8] Phillips documents the breakdown in teaching that occurs when teachers' and students' styles of communication clash.[9]

Multicultural reforms are also supported by a wealth of anthropological and social-psychological research on cultural and language patterns that discredits notions about the superiority or deficiency of various cultures.[10] In addition, research in ethnic and women's studies has retrieved a tremendous amount of knowledge about diverse groups. This research has been synthesized into new perspectives and theoretical frameworks that provide a wealth of material for transforming curricula.[11]

In the literature on multicultural education, one can find discussions that vary in complexity and depth. Some of Gay's discussions of multicultural teaching practice are quite comprehensive,[12] while others are fairly short and prescriptive.[13] One can also find formulations, which range widely in focus, of exactly what changes might be made in schools.

Five Approaches to Multicultural Education

Grant and Sleeter distinguish five different approaches to multicultural education, each of which details a somewhat different set of recommended changes.[14] The main purpose of the first approach, "teaching the exceptional and culturally different," is to help students achieve well within schools largely as they are by building bridges between students' backgrounds and the schools in order to make the curriculum more "user friendly." Bridges may consist of instructional strategies that build on students' learning styles, culturally relevant materials, or use of students' native language to teach standard English. A second approach, "human relations," attempts to build positive affective relationships among members of diverse racial and cultural groups and/or between males and females in order to strengthen each ·student's self-concept and to increase interpersonal harmony. This is generally done through lessons about stereotyping and individual differences and similarities, conflict-reduction programs, and use of cooperative learning. "Single-group studies" is an umbrella term for a third approach, which consists of programs or courses of study that focus on particular groups, such as ethnic studies, labor studies, or women's studies. This approach seeks to raise consciousness about a group by teaching its history and culture, as well as how that group has interacted with the dominant society. The "multicultural" approach promotes cultural pluralism by reconstructing the entire education process. Disciplinary content, for example, is reorganized around the perspectives and knowledge bases of diverse American racial and ethnic groups, both sexes, and diverse social classes. This approach questions the use of tracking and ability grouping, advocating heterogeneous grouping as much as possible, with high academic expectations for all students. Finally, education that is "multicultural and social reconstructionist" teaches students to analyze inequality and oppression in society and helps them develop skills for social action. This approach organizes curriculum around contemporary issues of social justice, using disciplinary knowledge to examine those issues and create ways of effecting change.

Multicultural education, however, though often formulated as "how-to's" in an effort to illustrate changes schools could make, cannot be reduced to any one list of "correct" practices. In the context of the Civil Rights struggle, multicultural education was initially part of a larger quest by oppressed racial groups for decision-making power and control over the education of their own children. Writings articulated agendas of concerns and recommendations for practice, but they emerged as part of a larger quest for self-determination. In the context of the 1990s, however, most educators, especially those who are white, tend not to associate multicultural education with social movements and power sharing. Rather, white educators often appropriate its language and some of its practices in order to "solve" racial issues without dismantling white dominance.[15] From the perspective of those who connect multicultural education with empowerment and self-determination, common school practices such as food fairs and celebrations of racial and ethnic heroes miss the point.

For example, I often observe white teachers talking among themselves about what they believe are appropriate materials or teaching strategies to use with a culturally diverse class. They may seek input from a consultant and/or a colleague of color, but the decision-making power about schooling stays with the classroom teacher, the building principal, and the administrative hierarchy. Virtually excluded from decision-making power are the students, their parents, and their community, particularly if the community is poor and/or of color. In the case of one school, I recall teachers adding lessons about individual differences and Native American culture but continuing to dodge the question of how much academic achievement they could actually expect of students. In conversations with African-American and Latino community members, I was told (and was not surprised to hear) that academic achievement was their main concern. By defining themselves as the "experts" and the literature on multicultural education as a collection of ideas to use selectively, many educators undermine the basic impulse for dialog, power sharing, and self-determination that gave rise to multicultural education in the first place.

Thus, what began in a movement for self-determination in practice very often is reduced to additions to "business as usual" that do not actually change schooling or shift decision-making power toward oppressed groups. Multicultural education fundamentally means dialog and power sharing and the need for dialog and power sharing is as great now as it was three decades ago. While organized social movements may not be as visible in the 1990s as they were in the 1960s, the issues and basic conditions of life for Americans of color as well as for poor whites have not changed much since then. The small gains in income, employment, and status won by people of color as well as by women in the early 1970s have eroded.[16] Megacorporations have exported jobs from the United States. As Chomsky and others have argued, they have pitted white male workers, who are accustomed to having access to decent jobs, against Americans of color and women who are viewed as taking jobs unfairly through affirmative action, and against Third World people who are depicted as uncivilized.[17] Of course, schools alone cannot solve these problems, but schools embody and reflect them. Historically, multicultural education developed as a movement grounded in organized action aimed at social justice and educational equality for everyone; today the need for such organized action is as great as it has been for decades.

New Multicultural Curricula

Over the past three decades, multicultural education has produced some tangible fruit, the most visible of which is curriculum. As a reform movement, multicultural education cannot be reduced to curriculum. However, since curricular materials have emerged as the focus of heated national debate, I will concentrate on them.

Much "multiculturalized" curriculum actually ignores the main themes in scholarship and the experiences of oppressed groups. This happens when curriculum developers begin with existing curriculum as the base and then simply add on references to nondominant groups. These references may take the form of stories, biographical information, historic events, or pictures. To the observer whose conceptual viewpoint is congruent with that of white mainstream America, such a curriculum may seem multicultural. But to the observer whose viewpoint is rooted in a different conceptual space (such as someone with an Indian worldview), the curriculum looks "white" although with additions of color.[18]

There is, however, an expanding array of curricular materials that draw substantively on scholarship by oppressed groups. For example, a few secondary-level textbooks for African-American history[19] and African-American literature[20] make use of African-American scholarship. There are also a few anthologies with substantial offerings that are multicultural[21] as well as curriculum guides for teachers that illustrate how to help children learn to grapple with issues of social justice.[22]

But as one moves into the realm of textbooks to be adopted for courses required of all students, one encounters a hotly political terrain. It is the degree to which debates surrounding multicultural education have entered this terrain that has prompted popular publications such as *Time*, *U.S. News and World Report*, and *The New York Times* to feature articles about multicultural education. Cornbleth and Waugh have noted that "not unexpectedly, two of the places where the America debate [debate about what it means to be 'American'] has emerged most boisterously are New York and California, the states with the largest numbers of immigrants and the widest variety of people."[23] I review briefly here some curriculum development efforts in three states—California, New York, and Oregon—that have been featured prominently in the national debates.[24]

During the mid-1980s, the state Superintendent of Public Instruction in California directed the state to revise various subject area frameworks. A committee approved by the State Board of Education drafted the California *History/Social Science Framework* that guided the adoption of a textbook series.[25] The *Framework* takes what Cornbleth and Waugh describe as a "modest" approach to multiculturalism, situating California's diverse population within the immigrant mold.[26] An anchoring idea of the *Framework* is that the United States is a nation of immigrants: everyone who is not an immigrant is a descendant of immigrants, and Native Americans are depicted as the first immigrants. As such, all Americans share a common national identity, including allegiance to symbols of U.S. citizenship. That citizenship extends "the promise of freedom and equality for all," although throughout its history "citizens have struggled to make sure that all Americans have the rights they need to fulfill this promise."[27] A textbook series published by Houghton Mifflin that fits within the *Framework* was adopted at the state level; most districts in the state use it.

However, adoption of the series was fought by parents in urban districts, as well as a cadre of others "who grew to include not only racial and ethnic minorities but also Muslims, Jews, Christians, gays, lesbians, and feminists."[28] Joyce King, an African-American scholar who argued against the *Framework*, has pointed out that "none of the history textbooks reviewed, including those that were eventually adopted, received higher than 'moderate' ratings for 'cultural diversity,' one of the *Framework*'s seventeen 'characteristics' for evaluating the texts."[29] Ultimately, adoption of this series of texts, which views multiculturalism as a common experience of immigration and assimilation, was orchestrated by a small, largely white group of academicians and political leaders including Diane Ravitch, Charlotte Crabtree, Bill Honig, and Lynne Cheney.[30] This *Framework* and textbook series does not fit clearly within any of the five approaches to multicultural education mentioned earlier in this chapter since the anchoring ideas draw most firmly from the experience of European immigrants; alternative voices and perspectives are added but are truncated and muted.

In the late 1980s New York State also began to write its own multicultural curriculum, but took a very different approach from that taken in California. A task force created by Commissioner Thomas Sobol drafted *A Curriculum of Inclusion*, which is a framework for subsequent curriculum development.[31] The task force was predominantly minority and drew substantively on the literature of multicultural education.[32] In 1990, *A Curriculum of Inclusion* was presented at a conference of textbook publishers in which texts were criticized for superficial multicultural content, and various speakers articulated the depth of diverse perspectives they would like to see in curriculum materials for teachers.[33] My presentation at the conference was a critique of forty-seven textbooks published in the 1980s and used in grades 1 through 8 in core academic subjects. I argued that most additions to textbooks to make them multicultural were far more cosmetic than substantive.[34]

In 1991, a second task force produced another report entitled *One Nation, Many Peoples: A Declaration of Cultural Interdependence*.[35] This report called for

the acknowledgement and study of racism and the continuing struggle to realize democratic ideals in everyday life. In so doing, the New York position recognizes structural inequities in U.S. society. Pluralism is not contained as in California, and diversity is not trimmed to fit the European immigrant experience, but neither is the conventional story of America directly confronted.[36]

To assist teachers in making their seventh and eighth grade U.S. history course multicultural, for example, the New York City school system had produced a supplementary curriculum guide of lessons and resource material that teachers are encouraged, but not required, to use.[37] The unit topics coordinate with those in standard history textbooks, but the activities help students examine events from the perspectives of many groups. Activities help students to critique policies in view of their impact on oppressed groups (such as the impact of expansionist policies on Native Americans and Mexicans). For example, in Activity 4 of Unit 4 the students are asked to contrast the Mexican viewpoint regarding Texas with that of the United States during the 1830s and 1840s. Activities throughout the curriculum guide regularly incorporate many cultural groups and multiple perspectives about events to encourage students to engage in critical thinking. The guide can be criticized for oversimplification because it suggests that there was one single U.S. viewpoint and one single Mexican viewpoint and because it fails to provide in-depth treatment of the histories of any oppressed group. Its critical stance, however, is a departure from the tendency of other history curricula to gloss over brutal policies of aggression. The New York supplementary curriculum guide illustrates the "multicultural and social reconstructionist" approaches to multicultural education.

Portland, Oregon, also published its own material to assist teachers in making their subject curricula multicultural. The first package of materials to receive distribution was the *African American Baseline Essays*, published in 1989.[38] This is a series of six commissioned essays by authors from six disciplines: art, music, literature, social studies, science, and mathematics. Each essay develops an Afrocentric perspective on the discipline, highlighting particularly the contributions of ancient Egypt to the development of knowledge in that discipline. An Afrocentric perspective means "placing African ideals at the center of any analysis that involves African culture and behavior."[39] It entails situating people of African descent within an African history and worldview. The essays provide teachers with background information they can use in their own teaching. Other baseline essays on Hispanics and Native Americans are nearing completion. These essays illustrate the "single-group studies" approach to multicultural education.

These three curricular projects, along with revisions of core curricula at several universities, have become the focus of debates about multicultural education in the 1990s. They have come into the public spotlight largely through the work of critics of multicultural education who are attempting to mobilize public opinion in support of a conservative conception of how children should be taught to regard America's diversity. In the next section I will comment on issues emerging from debates over these curricula.

Contemporary Criticisms of Multicultural Education

Although most of the literature on multicultural education in the United States supports and develops the concept, the amount of writing that criticizes it has escalated rapidly. Through a search of the literature I located two critiques published in journals in the 1970s, six in the 1980s, and fifty-one between 1990 and 1992 alone.[40]

Although critiques that take a conservative position greatly outnumber other critiques of multicultural education, the latter need to be mentioned. A handful of the critiques articulate a radical left position; these appear exclusively in scholarly literature and are written for an audience of theorists. They critique multicultural education as a field rather than targeting specific curriculum projects. Their main criticism is that the field downplays or simply ignores structural inequalities such as systemic racism, focusing instead on cultural differences and simplistic solutions to racism in education. For example, Olneck ties multicultural education to the Intergroup Education movement, arguing that both stress individualism and upward mobility of individuals rather than collective advancement of oppressed racial groups.[41] Since the criticisms of the radical left focus on theory more than on curriculum they will not be reviewed here.

Although little has yet been published, an anthropological critique of multicultural education is emerging. This criticism has been voiced mainly at professional conferences. The main concern of some educational anthropologists is that the concept of "culture" is not being used in the way that anthropologists use it and therefore much work in multicultural education offers simplistic analyses of minority students' underachievement and other problems related to race. But again, since anthropologists have not specifically targeted curriculum for criticism their views are not reviewed here.

The remaining critiques share common assumptions and concerns that will be reviewed. Some observers term these critiques "conservative," although some of the "conservative" critics describe themselves as "liberals." Other observers term the critiques "neonativist" since they echo the Americanization movement of earlier decades.[42]

What the conservative or neonativist critics define as multicultural education is not the scholarly literature on the subject, but rather specific curricular changes. Their most frequent targets are New York State's *A Curriculum of Inclusion*, New York City's first grade curriculum, Portland's *African American Baseline Essays*, Afrocentrism in general, and revisions of core curricula on several university campuses. They often uphold California's *History/Social Science Framework* as a version of multicultural education they support.

I will address here four charges made by conservative critics. First, they characterize multicultural education as the politically charged work of an extremist lunatic fringe of radicals who represent neither the public at large nor the majority of African Americans and Latinos. For example, an editorial in *U.S. News and World Report* characterized New York's *A Curriculum of Inclusion* as the product of a group of "prescreened worshipers at the altar of multiculturalism" who do not represent "the views of most blacks, immigrants, or New Yorkers in general."[43] Arthur Schlesinger, who served on and eventually dissented from the second New York task force, complained that "ethnic ideologues" and "unscrupulous hucksters" have "imposed ethnocentric, Afrocentric, and bilingual curricula on public schools, well designed to hold minority children out of American society."[44] Dinesh D'Souza described changes universities were making to accommodate diversity as the work of former radical student protesters of the 1960s who have now returned to the university as professors to complete their conquest of it.[45]

The second charge against multicultural education is that it places excessive emphasis on race and ethnicity, which conservative and neonativist critics regard as divisive and capable of tearing the United States apart. The critics view U.S. history as one of progress in learning to implement the ideals of Western political thought. These ideals champion the rights of individuals: "Class, race, religion, national origin or culture all disappear or become dim when bathed in the light of natural rights, which give men common interests and make them truly brothers."[46] Western ideals also presumably articulate universal principles of the good life, which are of a higher order than principles emanating from particular sociocultural experiences. Education should cultivate reason, enabling individuals to rise above their own particular group affiliations and participate in a common society; Western classics offer the best training for this honing of the mind and contemplation of universal principles. Some critics are worried that contemporary attention to ethnic origin reverses what they view as a progressive trend in U.S. history toward inclusion of everyone.

Some critics of writing on multicultural education are troubled by what they regard as excessive criticism of the West, which they believe calls Western political ideals into question. For example, can American slavery best be understood as a "holocaust" that needs to be examined because of what it reveals about how white supremacy was and still is institutionally embedded in social constructions? Or, should slavery be regarded as an unfortunate historic institution in which most societies participated but the effects of which have been virtually eliminated? These critics tend to take the latter position, arguing vehemently that the former position undercuts the West. For example, Schlesinger asserts: "Whatever the crimes of Europe, that continent is also the source—the *unique* source—of those liberating ideals of individual liberty, political democracy, the impartial rule of law, and cultural freedom . . . to which most of the world aspires."[47]

Few conservative critics deny that the United States is culturally diverse, and they propose a conception of multicultural education that fits with their belief in progress, individuality, and Western ideals. Diane Ravitch is perhaps the leading spokesperson for what she terms "pluralistic" as opposed to "particularistic" multicultural education.[48] Pluralistic multicultural education, exemplified by California's *Framework*, which Ravitch helped to draft, seeks commonalities across diverse groups and views U.S. history as a grand narrative of the extension of Western ideals to all Americans. Conservative critics laud its search for commonalities, contrasting it with New York's emphasis on multiple perspectives, which they regard as "private tribal truths."[49]

A third objection of conservative critics is that multicultural education is intellectually weak, substituting sentimentality and political dogma for sound scholarship. Their main target is Afrocentrism, with Portland's *African American Baseline Essays* receiving a good portion of their attention. The science essay has been criticized most strongly. Although disputing some of these criticisms, Portland is currently having the essay revised. But the larger problem critics have with Afrocentrism is that it "reject[s] European civilization outright—or take[s] credit for it."[50] They argue that this rejection is based on poor scholarship. Davidson argues, for example, that Afrocentrists are too "sunk . . . in a blanket rejection of Western civilization" to be swayed by evidence.[51] Schlesinger refers to Afrocentric curricula as "myth" passed off as "fact."[52]

New York's curriculum is also attacked as intellectually weak, a "hatchet job on existing academic standards," as Paul Gray put it in *Time* magazine.[53] Similarly, multicultural courses in higher education are also criticized as lacking scholarship. Lewis Feuer, for example, regards the aim of cultural diversity in higher education as being "to entrench a place for the superficial and mediocre," advocating "ideological apologia for backward peoples";[54] D. P. Bryden describes professors who teach multicultural courses as "dumb."[55] The problem as conservatives see it is that such courses replace what they regard as the intellectually sound study of the Great Books.[56]

A fourth criticism from the conservative perspective is that multicultural education attacks the problem of minority students' underachievement by advocating exercises in self-esteem rather than hard work and by substituting "relevance" of subjects studied for instruction in solid academics. For example, several critics point out that writers of color such as Richard Wright, Ralph Ellison, and Chinua Achebe profited intellectually from their study of Western classics, and that minority students today who are offered an intellectually weak multicultural curriculum are not served well.[57] Ravitch faults "particularistic" multicultural education for tracing minority students' underachievement to lack of self-esteem and for proposing to correct that lack by replacing the study of Europeans with the study of the children's own ancestral group. She argues that this line of reasoning is faulty because it places children's identity "on another continent or in a vanished civilization" rather than in contemporary America and because it does not emphasize achieving success by working hard.[58] She asks whether it makes more sense to teach ancient African number systems rather than modern mathematics, suggesting that Afrocentrists' prescriptions for teaching African-American children are flawed by their interest in ancient African culture.[59] Bilingual education is also criticized as retarding language minority children in their acquisition of English and hence in their cultural assimilation.

The Criticisms Reexamined

The conservative or neonativist critics regard multicultural education as the work of a dangerous radical fringe group, and position themselves as spokespersons for Americans of color as well as for Americans in general. Herein lie serious weaknesses of their entire critique, as well as an affront to the underlying premise of multicultural education, namely, that it emerged as educators of color attempted to articulate their own concerns about schooling and that it is based on sound scholarship.

The critics ignore a great deal of the literature on multicultural education, as well as the supporting research and theory from fields such as anthropology and social psychology. For example, a major concern of educators of color is how to promote high achievement among students of color. One approach they have used to explore this concern has been to identify schools and/or teachers who are exceptionally successful with students of color and to find out what factors seem to account for their success. Such studies that have been reported in the literature are being synthesized for educators.[60] Research findings are consistent with multicultural education literature, emphasizing, for example, (1) the need for teachers to become familiar with students' community culture and build on that, (2) the need to build on students' language base rather than attempting to replace it, (3) the benefit to students of a culturally relevant curriculum, and (4) the academic value of teachers' viewing parents as a resource from whom teachers can learn. By framing such practices only as builders of "self-esteem," critics manufacture a straw person to tear down. None of the conservative critiques reviewed above mentioned any of the scholarly work supporting multicultural education; about half of the radical left critiques reviewed some of it. It is ironic that the conservative critics fault multicultural curricula for weak scholarship, but often display this very weakness in their own critiques.

However, the conservative and neonativist critics mask their disconnection with established multicultural scholarship including ethnic studies by name-dropping and drawing selectively on quotations by well-known scholars of color. By far most critics are white, although conservatives of color are also enjoying the public spotlight.[61] To position themselves as colleagues of Americans of color, many of the white conservatives sprinkle their writings with names such as W. E. B. Du Bois, Carter Woodson, Frederick Douglass, and James Comer who, they imply, agree with their viewpoints. Consider, for example, the following passage:

Multicultural history in its militant vein promotes fragmentation, segregation, ghettoization—all the more dangerous at a time when ethnic conflict is tearing apart one nation after another. James Baldwin once said, "To create one nation has proved to be a hideously difficult task; there is certainly no need now to create two, one black and one white."[62]

In this passage, Schlesinger implies that he and Baldwin share a common version of multicultural education. But they do not, and there is no suggestion in Baldwin's writings that he would support Schlesinger over advocates of multicultural education. Yet, by linking their arguments with quotations from prominent scholars of color, the conservative and neonativist critics suggest that those scholars agree with them.

In fact, one can marshall evidence that conservative criticisms and renderings of multicultural education contradict the interests and positions of a large spectrum of Americans of color. For example, Joyce King, who participated in the committee that created the California *Framework*, actively dissented from its defining of all Americans as immigrants and its transmutation of the problem of racism into a problem of assimilation and ethnic conflict. In a discussion of the politics surrounding California's curriculum, she notes that minority communities in several cities, including East Palo Alto, Hayward, Oakland, San Jose, San Francisco, Los Angeles, and Berkeley, objected to the curriculum. In order to probe the perspectives of the African-American communities, she convened meetings with parents from those communities and African-American multicultural education specialists. In the discussions that ensued, these groups found Sylvia Wynter's Black Studies perspective[63] to be more useful to their own understanding of race relations in the United States and the educational needs of African-American students than the perspective adopted by the California Education Department and the State Board.[64]

Conservative critics as well as most white mainstream educators differ from most scholars in multicultural education and in ethnic studies regarding the nature of racial inequality today, and how to address it. Conservatives (and many whites) tend to frame their understanding of race relations around a theory of ethnicity that is based on an analysis of the experience of European ethnic groups in the United States and mainly examines the extent to which groups retain distinct cultures while becoming structurally assimilated into the dominant society. As Omi and Winant argued in their review of theoretical perspectives for examining race in the United States, "ethnicity theory assigned to blacks and other racial minority groups the roles which earlier generations of European immigrants had played in the great waves of the Atlantic migration of the nineteenth and early twentieth centuries."[65]

In the California social sciences curriculum, all groups are presented as immigrants, retaining to various degrees different cultural customs and holidays, and the story of the United States is presented as one of progress in extending rights to all citizens. Even African Americans were immigrants, although they arrived in chains; slavery was an institution many societies practiced, and one that ended in the United States with the Civil War. Reconstruction is skipped over; African Americans are described as facing largely the same problems after the Civil War as other immigrants, including lingering prejudice and discrimination.

Ethnicity theory suggests that, over time, "successive" groups will assimilate; the process of assimilation is facilitated by focusing on commonalities among Americans; and there is no need to change institutional or political structures to accelerate this process. Thus, adherents to ethnicity theory tend to regard traditional school practices and curricula as well suited to the assimilation of diverse children. Further, the traditional curriculum's foundation in Western liberal thought enables any citizen to learn to transcend the limits of sociocultural context and participate in society objectively. As Schlesinger put it, the United States is a nation in which people "escape from origins" and go about "casting off the foreign skin."[66] From this perspective, any inequalities in the broad society will be corrected over time by adhering to tradition and continuing to expect schools to eradicate cultural differences among groups. White ethnics assimilated as did Jews; African Americans are to be next in line, followed by Mexicans and Asians.[67] The conservative or neonativist critiques of multicultural education are framed around discussion of unity versus difference, defining equality as equal rights of individuals before the law rather than as political and economic equality across groups. That perspective allows critics to regard racism as "a great national tragedy" in U.S. history that has been largely overcome: "The American synthesis has an inevitable Anglo-Saxon coloration, but it is no longer an exercise in Anglo-Saxon domination."[68]

While conservative critics seem to conceptualize ethnic and racial conflict as stemming from excessive group pride, multicultural education scholars conceptualize it as stemming largely from systemic racism and other forms of exclusion and domination. Conservatives may not regard data showing that white Americans enjoy the highest standard of living in the world while African Americans rank 31st[69] as evidence of "Anglo-Saxon domination," but Americans of color tend to see it as precisely that. Further, Americans of color increasingly voice frustration over the eroding conditions of life many have experienced over the past twelve years, as jobs have been exported, social services cut, funding for scholarships cut, and support for expressions of racism strengthened. Continuing to adhere to past traditions means, for example, continuing policies of land theft and Native American genocide, continuing to regard Mexican Americans chiefly as expendable "cheap labor," and continuing to divert economic resources away from African-American communities while regarding them as culturally and morally depraved.[70] To answer the question of how to elevate the collective status of groups and how those groups can gain more control over their own futures, ethnicity theory is helpful only to Euro-Americans; it fails to critique white racism and it presumes that time will take care of inequality.

Race- and nation-based theories conceptualize racism as an integral part of U.S. institutions and their origins in Europe's development and global expansion, as much a part of the present as the past.[71] While European immigrants were able to blend in, non-Europeans look visibly distinct and cannot melt (or "cast off the foreign skin") even if they wish to do so. In addition, non-European groups have experienced oppressive colonial relationships with Europe and the United States, which have brought about great disparities in wealth and power among races and well-ingrained racist theories that render such relationships legitimate. To understand the experiences of any given racial group, one must begin with that group, rather than adding that group's experience onto a narrative constructed around Euro-Americans.

The text *The African American Experience*,[72] for example, begins with Africans and documents struggles and achievements central to understanding the history and present status of African Americans in the United States. Portland's *African American Baseline Essays* specifically develops themes derived from a study of people of African descent, including a strong cultural connection between African civilizations, African Americans, and people of African descent worldwide, and the strengths of people of African descent in the face of continued oppression. According to race- and nation-based theories, history teaches us that the status of peoples of color will not be improved by attempting to assimilate with whites, by letting time take care of things, and by allowing the white majority to control their fate. Instead, collective advancement must continue to be a struggle in the face of persistent white resistance.

Conservative critics attempt to discredit much of multicultural education by depicting it as political and unscholarly, which they contrast with the study of Western classics. For example, Sandra Stotsky wrote: "One of the most contentious issues in education today is what the words 'multicultural education' mean and whether the content of such programs serves academic or political ends."[73] According to Western liberal thought, proper intellectual training can enable an individual to transcend personal vested interest in order to speak dispassionately for the whole society. This is an intellectual process, not a political one.

According to scholars in ethnic studies, women's studies, and cultural studies, however, Western liberal thought is not apolitical. Rather, it is tied to the experiences of a segment of humanity, and needs to be understood as such. No body of knowledge is universal and apolitical; there is no single perspective about anything. Once we understand the limitations and politics embedded within bodies of thought, we can appreciate the wisdom therein without limiting our inquiry to a single perspective. An intellectually rigorous multicultural curriculum teaches students to identify assumptions, perspectives, vested interests, and viewpoints within multiple bodies of thought.[74]

What about new immigrants who often do not line up behind established minority groups' perspectives? Indeed, many do enter the United States expecting to assimilate. But what is often ignored in discussions of new immigrants is that they are entering a society that is most definitely not colorblind, and that has a long history of complex racial dynamics. Those immigrants who are not from Europe—currently the great majority of immigrants—may not expect to become entangled in race relations, but over time they do so. For example, a colleague who is from Latin America and looks Hispanic or Indian to U.S. Anglos, came to the United States with no thought of being a "minority." However, over time many Anglo Americans have treated her as a minority (and often as uneducated). She has gradually redefined her own identity and her perception of race and ethnicity in the United States, so that her thinking has become increasingly congruent with that of "minority" Americans.[75]

Implications for Educators

This discussion has focused largely on curriculum controversies. Two central questions emerge: (1) In your own school or school district, how much serious dialog takes place among diverse sociocultural groups? (2) To what degree do those who have historically been disenfranchised have power to define education policies and practices, including curriculum?

The teaching profession continues to be predominantly white. This means that perspectives about education originating in any other sociocultural community and intimate knowledge of such communities are not often found within the corps of education professionals. I have observed that white educators tend to agree with conservative criticisms of multicultural education unless they work hard to learn alternate perspectives. Further, by regarding themselves as "experts" on educational issues and believing that their own education has helped them to view matters objectively, white professional educators often do not see much point in serious dialog and power sharing with minority communities. Instead, they make decisions about what multicultural education might mean by dialoging with each other and drawing very selectively from the literature in that field.

Educators must begin by learning to listen to and learn from the students and their parents. They must also learn about the community from which the students come. This means inviting dialog and listening nondefensively. Sometimes students may say that they prefer group work to individual worksheets in situations where the teacher also sees cooperative learning as feasible and desirable. At other times, however, a teacher's ideas may be challenged, which can require painful self-examination or much follow-up learning. For example, an African-American high school student recently tried to explain to a white teacher that she was tired of reading white literature and wanted to read African-American literature. The teacher had difficulty understanding why and conceptualizing an alternative curriculum. Instead, she tended to dismiss the student as oversensitive. If the teacher were to listen to and take seriously the student's viewpoint, and also to listen to other African Americans discuss the same issue, she would begin to see a different perspective.

Luis Moll and his colleagues at the University of Arizona have developed a project called "funds-of-knowledge," in which teachers are trained to conduct extensive interviews with parents of their students in order to situate teachers as learners in a different sociocultural community from their own. Teachers arrange at least three visits in the home of at least one student. The main purpose of the visits is to enable the teacher to discover areas of knowledge the parents have in order to develop authentic collaboration in the construction of teaching that bridges cultures.[76] This kind of project is useful to teachers of any racial or ethnic background. My preservice students who complete a project that is similar to, although less extensive than, Moll's, seem to learn to "tune in to" a different perspective.

Educators should make a point of systematically reading professional literature by scholars of color, addressing specific questions such as the following: What kinds of practices have helped students of color learn mathematics successfully? Why do Latino educators usually insist that bilingual education is necessary and that it does not retard acquisition of English? Why do many Indian educators believe Indian children fare better in tribally controlled schools than in mainstream white schools? Reading professional literature does not substitute for dialog with people of color in one's own community, but it helps develop depth and support for what lay people know from their own experience.

Developing a multicultural school is a process of reconstructing relationships rather than adopting a program or a product. One school that illustrates this process is La Escuela Fratney in Milwaukee, an example of excellent multicultural education in action. It was established in 1988 through a grassroots effort, and the school has an active collaborative relationship with parents. The school's basic philosophy advocates high-quality multicultural, antiracist education; it offers a two-way Spanish-English bilingual program. The teachers create a good deal of the curriculum, which is oriented around helping children learn to examine issues from multiple points of view.[77]

Engaging in listening, learning, and dialog can help move educators beyond simplistic conceptions of multicultural education or tugs of war over "political correctness," and toward the creation of school practices that better serve a diverse society that has yet to eliminate racism, sexism, and institutionalized poverty.

I am very grateful to Joyce E. King and Ellen Swartz for their helpful and insightful comments on an earlier draft of this chapter.

NOTES

1. James A. Banks, *Multiethnic Education: Theory and Practice*, 2d ed. (Boston: Allyn and Bacon, 1988); Geneva Gay, "Multiethnic Education: Historical Developments and Future Prospects," *Phi Delta Kappan* 64 (1983): 560-563.

2. Banks, *Multiethnic Education: Theory and Practice*, pp. 30-31.

3. James A. Banks, "African American Scholarship and the Evolution of Multicultural Education," *Journal of Negro Education* 61, no. 3 (1992): 279.

4. James A. Banks, "Multicultural Education: Characteristics and Goals," in *Multicultural Education: Issues and Perspectives*, edited by James A. Banks and Cherry A. McGee Banks (Boston: Allyn and Bacon, 1989), p. 23.

5. Carl A. Grant, "Education That Is Multicultural: Isn't That What We Mean?" *Journal of Teacher Education* 29, no. 5 (1978): 45-48.

6. Jeannie Oakes, *Keeping Track* (New Haven, CT: Yale University Press, 1985).

7. Ray C. Rist, *The Invisible Children* (Cambridge, MA: Harvard University Press, 1978).

8. Carl A. Grant and Christine E. Sleeter, *After the School Bell Rings* (London: Falmer Press, 1986).

9. Susan U. Phillips, *The Invisible Culture* (New York: Longman, 1983).

10. See, for example, Shirley Brice Heath, *Ways with Words* (New York: Cambridge University Press, 1983); Luis Moll, "Bilingual Classroom Studies and Community Analysis: Some Recent Trends," *Educational Researcher* 21, no. 2 (1992): 20-24; Marietta Saravia-Shore and Steven F. Arvizu, eds., *Cross-Cultural Literacy* (New York: Garland, 1992); Barbara J. R. Shade, *Culture, Style, and the Educative Process* (Springfield, IL: Charles C. Thomas, 1989).

11. See, for example, Rodolfo Acuña, *Occupied America* (New York: Harper and Row, 1988); Paula Gunn Allen, *The Sacred Hoop* (Boston: Beacon Press, 1986); Molefi Kete Asante, *Kemet, Afrocentricity and Knowledge* (Trenton, NJ: Africa World Press, 1990); Paul Lauter, *Canons and Contexts* (New York: Oxford University Press, 1991).

12. Geneva Gay, "Curriculum Theory and Development in Multicultural Education," in *Handbook of Research on Multicultural Education*, edited by James A. Banks and Cherry A. McGee Banks (New York: Macmillan, forthcoming).

13. Geneva Gay, "Effective Teaching Practices for Multicultural Classrooms," in *Multicultural Education for the 21st Century*, edited by Carlos F. Diaz (Washington, DC: National Education Association, 1992), pp. 38-56.

14. Christine E. Sleeter and Carl A. Grant, *Making Choices for Multicultural Education*, 2d ed. (Columbus, OH: Merrill, 1994).

15. Christine E. Sleeter, *Keepers of the American Dream* (London: Falmer Press, 1992).

16. Derrick Bell, *Faces at the Bottom of the Well* (New York: Basic Books, 1992); Susan Faludi, *Backlash: The Undeclared War against American Women* (New York: Doubleday, 1991); Andrew Hacker, *Two Nations* (New York: Charles Scribner's Sons, 1992).

17. For development of this argument, see Noam Chomsky, "Domestic Policy: Change of Business as Usual," *Z Magazine* 6, no. 2 (1993): 30-42; Mahmut Mutman, "Under the Sign of Orientalism: The West vs. Islam," *Cultural Critique* 23 (1992-93): 165-198; Holly Sklar, "Crosscurrents: Young and Guilt by Stereotype," *Z Magazine* 6, no. 7/8 (1993): 52-61.

18. Ellen Swartz, "Cultural Diversity and the School Curriculum: Content and Practice," *Journal of Curriculum Theorizing* 9, no. 4 (1992): 73-88.

19. Sharon Harley, Stephen Middleton, and Charlotte M. Stokes, *The African American Experience: A History* (Englewood Cliffs, NJ: Globe, 1992).

20. *African American Literature* (Austin: Holt, Rinehart and Winston and Harcourt Brace Jovanovich, 1992).

21. Alan C. Purves, ed., *Tapestry: A Multicultural Anthology* (Paramus, NJ: Globe Book Co., 1993); Charles Tatum, ed., *Mexican American Literature* (New York: Harcourt Brace Jovanovich, 1990).

22. Louise Derman Sparks, *The Anti-Bias Curriculum* (Washington, DC: National Association for the Education of Young Children, 1989); Nancy Schniedewind and Ellen Davidson, *Open Minds to Equality* (Boston: Allyn and Bacon, 1983).

23. Catherine Cornbleth and Dexter Waugh, "The Great Speckled Bird: Education Policy-in-the-Making," *Educational Researcher* 22, no. 7 (1993): 31.

24. Catherine Cornbleth and Dexter Waugh, *The Great Speckled Bird: Multicultural Politics and Education Policymaking* (New York: St. Martin's Press, forthcoming).

25. History-Social Science Curriculum Framework and Criteria Committee, *History-Social Science Framework* (Sacramento: California Department of Education, 1988). The textbook series that was adopted is Beverly J. Armento, Gary B. Nash, Christopher L. Salter, and Karen K. Wixson, *Some People I Know, Across the Centuries*, and *America Will Be* (Boston: Houghton Mifflin, 1991).

26. Cornbleth and Waugh, "The Great Speckled Bird," p. 32.

27. Armento, Salter, and Wixson, *America Will Be*.

28. Cornbleth and Waugh, "The Great Speckled Bird," p. 33.

29. Joyce E. King, "Diaspora Literacy and Consciousness in the Struggle against Miseducation in the Black Community," *Journal of Negro Education* 61, no. 3 (1992), p. 322.

30. Cornbleth and Waugh, "The Great Speckled Bird."

31. Task Force on Minorities, *A Curriculum of Inclusion* (New York: New York State Education Department, 1989).

32. Leslie Agard-Jones, "Implementing Multicultural Education: The New York City Experience," *Multicultural Education* 1, no. 1 (1993): 13-15+.

33. The conference was held in Albany, New York, on January 9, 1990. The theme was "Winds of Change: A Forum on Multicultural Education."

34. Christine E. Sleeter and Carl A. Grant, "Race, Class, Gender, and Disability in Current Textbooks," in *The Politics of the Textbook*, edited by Michael W. Apple and Linda K. Christian-Smith (New York: Routledge, 1991), pp. 78-110.

35. Social Studies Review and Development Committee, *One Nation, Many Peoples: A Declaration of Cultural Interdependence* (Albany: New York State Education Department, June 1991).

36. Cornbleth and Waugh, "The Great Speckled Bird," p. 35.

37. New York City Public Schools, *United States and New York State History: A Multicultural Perspective* (New York: Board of Education of the City of New York, 1990).

38. *African American Baseline Essays* (Portland, OR: Portland Public Schools, 1989).

39. Molefi Kete Asante, *The Afrocentric Idea* (Philadelphia: Temple University Press, 1987), p. 6.

40. Christine E. Sleeter, "An Analysis of the Critiques of Multicultural Education," in *Handbook of Research on Multicultural Education*, edited by James A. Banks and Cherry A. Banks (New York: Macmillan, forthcoming).

41. Michael Olneck, "The Recurring Dream: Symbolism and Ideology in Intercultural and Multicultural Education," *American Journal of Education* 98, no. 2 (1990): 147-174.

42. Cornbleth and Waugh, "The Great Speckled Bird," pp. 31-32.

43. John Leo, "Multicultural Follies," *U.S. News and World Report* 111, no. 2 (1991): 12.

44. Arthur M. Schlesinger, Jr., *The Disuniting of America* (New York: Norton, 1992), p. 10.

45. Dinesh D'Souza, *Illiberal Education: The Politics of Race and Sex on Campus* (New York: Free Press, 1991).

46. Alan C. Bloom, *The Closing of the American Mind* (New York: Simon and Schuster, 1989), p. 27.

47. Schlesinger, *The Disuniting of America*, p. 127.

48. Diane Ravitch, "Multiculturalism: E Pluribus Plures," *American Scholar* 59, no. 3 (1990): 337-354.

49. Leo, "Multicultural Follies."

50. Nicholas Davidson, "Was Socrates a Plagiarist?" *National Review* 43, no. 3 (1991): 45.

51. Ibid., p. 46.

52. Arthur M. Schlesinger, Jr., "The Disuniting of America: What We All Stand to Lose if Multicultural Education Takes the Wrong Approach," *American Educator* 15, no. 3 (1991): 28.

53. Paul Gray, "Whose America?" *Time* 138, no. 1 (1991): 13.

54. Lewis Feuer, "From Pluralism to Multiculturalism," *Society* 29, no. 1 (1991): 21-22.

55. D. P. Bryden, "It Ain't What They Teach, It's the Way That They Teach It," *Public Interest* 103 (1991): 46.

56. D'Souza, *Illiberal Education*; Irving Howe, "The Content of the Curriculum: Two Views: The Value of the Canon," *Liberal Education* 77, no. 3 (1991): 8-9.

57. Schlesinger, *The Disuniting of America*; Howe, "The Content of the Curriculum."

58. Diane Ravitch, "Diversity and Democracy: Multicultural Education in America," *American Educator* 14, no. 1 (1990): 47.

59. Ravitch, "Multiculturalism: E Pluribus Plures."

60. For syntheses of research, see Etta Ruth Hollins, Joyce E. King, and Warren Hayman, eds., *Teaching Diverse Populations: Formulating a Knowledge Base* (Albany: State University of New York Press, 1994); Beverly McLeod, ed., *Language and Learning: Educating Linguistically Diverse Students* (Albany: State University of New York Press, 1994).

61. Dinesh D'Souza is an immigrant from India. Other conservatives of color who do not support multicultural education include Linda Chavez, *Out of the Barrio: Toward a New Politics of Hispanic Assimilation* (New York: Basic Books, 1991); Richard Rodriguez, *Hunger of Memory* (Boston: D. Godine, 1981); Shelby Steele, *The Content of Our Character* (New York: St. Martin's Press, 1990); Thomas Sowell, *Inside American Education* (New York: Free Press, 1993).

62. Arthur M. Schlesinger, Jr., "Writing, and Rewriting History," *New Leader* (December, 1991): 14.

63. Sylvia Wynter, *Do Not Call Us Negroes: How Multicultural Textbooks Perpetuate Racism* (San Jose, CA: Aspire Books, 1992). Wynter's perspective can be described as "a cultural model or epistemology with the potential for transmuting knowledge by challenging the 'prescriptive rules' of the American 'public culture,' which over the centuries have rigidly maintained racial harmony." Cornbleth and Waugh, *The Great Speckled Bird*.

64. King, "Diaspora Literacy and Consciousness in the Struggle against Miseducation in the Black Community."

65. Michael Omi and Howard Winant, *Racial Formation in the United States* (New York: Routledge and Kegan Paul, 1986), p. 20.

66. Schlesinger, *The Disuniting of America*, pp. 15, 112.

67. Joyce E. King, Personal communication, June 14, 1993.

68. Schlesinger, *The Disuniting of America*, pp. 19, 48.

69. Robin Wright, "Living Standard in U.S. Diverse: U.N.," *Kenosha (Wis.) News* 16 May 1993.

70. Ward Churchill, *Struggle for the Land* (Monroe, ME: Common Courage Press, 1993); Acuña, *Occupied America*.

71. Acuña, *Occupied America*; Bell, *Faces at the Bottom of the Well*; Ward Churchill, *Fantasies of the Master Race* (Monroe, ME: Common Courage Press, 1992); Omi and Winant, *Racial Formation in the United States*.

72. Harley, Middleton, and Stokes, *The African-American Experience*.

73. Sandra Stotsky, "Cultural Politics," *American School Board Journal* 178, no. 10 (1991): 26.

74. James A. Banks, "The Canon Debate, Knowledge Construction, and Multicultural Education," *Educational Researcher* 22, no. 5 (1993): 4-14.

75. Carmen Montecinos, "Multicultural Education That Is Social Reconstructionist: What Should Teachers Know?" in *Multicultural Education and Critical Pedagogy*, edited by Christine E. Sleeter and Peter McLaren (Albany: State University of New York Press, forthcoming).

76. Luis C. Moll, "Bilingual Classroom Studies and Community Analysis."

77. Priscilla Ahlgren, "La Escuela Fratney," *Teaching Tolerance* 2, no. 2 (1993): 26-31.

Introduction to Chapter XI

In the following chapter, Elliot Eisner explains why the humanities, including the arts, do not have a significant place in the curriculum in elementary and secondary schools in the United States. He then makes a compelling case, not only for the inclusion of subjects normally associated with the humanities but also for examining the possibility that even subjects outside the arena of the humanities (e.g., physics, chemistry) could be taught in a "humanistic" way.

We include Professor Eisner's chapter in this volume not simply to provide a platform for an advocate for the humanities, although there is nothing wrong with that. We also see his essay as giving further meaning to a theme that occurs elsewhere in this volume. He shows that a curricular change *that brings humanistic subjects to a more prominent place in the school will be of little consequence unless there is a corresponding* pedagogical *change that features humanistic teaching and learning. In this respect, Eisner points to the need for what amounts to a change in the "culture" of the school.*

Like others in this volume, he does not underestimate the difficulty of effecting such a change.

Elliot Eisner is Professor of Education and Art at Stanford University. This chapter first appeared in the Society's 83rd Yearbook, Part 2, The Humanities in Precollegiate Education, *edited by Benjamin Ladner.*

CHAPTER XI

Can the Humanities Be Taught in American Public Schools?

ELLIOT W. EISNER

The Context of Humanities Education

The saliency of the humanities in American schools is extremely low. The reasons are not particularly difficult to discern. In the first place, American schools embrace, whether they know it or not, a positivistic attitude toward education. This attitude looks with suspicion on forms of understanding that rely upon judgment, intuition, metaphor, and other nonquantitative and hence "imprecise" forms of disclosure. The humanities as typified by literature, history, and ethics are hard pressed to employ the kind of criteria that a positivist view of knowledge requires. In education we tend to get nervous about making decisions that depend upon judgments, preferring to rely upon those procedures that lead to "certain" answers. Ambiguity has never been a load that Americans have liked to carry. We have little tolerance for it in political leaders, but even less in education.

Second, American schools, especially at present, are preoccupied with the achievement of prespecified outcomes. This is not a new phenomenon but it has been exacerbated in recent years by the accountability movement in education. What this means for curriculum and for classroom practice is that the character of the journey is less important than arriving at the destination on time. Measured payoff in relation to conventionally defined competencies is the current theme song among educators; hence talk about so evanescent, ineffable, and difficult-to-measure outcomes as those achieved through humanistic studies receives less than an enthusiastic welcome. When one believes one has an angry or anxious public barking down one's neck, measured outcomes on noncontroversial skills appear much more sensible.

Third, American educators are influenced by a practical public which often finds it difficult to understand why so impractical a body of studies as the humanities should be given serious attention in the public schools. Given the high rate of unemployment, the widespread concern about basic skills, and the pressure to get rid of the frills, studies that seem to lead to few vocational outcomes and which, in any case, one cannot confidently evaluate are not given high priority.

Fourth, and related to the foregoing, is the educator's concern with time. In American culture, time is treated as a commodity. It is something we buy and sell. Given the pressure upon teachers to get students to perform up to standard, time cannot be squandered on what is not truly of importance. While time for physics, chemistry, biology, and calculus is seldom questioned, the same cannot be said for humanistic studies.

Fifth, most Americans still harbor the illusion that schooling is or should be a value-free enterprise. The humanities are riddled with values. They deal with issues that are controversial; they expose students to ideas and that might encourage them to become critical of the values that their families and community embrace. Hence, a course that deals with values, such as *Man: A Course of Study*, is first proscribed in Arizona and later has its funding cut by the Congress of the United States. What the public seems to want is a form of schooling that is designed to teach children to think, but not to become critical of the status quo. The humanities, dealing as they do with values rather than facts (in the eyes of the public at least), are troublesome in this regard.

Finally, the humanities as a general field has no effective professional constituency. Teachers of each of the fields or disciplines that typically constitute the humanities owe their allegiance to their own disciplines; hence, seldom are their common aims and the means appropriate for achieving them considered. In fact, given tight budgets and reduced time, the members of this humanistic family of fields often compete with each other for the few scraps that are left after the really important subjects are assigned time and resources.

The point of the foregoing narrative is not to depress the reader but to avoid engendering the illusion that because a yearbook of the

National Society for the Study of Education is devoted to the humanities in American schools, the humanities occupy a place having curricular significance in the schools or that light is soon to be found at
the end of the tunnel. I do not believe that this is the case; your eye-
sight may be keener than mine, but I see no light yet. In fact, I believe
that the pressures I have described have led to a deterioration of the
quality of schooling—and I do not mean a deterioration of test scores.
On the contrary, pressure to increase test scores *could* contribute to a
further decline in the quality of education *if* higher test scores are
secured at the cost of neglecting the very mental skills and curriculum
content that the humanities require. A public anxious about test scores
and a body of school administrators concerned about their jobs do not
augur well for programs that give flight to the spirit. We are still very
much on a "back-to-basics" kick in American education.

Humanities Education

So much for context. What is it that the humanities provide in
education?

To raise this question implies that we desire but frequently do not
have a positive conception of the humanities. For example, the National
Endowment for the Humanities lists the following as constituting the
humanities: history, ethics, law, philosophy, linguistics, archeology,
literature. . . .[1] It does not include the arts in its list. Nor does it provide
a discussion of the criteria used to select those particular fields and not
others. One might say we have in the National Endowment for the
Humanities an ostensive definition. Yet our mind yearns for something
more. We want to know what essential properties, if any, constitute
fields such as these and we want to know why the arts are excluded. We
want more than a list of fields; we want a principle that sheds light upon
them and that helps us rationalize the distinctions we make.

But because we are educators, we want not only to know what
counts as a humanistic study; we want also to know about the
distinctive educational import of humanistic studies. Indeed, if such
studies have no distinctive educational import, identifying the essential
properties of the humanities is of little use. It would be both arrogant
and foolish for me to write about the humanities as though no one had
given any thought to the subject prior to my writing. The variety of
conceptions of the humanities are as diverse as the disciplines and fields

of study that are said to constitute them. Yet, the various conceptions that have been advanced do share certain common qualities. First, there is a shared agreement that humanistic studies shed light on what it means to be a human being. While the natural sciences focus on the operations of the natural world, the humanities have something important to say about the cultural world so that through the study of the humanities one learns about man. Even more important, the student of the humanities learns something significant about himself. For example, Shakespeare's *Othello* has much to say about jealousy as experienced by its central character, but it says much more than that; it tells us about jealousy in general and it helps the competent reader understand through feeling what jealousy means in his or her own life. Somehow *Othello* becomes a vehicle, to be sure to be enjoyed in its own right, but also to help us reflect on our feelings of jealousy and on the frailties that all humans share.

The second function of the humanities that most conceptions of them describe is the contribution humanistic learning makes to our powers of critical appraisal. In some ways this is a necessary offshoot of the nature of humanistic content. We have not devised a way to determine within small errors of measurement the intellectual or aesthetic value of humanistic scholarship or of works of art. There is no scale, no yardstick, no measure that can be applied to such works to determine the value of what we encounter. Such judgments in the humanities require attention and sensitivity to nuance; they require appreciation for context; they require the ability to deliberate and judge. These processes are utterly fallible; they are swayed by argument, moved by rhetoric, and altered as time changes. It is precisely these features that make human judgment acute. Where an infallible yardstick exists, judgment is unnecessary. Participation in the questions that humanists ask requires one to sharpen one's critical sense. Upon this too there is consensus.

Attempting to encapsulate the defining features of the humanities, the Commission on the Humanities writes:

The essence of the humanities is a spirit or an attitude toward humanity. They show how the individual is autonomous and at the same time bound, in the ligatures of language and history, to humankind across time and throughout the world. The humanities are an important measure of the values and aspirations of any society. Intensity and breadth in the perception of life and power and richness in works of the imagination betoken a people alive as moral and aesthetic beings, citizens in the fullest sense. They base their education on sustaining principles of personal enrichment and civic responsibility. They are sensitive to beauty and aware of their cultural heritage. They can approach questions of value, no matter how complex, with intelligence and goodwill. They can use their scientific and technical achievements responsibly because they see the connections among science, technology, and humanity.[2]

Such an accolade might be faulted for what it fails to omit. Yet, its general thrust is consistent with the views of those who have attempted to provide a conception of the humanities. For some readers conceptions such as the foregoing may seem imprecise, too global, leaving too much to matters of taste and judgment. Yet would it not be peculiar to provide a definition or conception of a field whose very characteristics controverted the properties that it was designed to define? Definitions of the humanities are "imprecise" precisely because they are in keeping with what humanists do. They are definitions that invite deliberation, argument, counterpoint. It seems unreasonable to seek precise definitions in a field in which the drawing of precise lines is an anathema.[3]

I concur with the spirit of the Commission's efforts to say what the humanities are. Humanists regard knowledge as fallible, believe that no single method has a monopoly upon inquiry, believe that the fundamental human questions are ineluctably enduring and that over the course of human history some extraordinary human beings have made some remarkable efforts to answer those questions. Humanists place premium on the human's ability to be critically rational, that is, to reason deeply and sensitively about important human matters. And they believe that a dialectical engagement with the works of the humanities helps man not only to view the world in useful, illuminating ways, but also helps man learn something about himself.

How is it that one learns about oneself through the humanities? Consider first an example from music, and then one from literature. In the fifth movement of his Ninth Symphony, Beethoven slowly begins to build a pattern of rhythms that gain increasing momentum. This rhythmic sequence appears to crescendo when it is made to retreat to a more modulated dynamic range and then made to crescendo again. Moving toward still another crescendo, Beethoven suddenly introduces an unexpected cacophony that is immediately followed by a baritone voice singing the lines from Schiller's "Ode to Joy." The poem becomes the lyrics of a moving melodic theme that builds to a perfect finale within a huge symphonic score. By the time one reaches the coda, the dynamics, the rhythm, and the melodic line of this movement bring the listener rising to his feet. Feelings are experienced that one could not know prior to hearing the symphony. The musical forms that Beethoven creates reveal to the competent listener a new source of personal discovery. It is by virtue of the music that one aspect of the self and its capacity to respond is known.

In Arthur Miller's play, *Death of a Salesman*, Willy Loman, a middle-aged, ne'er-do-well salesman, creates a world of self-deception through which he avoids the reality of a declining career and of recognizing that his two sons are not what he wants them so desperately to be. It is only when he is confronted by the loss of his job, which was the hub of his life, and by pleas from his son, Bif, to see Bif as he really is, that reality breaks through.

Miller's play is a powerful vehicle that sheds light on the human tendency to bypass reality and to substitute for it a fantasy or a dreamlife that is often unproductive and unsatisfying. While few of us are as immersed in a private, illusory world as is Willy Loman, all of us share aspects of his life. Through Miller's work we are able to discover those aspects. We come to recognize some of our own weakness and come to share an affinity with Willy Loman. By distilling a human weakness and giving it a vivid presence, Miller affords us a means for discovering what we might not otherwise see in ourselves.

These contributions to self-discovery are, of course, indirect. The humanities do not aim at psychotherapy. Furthermore, to recognize oneself in the content that the humanities provide requires one to be able to read their messages; great humanistic works require great audiences. Yet the fact that such contributions are indirect does not diminish their significance. The humanities are both a lamp and a mirror. While neither a lamp nor a mirror guarantees insight, they do help make sight possible.

If we use as one defining characteristic of the humanities the capacity of a work to help us understand the nature of human nature, it seems to me that there is no field or discipline that could not be treated in a way that is humanistic in character. Physics and chemistry are normally not taught or thought of as being a part of the humanities, yet one could easily imagine how physics and chemistry, when put into historical context and treated as examples of intellectual history, could become humanistic studies. What do Kepler's epicycles tell us about Kepler and the times in which he lived?[4] What does the race of Watson and Crick with Pauling tell us about the role of human motivation and competition in scientific inquiry?[5] What moral obligations, if any, does a scientist have with respect to the uses of the ideas he or she creates? Such questions broaden the context of scientific understanding and give it a cast that is thoroughly humanistic in flavor. My point here is that even disciplines that appear to be outside the arena of the humanities can be placed within them if the focus and the approach to learning is humanistic in character.

The Arts and the Humanities

What about the arts? What claim, if any, can they make to being a part of the humanistic tradition rather than distinct from the humanities? There are, of course, traditional separations that have been made between the arts and the humanities. For example, the Commission on the Humanities writes:

Whether defined by questions, methods, or fields, the humanities employ a particular medium and turn of mind. The medium is language. Discourse sets in motion and supports reflection and judgment. The humanities have close ties not only with speech but especially with writing and the thought processes writing makes possible. Study in the humanistic disciplines is not limited to texts—oral cultures have reflected deeply on human experience and have achieved great wisdom—but it cannot proceed without creating and using texts.[6]

From a political perspective as well, the humanities have been separated from the arts. Congress saw fit to create two endowments: the National Endowment for the Arts and the National Endowment for the Humanities. On our own university campuses we often distinguish between the arts faculty and the humanities faculty, or the arts *and* humanities faculty and the science faculty. Tradition seems to lead politics, and the distinction, rarely defined, is built into our language and our way of doing business.

I have no trouble with such distinctions as long as one does not take them too seriously. If the distinction between humanistic and artistic work is simply a carry-over from an ancient legacy, and if such legacies make people comfortable, okay. But if the distinction implies a difference in social or intellectual status or in our conception of the source of the work—for example, intelligence as contrasted with talent—then the distinction is mischievous, or worse, misleading, and should be abandoned.[7]

The use of language, which appears to be crucial to the Commission, must be treated just as qualitatively or artistically in writing poetry and literature as a composer must treat sound, or a painter space and form. As for the idea that a humanistic work conveys ideas while the arts convey feeling, that distinction simply will not hold water. Works of visual art have as much to say about man and his world as any writer can convey or any historian can describe. The paintings of Francis Bacon and Georgio De Chirico, the sculpture of Marcel Duchamp, the drawings of Daumier, the music of Stravinsky, Wagner, Mahler, and Schoenberg are riddled with ideas about man, music, and the world. Hence, from a substantive point of view I can find no sound basis for distinguishing between the arts and the humanities when one focuses upon either their aims or their achievements. Both the works we call the humanities and those we call the arts are artifacts, man-made constructions, the off-spring of the human imagination, and they reveal aspects of the world in ways that are *sui generis* to their form. The works created within each of these historically inherited categories are achievements of the mind, produced by people of genius and are there to enhance the lives of those who can "read" them.

The Mission of Schools and Colleges for Teaching Humanities

It is precisely in the realm of helping students learn to read the arts and the humanities that the school has one of its most important but most neglected missions. I have already alluded to some of the factors that have militated against the teaching of the arts and the humanities in the schools. If one were really skeptical, one might seriously question whether the arts and the humanities can be taught in the majority of schools in the nation. Such skepticism has been expressed by those social theorists who see the school as an institution designed— intentionally or not—to sustain the inequities that currently exist in our society.[8] They claim that schools merely echo the messages of the larger social order and are used to prepare people who will be willing workers within an economic system that places little value on what is most precious about human beings—their capacity to use their rationality and to exercise free will. They claim that schools militate against the development of such competencies by enveloping students in an organizational structure that allows primarily for one-way communication, from the top down, and that makes horizontal communication difficult. Furthermore, the schools are said to emphasize a sociology of knowledge or a knowledge hierarchy that places a premium on being able to follow prescribed rules in order to arrive at known ends. In sum, these and other features of schooling produce what one writer calls a type of structural violence.[9] Such violence, he claims, is not direct, it is indirect; it pervades the culture of schooling silently, and therefore is even more insidious than if it were blatant, since in silence the aggressor is even more difficult to identify.

When one adds to such analyses the fact that most college graduates choosing teaching as a career come from the bottom quarter of the college graduating class, the prospects for teaching subjects in a manner consistent with the humane become even more problematic.[10] Unlike teaching simple arithmetic, punctuation, spelling, and the rules of grammar, the arts and the humanities demand attention to nuance; they place a premium on deliberation; they ask students not only to cope with ambiguity and uncertainty, but to enjoy them. Can teachers who are likely to be among the least able intellectually and who work in an environment in which the arts and humanities are regarded as marginal, create the kind of classrooms and provide the kind of curriculum that will truly be in harmony with the spirit of the arts and humanities? Put another way, can teachers who themselves have little understanding of what the humanities are and do, help the young learn to appreciate them?

From my point of view the likelihood of achieving such goals is dim—*unless* there is a turnaround in what universities emphasize and a change in the public's view of the mission of the school.

I indicated above that those currently entering the teaching profession are among the least intellectually able of their cohorts. According to the best data available these are the facts. But I would be only marginally more sanguine about the humanities in the schools if it were those in the first rather than in the fourth quartile who were entering the teaching profession. This is due to the fact that regardless of the intellectual level of prospective teachers, university programs, like programs in elementary and secondary schools, are not characterized by a deep commitment to the spirit of the arts and humanities. Most colleges and universities are essentially extensions of secondary education; they have a wider curriculum, to be sure, but they provide the same climate of expectations for students. As a result, note-taking and "cramming" by students sitting in large lectures has unfortunately become characteristic. In research-oriented universities the premium paid to good teaching is small, and in land-grant universities that have no clear research orientation, the size of classes, except in the most exotic of specializations, makes the kind of deliberation and critical analysis characteristic of humanistic inquiry all but impossible to achieve. When accompanied by a preoccupation among students with grade-getting and careerism, it matters less than it would otherwise who elects to go into education as a career. In addition, the impact of misguided but well-intentioned missives from prestigious private universities to American secondary schools is difficult to underestimate. Most such prestigious institutions are unhappy with the quality of their entering freshmen; they complain about their lack of adequate preparation and decry what has come to be called "grade inflation." Yet the solutions that they prescribe—tougher standards, harder courses, more homework—are almost always prescribed without a shred of philosophical context or empirical justification. The quick-fix, get-tough policy they prescribe is so denuded of theory that those same academics would raise the roof if similar nostrums were prescribed by others for the improvement of teaching in their own fields. The recommendations for educational improvement that have appeared have, on the whole, been contrary to the spirit that I believe resides at the heart of humanistic learning. Indeed, if one were to cast blame for some of the weaknesses of American primary and secondary schools, I would want to lay some of that blame on the doorstep of the university.

New Dimensions of Schooling for Humanistic Learning

Yet I am not willing to give up the aspiration to create schools whose programs and whose climate are humane in spirit. Education is, after all, an optimistic enterprise. What would it take to create schools in which humanistic learning could flourish? The answer to that question leads us to the major dimensions of schooling that would need to be changed if such an aim were to be achieved. These dimensions include (a) the character of the curriculum, (b) the structure or organization of school, (c) the competencies of the teacher, and (d) the conduct of evaluation programs. It is on these dimensions that I will focus in the remainder of this chapter. In focusing upon these dimensions of schooling I do not claim that they exhaust all of the dimensions that could be considered. Nevertheless, the ones I have identified, to my way of thinking, are the most important. One other caveat. Although I have distinguished among these dimensions for analytic purposes, in fact, these dimensions are intertwined: what is taught, at base, cannot be separated from how something is taught; the curriculum and the organizational structure of the school shape each other.

THE CHARACTER OF THE CURRICULUM

As far as the curriculum is concerned, I have already indicated that any subject, if treated as an aspect of man's intellectual history and taught in a spirit of deliberation, would be a humanistic study. The sciences, which are most often contrasted with the arts and the humanities, could be taught in a way that illuminates man's struggle to understand nature; they could be taught as a human quest characterized by all of the foibles that humans possess—self-doubt, jealousy, ambition, weakness; they could be taught for their moral implications. The sciences could be taught with special attention to the public status of their processes and claims, to the social burdens of some of their conclusions, and they could be taught with an eye to the responsibilities of the public to the scientist and to the social conditions that make scientific inquiry possible. The point here is that even those areas of the curriculum that appear most remote from the humanities could be studied for their humanistic potential.

Yet, notwithstanding this potential, insofar as the humanities shed light on what is most human about man, there are studies that take that subject matter as their major focus. Perhaps nowhere is this more vivid than in literature, drama, and poetry. The world of literature is replete with material that helps the competent reader to participate empathetically in the lives of others, and through such participation to know what cannot be known directly. Literature does this not only through the topics or themes writers choose to attend to, but because of the way in which its characters are revealed, the atmosphere that is created, the plot that is made to unfold, the way in which a theme is embedded within the story. These devices make literature and drama powerful modes of psychological transportation. The book, as vehicle, can be an escape from "reality" or a means of access to it; it can lead one away from significant human issues or it can present them vividly to our consciousness. What we regard as great books written by great writers emphasize the significant, not the trivial. They help us see more clearly the world in which we live. They do not lead us away from that world. Even *Alice in Wonderland* is referenced to humankind.

STRUCTURE AND ORGANIZATION

If students are to have access to such works, at least two conditions must be present. First, students must be sufficiently skilled in reading to find such works meaningful. Second, opportunities for reading and discussing such works must be available. As far as the former is concerned, reading skills are not wholly independent of subject matter. If students are to develop the skills needed to read literature, they need opportunities to read literature. The idea that students can develop such skills on nonliterary material and then apply them to literature or poetry underestimates the extent to which different written forms make different intellectual demands upon students. The acquisition of reading skills and the content to be read are not independent activities. With respect to the school curriculum, this implies that a program of study be defined in which a significant array of humanistic literature, including poetry, be available as an ongoing part of the school day, that such material be selected so as to be compatible with the existing reading competencies of students, and that such material serve as the basis for discussion.

The importance of discussion in helping students—even young students—penetrate the surface of what they have read should not be underestimated. Reading need not be a solitary activity. Common reading and the encouragement of diverse but relevant interpretations and implications of what has been read are of paramount importance for eliciting the full educational value of reading and for illuminating what is significant but subtle in the work. Discussion has become a dying art in our culture, despite the fact that when it goes well it is a stunning example of the capacities of the mind. Novels, poetry, works of visual art and music, these can be sources of such celebration. What school programs need are the time, space, and support for such activities to occur.

The importance of time in learning has been most recently highlighted by researchers studying what has come to be called "time on task."[11] Put simply, the more students are actually engaged in tasks that have academic importance, the greater the likelihood they will learn what is being taught. Put conversely, if students are not given an opportunity to learn something, it is not likely that they will learn it. Such research conclusions appear to belabor the obvious; nevertheless, these conclusions are educationally important: if students are to reap the benefits of what the humanities have to provide, the curriculum of the schools should provide them with time and access to humanistic content. Given such a conclusion, it behooves school administrators to get some sense of the quality and quantity of the opportunities for learning that students are afforded. One ought not to assume that English I or that "reading" from 9:15 to 10:30 A.M. implies that material from the humanities will be read or that it will be discussed in the manner alluded to above.

The skills needed to discuss the important ideas found within books, music, and the visual arts and the ability to analyze such works can be developed by teachers who themselves know how to lead such discussions and to critique relevant humanistic work. Yet, on the whole such skills are rare for reasons related to the ones I described earlier. These reasons relate to our antipathy toward discussion and critical analysis in schools; it simply is not a salient feature of what children or teachers do there. The primacy of achievement over inquiry is not new. Thelen wrote about it over two decades ago.[12] Unfortunately, things have not changed. As long as one is centered upon reaching fixed goals in a systematic way, the quality of the journey and the uncertain destination that genuine inquiry often creates are bound to suffer.

But school climate and the general expectations affecting the teacher—expectations of students, administrators, and parents—are not the only reasons why the kind of critical discussion on topics that pervade humanistic subject matter, or subject matters that are humanistically treated, is not characteristic of school classrooms. Teachers themselves are seldom taught how to lead discussions, how to dissect and help students analyze issues, how to penetrate the surface features of argument and to locate the author's starting point. It might seem remarkable, but few teacher training programs provide courses, or even significant sections of courses, on the conduct of class discussions. The difference between open and closed questions, the uses of probes, the application of skills needed to draw out students, or to elicit alternative views on the same issue are virtually absent in the repertoire of skills prospective teachers are asked to develop. The reasons for such neglect are obvious: such skills are not considered important because such processes are not considered important within the classroom. Indeed, in the past two decades the apotheosis of pedagogical virtue has been and still is something called individualized instruction. The educational ideal is a single track for each student who works in his own lockstep fashion by himself until he reaches an objective set by someone else. These locksteps are often color-coded so that the child can see the progress he has made and can compare his progress to others. The ideas that students can actually face each other and discuss what they had read, seen, or heard simply has no saliency in contemporary images of good educational practice. "Individualize" has come to mean "alone."

I hope it is clear from the foregoing how intimately related are the curricular and the pedagogical: what one teaches cannot be easily separated from how one teaches. This lesson was first taught to us by artists; form *is* content.

But before we leave the curricular and the pedagogical, I believe it is important for the reader not to come away with the conclusion that the content of the humanities is simply the classical disciplines or the great humanistic works. I believe that the contemporary world that students inhabit provides an enormously rich source of material for humanistic inquiry. I speak here of television, the mass-printed media, the architecture of shopping centers and local communities, the advertising that surrounds virtually all Americans. These sources, sources that have been called the vernacular arts, provide much in the way of issues, ideas, and themes that can be related directly to the kind of life human beings lead, to the forces and factors that influence their lives, and to the values that these sources reflect, engender, and reward. There is much to be learned from the very material that artists and writers have used as substance for their own work. There is no good educational reason why the study of contemporary life should not be used to develop the kind of skills and insights that one seeks in humanistic learning.

THE COMPETENCY OF THE TEACHER

The features of schooling needing attention if the humanities are to thrive include the competencies the teacher brings to teaching. As I have already indicated, the curricular and pedagogical are not easily separated. How one teaches colors what one teaches; indeed, the messages that students secure from teachers often have more to do with how teachers go about their tasks than what precisely it is that they are teaching. Consider for a moment the fact that teachers who care deeply about their subject matter and who express that caring to students are likely to generate a level of interest in that subject that can be secured in few other ways. The teacher who is genuinely excited by the ideas he or she treats in class, who does not feign enthusiasm, tells students indirectly that there is something here in this field that is worth knowing.

The difficulty, of course, that one encounters with teacher enthusiasm and commitment as valuable pedagogical traits is that these traits are extremely difficult to engender in teacher training programs. This does not diminish their significance; it simply diminishes the possibility of developing them in programs that prepare teachers.

The type of skills—rather than traits—that can be developed that are relevant to humanistic learning in schools focuses upon the ability of teachers to analyze materials that are read, seen, or heard with respect to themes and issues that are significant but subtle. The skills of interpretation, the ability to employ metaphor in the explication of text and image, the skills needed to elucidate relationships between particular humanistic works and, say, the historical context in which the work was created, are skills that should be secured during the course of a university liberal education. It should be remembered that the amount of time prospective teachers study within departments and schools of education prior to professional certification is very small—on the order of 15 percent of their courses taken are in education. In any case, the skills I am describing as relevant to humanities are best exemplified, practiced, and developed within history, literature, art, and other such courses. Helping students understand, for example, the historical context within which scientific discovery occurs is or should be a concern of departments of science. Put in more general terms, to teach the humanities well requires an undergraduate education in which the kinds of intellectual processes relevant to humanistic learning are cultivated. These processes are, in my view, best developed by faculties outside of schools and departments of education. It is not likely that professors of education will be able to develop skills that have been neglected in 85 percent of the undergraduate courses in which prospective teachers have been enrolled.

The implication of the foregoing is that without the support of the university faculty as a whole, it is unlikely that subjects will be studied by elementary and secondary school students in ways that make them humanistic in character. How teaching and learning take place in the college curriculum needs attention. Whether faculties outside of education will be willing to examine their own courses with respect to the manner in which they are taught remains to be seen. Since on many university campuses the department or school of education has low status, it might very well be the case that change must start elsewhere. The office of the president of the university is often a good place to begin.[13]

USING EVALUATION APPROPRIATELY

Another area that needs attention in schools if humanistic learning is to be cultivated, deals with the ways in which students are evaluated. In standard curriculum theories, evaluation procedures are to follow from the objectives that have been formulated for the curriculum. Evaluation is the means through which one determines if the objectives that have been set are achieved. This approach to evaluation is, of course, the standard means-ends model of curriculum planning: one first formulates ends, then implements means to achieve those ends, and finally evaluates to determine if the ends have been achieved.

In the real world, however, it is often the evaluation method that determines which ends students will pay attention to. Students can afford to neglect lofty goal statements, but they cannot afford to neglect the ways in which they will be evaluated. When evaluation procedures reward forms of study that contradict what the humanities prize—the ability to make rational judgments, the ability to critique incisively, the ability to see things in context, the ability to recognize and appreciate nuance, and so forth—such procedures diminish humanistic learning. When evaluation procedures give students the idea that meaningful humanistic learning consists of remembering bits and pieces of disconnected information in order to meet the demands of those who write test items, the evaluation interferes with what the humanities have to contribute to students. Unfortunately, much of testing has such consequences. To ameliorate our discomfort with subjectivity, we employ assessment methods that are characterized by precision, certainty, and attention to fragmented content.

On the positive side, we need to create evaluation tasks that do ask students to recognize and appreciate nuance, that ask them to evaluate relationships within and between the fields they study, that ask them to use their own subjectivity to interpret the material they read, see, and hear. In short, we need to move in a direction that is virtually 180 degrees away from the direction in which evaluation in the schools has been moving during the past decade.

Alas, it is much easier to describe our educational needs than to meet them through planned educational change. The schools are fettered to a social ecology that supports their existing practices. When those practices are antithetical to the humanities, the future of the humanities in the schools cannot look promising. Yet some goals are worth fighting for even when the odds of winning are small. Surely the contribution the humanities might make to the education of the young is one of them.

NOTES

1. Commission on the Humanities, *The Humanities in American Life: Report of the Commission on the Humanities* (Berkeley: University of California Press, 1980).

2. Ibid., p. 3.

3. When Aristotle wrote his *Ethics* he said: "Our discussion will be adequate if it has as much clearness as the subject matter admits of, for precision is not to be sought for alike in all discussions, any more than in all the products of the crafts . . . for it is the mark of an educated man to look for precision in each class of things just so far as the nature of the subject admits; it is evidently equally foolish to accept probable reasoning

from a mathematician and to demand from a rhetorician scientific proofs." Aristotle, *Nicomachean Ethics*, Book I, Part III.

4. For a lucid discussion of the context of scientific discovery, see Arthur Koestler, *The Act of Creation* (New York: Macmillan, 1964).

5. For a discussion of the human drama surrounding the discovery of DNA, see James D. Watson, *The Double Helix* (New York: Atheneum, 1968).

6. Commission on the Humanities, *The Humanities in American Life*, p. 2.

7. For many in American culture, artistic productivity is the offspring of talent, not intelligence. It is illuminating to note what John Dewey had to say about this issue as far back as 1934. See John Dewey, *Art as Experience* (New York: G. P. Putnam's Sons, 1934, reprinted 1958), p. 46, and Elliot W. Eisner, *Cognition and Curriculum: A Basis for Deciding What to Teach* (New York: Longman, 1982).

8. For example, see Samuel Bowles and Herbert Gintis, *Schooling in Capitalist America* (New York: Basic Books, 1976).

9. Johnan Galtung, "On Peace Education," in *Handbook on Peace Education*, ed. Christopher Wolf (Frankfurt am Main: International Peace Research Association, 1974).

10. Phillip C. Schlechty and Victor S. Nance, "Do Academically Able Teachers Leave Education? The North Carolina Case," *Phi Delta Kappan* 63 (October 1981): 106-112.

11. For a review of research on time on task, see Barak V. Rosenshine, "Content, Time, and Direct Instruction," in *Research on Teaching: Concepts, Findings, and Implications*, ed. Penelope L. Peterson and Herbert J. Walberg (Berkeley, Calif.: McCutchan Publishing Corp., 1979), pp. 26-56.

12. Herbert A. Thelen, *Education and the Human Quest* (New York: Harper, 1960).

13. I am pleased to say that at Stanford University, President Donald Kennedy has led the way to engage faculty in the systematic study of education at the secondary school level. Such engagement could have a ripple effect with respect to the analysis of pedagogical activity within the University. In addition, at Stanford there is a center for faculty opportunities to make video tapes of faculty teaching.

Name Index

Achebe, Chinua, 269
Acuna, Rodolfo, 277, 280
Adler, Mortimer, 111
Agard-Jones, Leslie, 278
Ahlgren, Patricia, 280
Ainley, John, 47
Airasian, Peter W., 90, 91, 107, 109, 110
Allen, Paula Gunn, 277
Anderson, Thomas, 146, 166
Angus, I., 108
Anrig, Gregory, 82
Apple, Michael W., 208, 229, 279
Applebee, Arthur W., 139
Aristotle, 299
Armento, Beverly, 278
Armbruster, Bonnie, 146, 148, 149, 166, 167
Arnold, Matthew, 3, 12, 13, 14, 22, 24, 108, 109
Arvizu, Steven F., 277
Asante, Molefi Kete, 277, 279
Atkinson, Richard C., 228
Au, Kathryn, 211, 229

Bacon, Francis, 290
Bagley, Ayers, 23
Bagley, William C., 116, 138
Bailey, Charles, 22, 25
Baldridge, J. Victor, 230
Baldwin, James, 271
Ball, Deborah, 164, 168
Banks, Cherry A. McGee, 277, 279
Banks, James, 258, 259, 277, 279, 280
Barker, R. G., 44, 47
Barr, Rebecca, 150, 151, 166, 168
Beck, M. D., 89, 90
Becker, Howard S., 210, 229
Beethoven, Ludwig van, 287
Bell, Daniel, 128, 139
Bell, Derrick, 278
Bell, Robert, 108
Bell, Terrel H., 129
Bellack, Arno, 207, 229
Belland, John, 196
Benne, Kenneth, 230
Bennett, William J., 132, 133
Bennis, Warren G., 230
Bernauer, James S. J., 111
Bettelheim, Bruno, 129, 139

Blinderman, Charles, 24
Bloom, Alan, 279
Bloom, Benjamin S., 31, 44, 46, 47, 81, 91, 107, 111
Bobbitt, Franklin, 20
Boguslaw, Robert, 138
Bowers, C. A., 178, 196
Bowles, Samuel, 300
Boyer, Ernest, 25, 111
Braun, K. P., 110
Braun, Robert J., 108, 110
Bridge, Connie, 153, 168
Broadfoot, Patricia, 108
Broudy, Harry S., 213, 230
Brown, John S., 228
Brown, K. P., 99
Bruner, Jerome, 31, 46, 118, 119, 138, 229
Bryan, William Jennings, 123

Cairns, Dorian, 109
Campbell, Donald T., 79, 107, 221, 231
Campbell, J. Olin, 228
Cardenas, Jose, 110
Carlyle, Thomas, 3
Carroll, John B., 31, 46
Carroll, Lewis, 103, 111
Carlson, Richard O., 230
Carpenter, Thomas P., 167, 228
Caswell, Hollis L., 125
Chall, Jeanne, 139, 146, 166
Charters, W. W., 20
Chavez, Linda, 280
Chesler, Mark A., 231
Cheyney, Lynne, 264
Chin, Robert, 230
Chomsky, Noam, 262, 278
Christian-Smith, Linda, 279
Churchill, Ward, 280
Clark, M., 99, 110
Clark, Richard, 128, 139
Cohen, David, 24, 179, 196
Comer, James, 271
Conant, James B., 30, 42, 45, 46
Conard, Sue, 139
Corbett, Mary K., 167
Cornbleth, Catherine, 263, 264, 278, 279, 280
Corse, L. B., 109

301

Subject Index

Advisory Panel on the SAT Test Score Decline, findings of, regarding cognitive level of textbooks, 129

American Association of University Professors (AAUP), Commission of, on Academic Freedom and Pre-College Education, 129

American Historical Association, Commission of, on Social Studies, 124

American Library Association, *Newsletter of, on Intellectual Freedom*, 126

Anti-intellectualism in American Life (Hofstadter), 123, 124

Arts, the, as part of humanistic studies, 289-90

Association for Supervision and Curriculum Development (ASCD), 79

Berea (Ohio) City School District, use of systematic monitoring system in, 221-28

Biological Sciences Curriculum Study (BSCS), modular approach of, in text materials, 126-27

Building America series, attacks on, 124-26

California Board of Education, rejection of science and mathematics textbooks by, 130

Cardinal Principles Report (1918), 20

Censorship, attack on Rugg textbooks and the *Building America* series as examples of, 123-26; problem of, in relation to textbooks and collateral materials, 122-33; watering down of curriculum as a consequence of, 126-29

Center for Law and Education, 236, 243, 248

Center for Study of Reading (University of Illinois, Urbana-Champaign), studies of, of textbooks in relation to content of standardized tests, 148-49

CityWorks program in Rindge School of Technical Arts: activities in, 238-40; attitudes of students toward, 250-51; changed attitudes of vocational education teachers in, 249-50; criticism of, 248; development of plan for, 156-57; features of, 237-40; goal of projects in, 239; Hands and Minds Collaborative

in, 248; multidisciplinary courses (City-Life and CitySystems) as part of, 239; potential clientele for, 244; strategies used in, to involve vocational education teachers in program development, 246-48; the city as the "text" in, 237; writing activities in, 239

College Entrance Examination Board, 76, 77, 82, 102

Committee of Ten, report of, 15-16

Commission on the Humanities, 286, 287, 289, 290

Common Curriculum, recommendations regarding, in secondary schools, 43-44

Communication networks, affordances and constraints in students' use of, 189-91

Computer Assisted Instruction (CAI), affordances and constraints in students' use of, 191; studies of effects of, on learning, 181-82

Computer technology, concerns marking introduction of, 173-74

Computers: studies of students' use of, 181-82; studies of teachers' use of, 182-84

Conceptual maps for curriculum: analysis of four examples, of, 58-62; multiple ways of knowing as example of, 62-69; use of, in curriculum planning, 52-55

Conflicting Conceptions of Curriculum (Eisner and Vallance), 56-57

Continuous Achievement Monitoring (CAM), evaluation of program using, in Pittsburgh, PA, 94-105

Critical analysis, absence of, in school programs, 295-96

Culture of schools, institutional dimensions of, 207-10

Curricular balance, lack of, in secondary schools, 39-40

Curricular content, variability in, among schools, 36-39

"Curricular Language and Classroom Learning" (Huebner), 57-58

Curricular traditions, challenge to, when significant innovations are proposed, 202-3

Curriculum: allegiance to disciplines as a constraint on planning of, 53-54;

RECENT PUBLICATIONS OF THE SOCIETY

1. The Yearbooks

97:1 (1998) *The Adolescent Years: Social Influences and Educational Challenges.* Kathryn Borman and Barbara Schneider, editors. Cloth.

97:2 (1998) *The Reading-Writing Connection.* Nancy Nelson and Robert C. Calfee, editors. Cloth.

96:1 (1997) *Service Learning.* Joan Schine, editor. Cloth.

96:2 (1997) *The Construction of Children's Character.* Alex Molnar, editor. Cloth.

95:1 (1996) *Performance-Based Student Assessment: Challenges and Possibilities.* Joan B. Baron and Dennie P. Wolf, editors. Cloth.

95:2 (1996) *Technology and the Future of Schooling.* Stephen T. Kerr, editor. Cloth.

94:1 (1995) *Creating New Educational Communities.* Jeannie Oakes and Karen Hunter Quartz, editors. Cloth.

94:2 (1995) *Changing Populations/Changing Schools.* Erwin Flaxman and A. Harry Passow, editors. Cloth.

93:1 (1994) *Teacher Research and Educational Reform.* Sandra Hollingsworth and Hugh Sockett, editors. Cloth.

93:2 (1994) *Bloom's Taxonomy: A Forty-year Retrospective.* Lorin W. Anderson and Lauren A. Sosniak, editors. Cloth.

92:1 (1993) *Gender and Education.* Sari Knopp Biklen and Diane Pollard, editors. Cloth.

92:2 (1993) *Bilingual Education: Politics, Practice, and Research.* M. Beatriz Arias and Ursula Casanova, editors. Cloth.

91:1 (1992) *The Changing Contexts of Teaching.* Ann Lieberman, editor. Cloth.

91:2 (1992) *The Arts, Education, and Aesthetic Knowing.* Bennett Reimer and Ralph A. Smith, editors. Cloth.

90:1 (1991) *The Care and Education of America's Young Children: Obstacles and Opportunities.* Sharon L. Kagan, editor. Cloth.

89:2 (1990) *Educational Leadership and Changing Contexts of Families, Communities, and Schools.* Brad Mitchell and Luvern L. Cunningham, editors. Paper.

88:1 (1989) *From Socrates to Software: The Teacher as Text and the Text as Teacher.* Philip W. Jackson and Sophie Haroutunian-Gordon, editors. Cloth.

88:2 (1989) *Schooling and Disability.* Douglas Biklen, Dianne Ferguson, and Alison Ford, editors. Cloth.

87:1 (1988) *Critical Issues in Curriculum.* Laurel N. Tanner, editor. Cloth.

87:2 (1988) *Cultural Literacy and the Idea of General Education.* Ian Westbury and Alan C. Purves, editors. Cloth.

Order the above titles from the University of Chicago Press, 11030 S. Langley Ave., Chicago, IL 60628. For a list of earlier Yearbooks still available, write to the Secretary, NSSE, 5835 Kimbark Ave., Chicago, IL 60637.

2. The Series on Contemporary Educational Issues

This series has been discontinued.

The following volumes in the series may be ordered from the McCutchan Publishing Corporation, P.O. Box 774, Berkeley, CA 94702-0774. Phone: 510-841-8616; Fax: 510-841-7787.

Academic Work and Educational Excellence: Raising Student Productivity (1986). Edited by Tommy M. Tomlinson and Herbert J. Walberg.

Adapting Instruction to Student Differences (1985). Edited by Margaret C. Wang and Herbert J. Walberg.

Choice in Education (1990). Edited by William Lowe Boyd and Herbert J. Walberg.

Colleges of Education: Perspectives on Their Future (1985). Edited by Charles W. Case and William A. Matthes.

Contributing to Educational Change: Perspectives on Research and Practice (1988). Edited by Philip W. Jackson.

Educational Leadership and School Culture (1993). Edited by Marshall Sashkin and Herbert J. Walberg.

Effective Teaching: Current Research (1991). Edited by Hersholt C. Waxman and Herbert J. Walberg.

Improving Educational Standards and Productivity: The Research Basis for Policy (1982). Edited by Herbert J. Walberg.

Moral Development and Character Education (1989). Edited by Larry P. Nucci.

Motivating Students to Learn: Overcoming Barriers to High Achievement (1993). Edited by Tommy M. Tomlinson.

Radical Proposals for Educational Change (1994). Edited by Chester E. Finn, Jr. and Herbert J. Walberg.

Reaching Marginal Students: A Prime Concern for School Renewal (1987). Edited by Robert L. Sinclair and Ward Ghory.

Restructuring the Schools: Problems and Prospects (1992). Edited by John J. Lane and Edgar G. Epps.

Rethinking Policy for At-risk Students (1994). Edited by Kenneth K. Wong and Margaret C. Wang.

School Boards: Changing Local Control (1992). Edited by Patricia F. First and Herbert J. Walberg.

The two final volumes in this series were:

Improving Science Education (1995). Edited by Barry J. Fraser and Herbert J. Walberg.

Ferment in Education: A Look Abroad (1995). Edited by John J. Lane.

These two volumes may be ordered from the Book Order Department, University of Chicago Press, 11030 S. Langley Ave., Chicago, IL 60628. Phone: 312-669-2215; Fax: 312-660-2235.